Writing Europe in Renaissance France

Edinburgh Critical Studies in Renaissance Culture

Series Editors: Lorna Hutson, Katherine Ibbett, Joe Moshenska and Kathryn Murphy

Titles available in the series:

Open Subjects: English Renaissance Republicans, Modern Selfhoods and the Virtue of Vulnerability
James Kuzner

The Phantom of Chance: From Fortune to Randomness in Seventeenth-Century French Literature
John D. Lyons

Don Quixote in the Archives: Madness and Literature in Early Modern Spain
Dale Shuger

Untutored Lines: The Making of the English Epyllion
William P. Weaver

The Girlhood of Shakespeare's Sisters: Gender, Transgression, Adolescence
Jennifer Higginbotham

Friendship's Shadows: Women's Friendship and the Politics of Betrayal in England, 1640–1705
Penelope Anderson

Inventions of the Skin: The Painted Body in Early English Drama, 1400–1642
Andrea Ria Stevens

Performing Economic Thought: English Drama and Mercantile Writing, 1600–1642
Bradley D. Ryner

Forgetting Differences: Tragedy, Historiography and the French Wars of Religion
Andrea Frisch

Listening for Theatrical Form in Early Modern England
Allison Deutermann

Theatrical Milton: Politics and Poetics of the Staged Body
Brendan Prawdzik

Legal Reform in English Renaissance Literature
Virginia Lee Strain

The Origins of English Revenge Tragedy
George Oppitz-Trotman

Crime and Consequence in Early Modern Literature and Law
Judith Hudson

Shakespeare's Golden Ages: Resisting Nostalgia in Elizabethan Drama
Kristine Johanson

Refusing to Behave in Early Modern Literature
Laura Seymour

Shakespeare's Virtuous Theatre: Power, Capacity and the Good
Kent Lehnhof, Julia Reinhard Lupton and Carolyn Sale

Writing Europe in Renaissance France: Travels in Reality and Imagination
Niall Oddy

Visit the Edinburgh Critical Studies in Renaissance Culture website at www.edinburghuniversitypress.com/series/ECSRC

Writing Europe in Renaissance France

Travels in Reality and Imagination

Niall Oddy

EDINBURGH
University Press

Edinburgh University Press is one of the leading university presses in the UK. We publish academic books and journals in our selected subject areas across the humanities and social sciences, combining cutting-edge scholarship with high editorial and production values to produce academic works of lasting importance. For more information visit our website: edinburghuniversitypress.com

© Niall Oddy 2024, 2025

Edinburgh University Press Ltd
13 Infirmary Street
Edinburgh EH1 1LT

First published in hardback by Edinburgh University Press 2024

Typeset in 10.5/13 Adobe Sabon by
Cheshire Typesetting Ltd, Cuddington, Cheshire

A CIP record for this book is available from the British Library

ISBN 978 1 3995 2261 8 (hardback)
ISBN 978 1 3995 2262 5 (paperback)
ISBN 978 1 3995 2263 2 (webready PDF)
ISBN 978 1 3995 2264 9 (epub)

The right of Niall Oddy to be identified as the author of this work has been asserted in accordance with the Copyright, Designs and Patents Act 1988, and the Copyright and Related Rights Regulations 2003 (SI No. 2498).

Contents

Acknowledgements vi
Series Editors' Preface viii

Introduction: Europe in Renaissance France 1

1. Bird's-Eye Views 15

2. Views from Brazil 43

3. Views from Constantinople 62

4. Views from Malta 86

5. Views from Geneva 113

Conclusion: Writing Europe, Writing France 135

Bibliography 141
Index 155

Acknowledgements

My thanks must go first of all to Kathryn Banks. She first inspired an interest in Renaissance culture and later suggested I read Montaigne's essays on the 'New World', which sparked a curiosity about who the 'us' was to whom he was referring. Over a decade later, this book represents the culmination of a project to answer that question. Kathryn supported my journey through undergraduate and MA level and then the PhD. I am grateful for all her help, advice and encouragement.

I am also thankful to John O'Brien, who co-supervised my PhD dissertation, for his support and interest in my work. He pushed me to grapple with the big picture, as well as getting stuck into the details of the material I was researching. Both John and Kathryn provided feedback on numerous drafts and helped to shape my thinking.

I have been very fortunate to have received financial support, without which I would have been unable to pursue postgraduate studies. The PhD research out of which this book has developed was funded by an AHRC Doctoral Scholarship. I am grateful to the Society for Seventeenth Century French Studies (now the Society for Early Modern French Studies) for the award of an Amy Wygant Research Bursary, which allowed me to conduct research in Paris. I must also express my thanks for funding received for research trips from Durham University's Institute of Medieval and Early Modern Studies, Faculty of Arts and Humanities, School of Modern Languages and Cultures, and the St Mary's College Society.

Much of this book was written in libraries. Working in a distance learning university has made me especially grateful for the SCONUL access scheme. Staff at the Literary and Philosophical Society of Newcastle upon Tyne, the Robinson Library at Newcastle University and the British Library at Boston Spa have been particularly helpful.

My thanks go to Katherine Ibbett, the series editors and the anonymous reviewers for prompts and suggestions that have made this a much better book. Thanks too to Richard Maber and Richard Scholar for their feedback and encouragement.

For emotional and practical support (and necessary distraction) at various times, I thank my family (Lindsey, Martin and Ryan), Janet Dixon-Dawson, Justine T. Wolfenden, Santiago Fouz Hernández and Sam Hudson. Thanks to Elayne Chaplin for providing me with the opportunity of meaningful work.

I was blessed to have counted Brian Santry as a friend. I am thankful for his hospitality during my research trips to Dublin and for our conversations. *Ar dheis Dé go raibh a anam dílis.*

Finally, I thank Catherine Ellis, my partner in cross-cultural travel, who has shared my journeys to Europe of the sixteenth and twenty-first centuries. Without her help this book would be poorer and without her support it might never have been finished. A good egg, a lover of languages and cultures (especially food cultures), she teaches me so much. There is no one else with whom I'd rather share our little patch of this fragile planet.

Series Editors' Preface

Edinburgh Critical Studies in Renaissance Culture may, as a series title, provoke some surprise. On the one hand, the choice of the word 'culture' (rather than, say, 'literature') suggests that writers in this series subscribe to the now widespread assumption that the 'literary' is not isolable, as a mode of signifying, from other signifying practices that make up what we call 'culture'. On the other hand, most of the critical work in English literary studies of the period 1500–1700 which endorses this idea has rejected the older identification of the period as 'the Renaissance', with its implicit homage to the myth of essential and universal Man coming to stand (in all his sovereign individuality) at the centre of a new world picture. In other words, the term 'culture' in the place of 'literature' leads us to expect the words 'early modern' in the place of 'Renaissance'. Why, then, 'Edinburgh Critical Studies in *Renaissance Culture*'?

The answer to that question lies at the heart of what distinguishes this critical series and defines its parameters. As Terence Cave has argued, the term 'early modern', though admirably egalitarian in conception, has had the unfortunate effect of essentialising the modern, that is, of positing 'the advent of a once-and-for-all modernity' which is the deictic 'here and now' from which we look back. The phrase 'early modern', that is to say, forecloses the possibility of other modernities, other futures that might have arisen, narrowing the scope of what we may learn from the past by construing it as a narrative leading inevitably to Western modernity, to 'us'. *Edinburgh Critical Studies in Renaissance Culture* aims rather to shift the emphasis from a story of progress – early modern to modern – to a series of critical encounters and conversations with the past, which may reveal to us some surprising alternatives buried within texts familiarly construed as episodes on the way to certain identifying features of our endlessly fascinating modernity. In keeping with one aspect of the etymology of 'Renaissance' or 'Rinascimento' as 'rebirth', moreover, this series features books that explore and interpret anew elements of the critical encounter between writers of the period 1500–1700 and texts of Greco-Roman literature, rhetoric, politics, law, oeconomics, *eros* and friendship.

The term 'culture', then, indicates a licence to study and scrutinise objects other than literary ones, and to be more inclusive about both the forms and the material and political stakes of making meaning both in the past and in the present. 'Culture' permits a realisation of the benefits to be reaped after two decades of interdisciplinary enrichment in the arts. No longer are historians naïve about textual criticism, about rhetoric, literary theory or about readerships; likewise, literary critics trained in close reading now also turn easily to court archives, to legal texts, and to the historians' debates about the languages of political and religious thought. Social historians look at printed pamphlets with an eye for narrative structure; literary critics look at court records with awareness of the problems of authority, mediation and institutional procedure. Within these developments, modes of research that became unfashionable and discredited in the 1980s – for example, studies in classical or vernacular 'source texts', or studies of literary 'influence' across linguistic, confessional and geographical boundaries – have acquired a new critical edge and relevance as the convergence of the disciplines enables the unfolding of new cultural histories (that is to say, what was once studied merely as 'literary influence' may now be studied as a fraught cultural encounter). The term 'Renaissance' thus retains the relevance of the idea of consciousness and critique within these textual engagements of past and present, and, while it foregrounds the Western European experience, is intended to provoke comparativist study of wider global perspectives rather than to promote the 'universality' of a local, if far-reaching, historical phenomenon. Finally, as traditional pedagogic boundaries between 'Medieval' and 'Renaissance' are being called into question by cross-disciplinary work emphasising the 'reformation' of social and cultural forms, so this series, while foregrounding the encounter with the classical past, is self-conscious about the ways in which that past is assimilated to the projects of Reformation and Counter-Reformation, spiritual, political and domestic, that finally transformed Christendom into Europe.

Individual books in this series vary in methodology and approach, sometimes blending the sensitivity of close literary analysis with incisive, informed and urgent theoretical argument, at other times offering critiques of grand narratives of the period by their work in manuscript transmission, or in the archives of legal, social and architectural history, or by social histories of gender and childhood. What all these books have in common, however, is the capacity to offer compelling, well-documented and lucidly written critical accounts of how writers and thinkers in the period 1500–1700 reshaped, transformed and critiqued the texts and practices of their world, prompting new perspectives on what we think we have learned from them.

Lorna Hutson, Katherine Ibbett, Joe Moshenska and Kathryn Murphy

Introduction:
Europe in Renaissance France

In our country, Europe occasionally appears and then disappears again.[1]

Yuri Andrukhovych

What is Europe?

There is a story told about Europe's ever closer union. It is a long history of increasing integration and a growing sense of pancontinental identity, culminating in the expansion of the European Union in the twenty-first century. As with so many features associated with the modern world – capitalism, globalisation, nation states, science – our contemporary understanding of Europe is often regarded as first emerging in the early modern period. The Reformation, which shattered the medieval notion of Christendom, and the consolidation of nations allowed for the political and secular development of the continent that underpins how European states function today as independent and cooperative political actors. The transformations that took place in society over the period broadly construed as 'the Renaissance' increased the status of Europe from a neutral geographical marker of space to an object of allegiance which stood for a set of values. Awareness of the so-called 'New World' of the Americas and the expansion of the Muslim Ottoman Empire into the continent sharpened a sense of what Europeans shared. At the same time, improvements in cartographic accuracy and the spread of the printing press facilitated the circulations of maps and books of geography, resulting in greater use of the word 'Europe' and a perception of it as distinct from and superior to the rest of the world.

This argument that Europe emerged in the Renaissance as a marker of a political and cultural identity is commonplace.[2] It is situated within the broader view of Europe that regards the continent as a significant idea in contemporary political and cultural life and that seeks to determine how this idea developed historically over the *longue durée*.³ However, the view of contemporary Europe as peaceful, cosmopolitan and unified faces increasing scrutiny in the light of resurgent nationalisms, as epitomised in the withdrawal of the United Kingdom from the European Union. The crux of the issue when dealing with Europe is to what exactly we are referring. When we talk about Europe, are we talking about the European Union or about another concept? Is that concept defined geographically, politically, culturally or by some combination of these aspects? The usage of the term varies from context to context, situation to situation, person to person. Europe through the eyes of a Europhile British person looks different through Eurosceptic eyes. Europe looks different again through the eyes of a Euromaidan protestor in Kyiv in November 2013. Europe is socially and culturally produced, and mediated by identitarian concerns of nation, culture, religion, ethnicity and profession.

Historical scholarship is taking an increasing interest in the contingent nature of Europe, better understood as a range of competing ideas and discourses, rather than as a linear narrative.[4] Roberto Dainotto's study of eighteenth- and nineteenth-century ideas of Europe examined counter-narratives of the continent that were written in light of a definition of Europe that marginalised the south of the continent.[5] Katharina Piechocki's examination of early modern geographic thought has shown how unclear and contested the boundaries of Europe were.[6] Isabella Walser-Bürgler's work on Europe in Neo-Latin literature has emphasised the importance of language choice in the multilingual early modern world.[7] *Writing Europe in Renaissance France* considers material written in the French vernacular to examine how early modern representations of Europe were shaped in a time of increasing national sentiment. It responds to Piechocki's assertion that 'Europe is an astonishingly unexamined continent' and to her call to 'historicize the idea of a continent, subjecting it to careful, interdisciplinary scrutiny'.[8]

France and Europe

In his essay on the Spanish conquests in the New World, 'Des coches' ('Of Coaches'), Michel de Montaigne wrote, 'Nostre monde vient d'en trouver un autre' ('Our world has just discovered another one').[9] He does not explicitly define the contours of 'our world'. It is left to the reader's interpretation to judge who is included and to where it refers. As Montaigne wrote in French, it might be surmised that his world was a Francophone one. Yet the encounter with the New World to which he is referring involved the Spanish and the Portuguese on an earlier and bigger scale than the French, and his essay deals with the Spanish at length. Montaigne's world, then, might be labelled the Old World or Europe. It might even stretch to include Asia and Africa, the extent of the known world before awareness of the Americas.[10] Timothy Hampton reads 'Des coches' as part of his study on nationhood in French Renaissance literature and argues that it is an attempt to define a location, France, from which to articulate a collective identity that allows him to judge the atrocities of the Spanish in the New World, a community to which he feels a shared cultural connection in spite of his revulsion.[11] Hampton refers to what he calls the 'European subject', although Montaigne does not use the word 'European' or even 'Europe' in 'Des coches'. In fact, Montaigne uses the word 'Europe' only once in his *Essais* (*Essays*).[12] The key words in 'Des coches' are 'nous' ('we/us'), referring to an unspecified group of people, and 'monde' ('world'), a term of geographical and cultural import. Montaigne is engaging in geographical and cultural thinking in a speculative and ambivalent manner, articulating a community and a place that on occasion seems synonymous with France yet elsewhere seems broader. This ambivalence reflects that the boundaries of place and between peoples were in flux when Montaigne was writing. His essay displays the interplay and the uncertainty between the different communities and places to which he imagines an allegiance. Yes, the early modern period was a time when the boundaries of nations were consolidating, but they remained mutable throughout and they were not the only boundaries that were under constant negotiation. Montaigne's 'Des coches' grapples with the boundaries of nationhood and the larger cultural-geographical world to which France belonged.

Writing Europe in Renaissance France explores the intersection of France and Europe, examining how reflections on the continent related to reflections on the nation. I argue that thinking about Europe developed as part of a broad scrutiny of the boundaries of place and peoples that took place across multiple disciplines and genres. This book investigates the writings of cartographers, geographers, historians, diplomats, spies, travellers, pastors, poets and writers of fiction. Interest in Europe crossed contexts and was shaped by a range of concerns, including French national identity. In his work on early modern France, Michael Wolfe has emphasised the 'ineluctable patterns of conflict over French identity' and the 'perennial problems relating to the interplay of politics, religion, gender, class, and order'.[13] *Writing Europe in Renaissance France* demonstrates that ideas of Europe were also part of this web of problems. It argues that Europe developed as a concept in conjunction with nationhood and other categories of belonging, not as an alternative to the nation state.

The rise of national consciousness in the sixteenth century coincided with the increased use of the word 'Europe'.[14] Prior to the Renaissance, 'Europe' was a rather specialised term which tended to denote space and was found mostly in scholarly works on geography.[15] 'Christendom' was a much more frequent frame of reference with significant emotional impact, indicating a unity held together by the shared culture of Christianity, the common Latin language and the headship of the pope.[16] The notion of Christendom was severely weakened by the Reformation and the rise of confessionalism, as well as by the increasing power of, and loyalties to, states.[17] 'Europe' developed as a possible synonym. Yet the word 'Christendom' continued to be used, even when it referred to a unity of Christian countries that existed only in theory. Discourses about Christendom were elaborated in relation to discourses about Europe. Given the slipperiness of both terms and the boundaries to which they referred, the use of one in a given context reflected a particular preference and, as such, a specific engagement in an ongoing debate about what Europe and Christendom meant. It was a debate that influenced and was influenced by discourses of nationhood, as thinkers pondered the place and status of a nation within Christendom, within Europe and in relation to other nations.

Renaissance France offers an especially revealing case study for the subject of Europe and nationhood. Under François I (r. 1515–47), France was vying for supremacy in the continent with Habsburg Spain and had begun colonising missions in North America. By the final decades of the sixteenth century, civil war had brought France close to political collapse. Nationhood was, therefore, a particularly prominent source of instability and anxiety in France.[18] Benedict Anderson's formulation of nations as 'imagined communities' has been extremely influential in studies of nation-building and has been a spur for scholars to consider the work of literature in *imagining* the nation.[19] The crisis of Renaissance France arguably meant that constructions of nationhood required acts of imagination. Studies by Timothy Hampton and Marcus Keller have shed light on how sixteenth-century literary texts engaged in a highly charged atmosphere of ideological contestation over the boundaries and meanings of France.[20] *Writing Europe in Renaissance France* seeks to broaden these insights by placing reflections on the nation and on Europe in the interconnected and overlapping discursive contexts in which they functioned.[21] Thinking about France related to thinking about Europe and about other geographical and cultural concepts – Christendom, Catholicism, Reformed Christianity – through which individuals understood their world and which were constantly conceived in dialogue, negotiation or competition with one another. This thinking was also carried out across multiple contexts. This book analyses a range of different types of texts to reveal the diversity of thinking about Europe in Renaissance France across different domains.

Imagined Geographies

Writing Europe in Renaissance France is written in the wake of the so-called 'spatial turn' in the humanities and social sciences which treats space as a theoretical category.[22] The term 'spatial literary studies' refers to an emerging body of work that embraces a diverse range of methods and approaches to examine representations of space and place in literature.[23] Several studies have explored the connections of literature with geography, cartography and space in sixteenth-century France.[24] Philippe Desan has argued that consciousness of space became relativised in the Renaissance, that is, space and place were understood in relation to the position of the individual interpreter.[25] Writers were important to this development in that narration was effectively a claiming of space, of the place of the writer's (or fictional character's) body in the world. Indeed, if the difference between space and place is understood in terms of the investment of meaning, that is, a place is a space to which humans have ascribed meaning, then it is clear that literature and other forms of writing have roles to play in making spaces into places.[26]

Moreover, spatial literary criticism considers both real and imagined places and, in the words of Robert Tally, 'often calls into question the facile distinction between real and imaginary places'.[27] Europe is an ideal object for this sort of analysis. As Martin Lewis and Kären Wigen have demonstrated in their work on the 'myth of continents', the basic geographical divisions of the world are cultural constructs.[28] In that sense, the boundary between Europe and Asia is at least as much the product of imagination as it is real. A continent covers such a vast space that it cannot be directly comprehended and experienced in its entirety. In thinking about a continent, then, one is engaging in an act of imagination.[29] Examining literary works in relation to other discourses, as this book does, foregrounds the role of the imagination in conceiving of Europe and brings the stylistic, aesthetic and representational concerns of literary studies to bear on historical study.

Of course, the categories of the 'literary' and 'non-literary' belong to our present time and not to the Renaissance. The essential aesthetic dimension of literature is an eighteenth-century conception. And that is not to say that 'literature' can be easily defined today; Terence Cave has noted that literature is 'a category with blurred edges, a set of variously related cultural practices'.[30] While I on occasion refer to the literary and the non-literary, I do so in a general way. Grouping writers as diverse as Rabelais, Ronsard and Montaigne together as writers of 'literature' reveals nothing of *how* they explored questions of Europe. Rather, I will pay attention to the more salient features that determine how a text generates meanings, for example, the use of fictive elements. Genre, too, I understand loosely, following Rosalie Colie in regarding genres in the Renaissance not as a rigid system but as 'ideas of form, established by custom and consensus' which writers felt free to follow, reject or adapt.[31]

While New Historicism casts a long shadow over scholarship that reads literary works alongside non-literary ones, *Writing Europe in Renaissance France* has been influenced more directly by Terence Cave's method of pre-history, which advocates reading literature in relation to intellectual history by understanding a text as a particular and individual response to historical phenomena.[32] A pre-history rejects a teleological model of history and is thus pertinent to a study of Europe, where there is the danger of understanding the early modern past with the hindsight of the present.[33] The pre-historical method is attentive to comprehending literary works 'in the present tense of their articulation'.[34] Hence, literary works can be useful to the study of history as their very individuality emphasises the unique over the general, making them suitable sources of authentic past experience.

The examination of representations of Europe undertaken in this book draws on the concept of imagined geography, which has developed from Edward Said's work in his seminal *Orientalism*. Said used the term 'imaginative geography' to refer to the perception of the Orient in the western imagination.[35] He draws on Gaston Bachelard's work on the 'poetics of space' to argue that space is given emotional meaning beyond any objective reality. Imaginative geography also underscores the arbitrary nature of spatial boundaries: '[a] group of people living on a few acres of land will set up boundaries between their land and its immediate surroundings and the territory beyond, which they call "the land of the barbarians"'.[36] In this way, 'geographic boundaries accompany the social, ethnic, and cultural ones', and divide 'our' land from 'theirs'.[37] Imaginative, or imagined, geographies, then, are ways of representing spaces and places culturally and symbolically that circulate in academic, administrative and cultural outputs to shape how a space/place is understood. The concept has been used across scholarly disciplines, including geography and history, as a means of examining how geographies are produced.³⁸

Said's *Orientalism* has had a powerful impact on the development of postcolonial studies, a body of work which began as a critique of European colonialism. While Said was concerned with how the west represents the east, it is clear that such discourses are as much about self-understanding as they are othering outsiders. When the ancient Greek rhetorician Isocrates wrote that 'Europe became stronger than Asia' (*Panathenaicus* 47), he was representing Asia and representing Europe by imagining their affective geographies in the light of one another.³⁹ 'It is Europe that articulates the Orient', Said claimed.⁴⁰ Europe also articulates itself and, therefore, a postcolonial gaze ought to subject Europe to examination, as Dipesh Chakrabarty has argued in *Provincializing Europe*, since Europe is a figure 'of imagination whose geographical referents remain somewhat indeterminate'.⁴¹ *Writing Europe in Renaissance France* conducts this examination of Europe for the period that witnessed the continent's first global encounters with the rest of the world, when the geographical referents of the continent became a pressing concern. The awareness of the previously unknown Americas destroyed the prior conception of the world as a single landmass in favour of a world divided into the four parts of Europe, Asia, Africa and America, which increased the importance of a continent as an idea.⁴² Voyages of discovery and the rediscovery of Ptolemy's *Geographia* fuelled the development of geography and cartography, with more and more publications on these subjects, meaning that the average reader would be more likely to encounter the word 'Europe'.⁴³ Europe in this period, writes Roberto Dainotto, 'was in everyone's mind'.⁴⁴ And as Europe was in people's minds in large part as a result of imperial expansion and colonial violence, the concept is bound up with what Walter Mignolo has called the 'darker side of the Renaissance'.⁴⁵

Angles of Vision

While in the Renaissance Europe was busy articulating the world and articulating itself, it was not articulating itself in one way only. Just as Said in *Orientalism* is concerned with the European practice of representation, *longue durée* studies of the idea of Europe tend to examine a shared way of understanding the continent. Michael Wintle, for instance, has argued that there 'was a European view of the world, certainly from the Renaissance onwards, which was more distinguished by its shared features than by its internal divisions'.⁴⁶ In contrast, the present book is concerned with Europe's internal divisions and with French views of the world. French writers articulated an imagined geography of Europe as 'ours', as distinct from the rest of the world, yet when they wrote of 'nostre Europe' ('our Europe') they did so from a particular position. Montaigne's 'j'estime tous les hommes mes compatriotes, et embrasse un Polonois comme un François' ('I consider all men my compatriots and embrace a Pole like a Frenchman')[47] might sound like a cosmopolitan, maybe even European, impulse, yet it is shaped by Montaigne's national context, Henri III having been King of Poland prior to ascending to the French throne.[48] The book's focus on France offers fresh perspectives and new sources with which to analyse Europe. By examining individual conceptions of the continent across different text types, *Writing Europe in Renaissance France* highlights the distinctive role of genre in imagining geography in different ways.

As well as national consciousness and genre, the book shows how representations of Europe were inflected by travel, both real and imagined. Europe might mean one thing to a French Catholic in Paris and something different to a French Catholic in Brazil. Europe might mean something different still to a French Catholic writing about Brazil without ever travelling there. In this sense, *Writing Europe in Renaissance France* responds to work in global history that has investigated new and diverse formulations of space.[49] Sebastian Conrad has argued that 'as important as the quest for alternative spatial units may be, the real challenge consists in shifting between, and articulating, different scales of analysis, rather than sticking to fixed territories'.[50] The local, the regional, the national and the transnational all impact the global, and each of these scales impacts the others. *Writing Europe in Renaissance France* complements macro-histories of the idea of Europe by bringing the national scale into focus. It also places the national within its global contexts, examining the imagined geographies of France and Europe in relation to thinking about Brazil, the Ottoman Empire, the Mediterranean and Geneva. In the sixteenth century these were among the places outside France to have had the most significant impact on shaping French geographical thinking. Studies of Europe from the point of view of other nations would chart different geographies; East Asia, for instance, was more significant in Iberian imaginaries than in Francophone ones.

Chapter 1 considers the bird's-eye view of Europe offered in *La Cosmographie de Pierre Apian* (*The Cosmography of Peter Apian*). This universal cosmography, which mapped regions and towns according to Ptolemaic coordinates of latitude and longitude, defined Europe as spatially smaller than Asia, Africa and America, but superior in its virtues. I read this text alongside the larger cosmography of Sebastian Münster, which included descriptions of the world's many regions and nations, and was available in France in a Latin edition. These examples of the genre of cosmography are compared with a work of comic imaginative fiction by Rabelais, the *Quart Livre* (*Fourth Book*) of 1552. I argue that Rabelais engaged critically and creatively with the language and stylistic features of contemporary cosmographical writing in order to unsettle the knowledge such works produced. In doing so, he used the medium of fiction to offer a different view of Europe. Where the cosmographies represent Europe as superior to the rest of the world, marked out by the shared customs of its people and the fertility of its landscape, the much bleaker perspective in Rabelais' *Quart Livre* is of a fragmented continent mired in national and religious conflicts.

Chapter 2 examines how Europe was represented from the perspective of the New World through an analysis of André Thevet's account of his voyage to Brazil, *Les Singularitez de la France antarctique* (*The Singularities of Antarctic France*), and Montaigne's 'Des cannibales' ('Of Cannibals'), which includes the only instance of the word 'Europe' in his *Essais*. I argue that in 'Des cannibales' Montaigne, who never travelled to the Americas, offers a productive response to the idea of Europe generated by discourses of conquest. Thevet relates a set of ideas – savagery, civility, Christianity – to the term 'Europe', thereby constructing an idea of Europe as a superior culture, which serves to justify overseas expansion. Montaigne challenges the meanings of the lexis that underpin Thevet's view and, in doing so, enacts a much more uncertain interpretation of Europe that casts doubt on the value of imagining geography.

Chapter 3 turns to Constantinople to ask how the Ottoman Empire shaped representations of Europe. It compares the political treatises of François Savary de Brèves, French ambassador to Constantinople from 1592 to 1605, with the poetry of Ronsard who travelled to the Ottoman capital only in his imagination. Where Ronsard's verse depicts a civilisational clash between Europe and the Ottoman Empire, Savary de Brèves offers a fluid and pragmatic understanding of east–west relations. The two, though, share a common concern with French national interest, Savary de Brèves as a diplomat and Ronsard as a court poet.

Chapter 4 moves to the Mediterranean Sea to consider the case of Malta. The increasing interest in documenting and categorising the world, as more and more came to be known about it, made the question of whether the islands in the Mediterranean Sea were African or European a vexed one. The chapter turns first to the universal cosmographies written in French by André Thevet and François de Belleforest to see how this question was answered. Though the inhabitants of

Malta were acknowledged to be Christians, they were considered culturally closer to the people of Africa and so the island was delimited as African. This highlights the significance of ethnicity and the imagined geography of Africa in constructing perceptions of Europe. The chapter then compares the cosmographies with two travel accounts, Thevet's *Cosmographie de Levant* (*Cosmography of the Levant*) and the spy Nicolas de Nicolay's *Les Quatre Premiers Livres des navigations et peregrinations orientales* (*The First Four Books of Oriental Navigations and Peregrinations*). I show how geography is imagined differently in travel accounts, arguing that Europe was a much less significant category to travellers to Malta than to cosmographers.

Chapter 5 examines the impact of the Protestant Reformation on ideas of Europe through the writings of two Frenchmen who, on account of their religion, were exiled to Calvinist Geneva, Jean de Léry and Agrippa d'Aubigné. Léry's *Histoire d'un voyage faict en la terre du Brésil* (*History of a Voyage Made to the Land of Brazil*) and d'Aubigné's *Histoire universelle* (*Universal History*) show how perspectives on Europe were shaped by religious civil war. Both Léry and d'Aubigné appeal to their faith and to their country in a double discourse of competing, and ultimately irreconcilable, narratives of cultural belonging. Forced to choose between religion and nation, they both opted for the former. Their texts register a sense of loss and reject Christendom and Europe as meaningful ideas, regarding the continent as irrevocably fragmented.

Writing Europe in Renaissance France draws a conceptual map of what Europe looked like from these different points on the globe. It demonstrates that ideas about Europe were shaped by real and imagined journeys to these locations.[51] By considering Europe from these different vantage points, this book offers a new way of looking at Europe through a national lens and of looking at Renaissance France through a European lens. Concerns about Europe were shared across the continent, but the ways these concerns were manifested in the French vernacular were specific to Renaissance France. And yet there was not one way of imagining Europe in Renaissance France. The analysis of texts across the genres of literature, history, geography, travel and politics is designed to widen the range of sources that are used to study the history of the idea of Europe.[52] In doing so, it offers insight into the diffuse nature of thinking about Europe across the range of discursive contexts in which the concept appeared. And it shows how these contexts shaped diverse formulations of the imagined cultural, political and geographical boundaries of the French nation and of Europe.

Notes

1. Yuri Andrukhovych, 'The Star Absinthe: Notes on a Bitter Anniversary', in *The White Chalk of Days: The Contemporary Ukrainian Literature Series Anthology* <https://www.whitechalkofdays.com/the-star-absinthe-notes-on-a-bitter-anniversary> [accessed 4 May 2023].
2. For instance, John Hale has written of the 'discovery of Europe' in this period (*The Civilization of Europe in the Renaissance* (London: HarperCollins, 1993), p. 3). Jerry Brotton argues that Europe started to become associated with a political and cultural identity in the fifteenth and sixteenth centuries (*The Renaissance Bazaar: From the Silk Road to Michelangelo* (Oxford: Oxford University Press, 2002), p. 11). Similarly, the German historian Winfried Schule suggests the notion of Europe as a cultural and religious system can be traced to the sixteenth century ('Europa in der Frühen Neuzeit – Begriffsgeschichtliche Befunde', in *'Europäische Geschichte' als historiographisches Problem*, ed. by Heinz Duchhardt and Andreas Kunz (Mainz: Philipp von Zabern, 1997), pp. 35–65). For an alternative view, see Peter Burke, 'Did Europe Exist before 1700?', *History of European Ideas*, 1 (1980), 21–29; Burke argues that there was not a clear idea of Europe before the eighteenth century.
3. Such was the approach taken by Denys Hay in his classic study that examined material from antiquity to the seventeenth century, *Europe: The Emergence of an Idea*, 2nd edn (Edinburgh: Edinburgh University Press, 1968). Lucien Febvre, one of the founders of the *Annales* school of history, took an even longer view from the ancient Greeks to the twentieth century in his 1944–45 lecture course at the Collège de France, posthumously published as *L'Europe: Genèse d'une civilisation*, ed. by Thérèse Charmasson and Brigitte Mazon (Paris: Perrin, 1999). More recent studies also trace the development of Europe from the classical period to the present day, including Gerard Delanty, *Inventing Europe: Idea, Identity, Reality* (Basingstoke: Macmillan, 1995), Michael Wintle, *The Image of Europe: Visualizing Europe in Cartography and Iconography throughout the Ages* (Cambridge: Cambridge University Press, 2011), and Shane Weller, *The Idea of Europe: A Critical History* (Cambridge: Cambridge University Press, 2021).
4. For example, *Finding Europe: Discourses on Margins, Communities, Images*, ed. by Anthony Molho and Diogo Ramada Curto (New York: Berghahn, 2007), and *Contesting Europe: Comparative Perspectives on Early Modern Discourses on Europe, 1400-1800*, ed. by Nicolas Detering, Clementina Marsico and Isabella Walser-Bürgler (Leiden: Brill, 2020).
5. Roberto M. Dainotto, *Europe (in Theory)* (Durham, NC: Duke University Press, 2007).
6. Katharina Piechocki, *Cartographic Humanism: The Making of Early Modern Europe* (Chicago: University of Chicago Press, 2019).
7. Isabella Walser-Bürgler, *Europe and Europeanness in Early Modern Latin Literature: 'Fuitne Europa tunc unita?'* (Leiden: Brill, 2021). Nicolas Detering has considered the discourse on Europe in vernacular German material of the seventeenth and early eighteenth centuries in *Krise und*

Kontinent: Die Entstehung der deutschen Europa-Literatur in der Frühen Neuzeit (Cologne: Böhlau Verlag, 2017).
8. Piechocki, p. 5.
9. Michel de Montaigne, *Les Essais*, ed. by Pierre Villey and V. L. Saulnier (Paris: Presses Universitaires de France, 2004), p. 908. All translations are my own except where otherwise specified.
10. Marcus Keller, 'France, Europe, and the Orient in the *Essays*: Montaigne's Dialectics', in *The Dialectics of Orientalism in Early Modern Europe*, ed. by Marcus Keller and Javier Irigoyen-García (London: Palgrave Macmillan, 2018), pp. 121–36 (p. 127).
11. Timothy Hampton, *Literature and Nation in the Sixteenth Century: Inventing Renaissance France* (Ithaca, NY: Cornell University Press, 2001), pp. 195–226.
12. In the chapter 'Des cannibales'. See Chapter 2 of the present book.
13. Michael Wolfe, 'Introduction: Becoming French in Early Modern Europe', in *Changing Identities in Early Modern France*, ed. by Michael Wolfe (Durham, NC: Duke University Press, 1997), pp. 1–21 (pp. 15–16).
14. On the historical development of French national consciousness, see Colette Beaune, *Naissance de la nation France* (Paris: Gallimard, 1985).
15. On the medieval use of the term 'Europe', see Hay, pp. 37–55.
16. A useful overview of the notion of Christendom can be found in Hay, pp. 16–36.
17. The destruction of Christendom is the framing narrative of Mark Greengrass's history of Europe from 1517 to 1648: *Christendom Destroyed: Europe 1517–1648* (London: Allen Lane, 2014).
18. See, for example, Myriam Yardeni, *La Conscience nationale en France pendant les guerres de religion (1559–1598)* (Louvain: Nauwelaerts, 1971), and Henry Heller, *Anti-Italianism in Sixteenth-Century France* (Toronto: University of Toronto Press, 2003). On how early modern French cultural anxieties related to colonial ventures, see Sara Melzer, *Colonizer or Colonized? The Hidden Colonial Stories of Early Modern French Culture* (Philadelphia: University of Pennsylvania Press, 2012).
19. Benedict Anderson, *Imagined Communities: Reflections on the Origin and Spread of Nationalism*, rev. edn (London: Verso, 2006). The seminal study of literary constructions of nationhood is Richard Helgerson, *Forms of Nationhood: The Elizabethan Writing of England* (Chicago: University of Chicago Press, 1992).
20. Hampton; Marcus Keller, *Figurations of France: Literary Nation-Building in Times of Crisis (1550-1650)* (Newark: University of Delaware Press, 2011).
21. Previous work on ideas of Europe in Renaissance France tends to limit the scope of the study to Europe. See *La Conscience européenne au XVe et au XVIe siècle: Actes du colloque international organisé à l'École Normale Supérieure de Jeunes Filles (30 septembre – 3 octobre 1980)* (Paris: École Normale Supérieure de Jeunes Filles, 1982); *Conceptions of Europe in Renaissance France: Essays in Honour of Keith Cameron*, ed. by David Cowling (Amsterdam: Rodopi, 2006).
22. See *The Spatial Turn: Interdisciplinary Perspectives*, ed. by Barney Warf and Santa Arias (London: Routledge, 2009).

23. The diversity of the field can be seen in two edited collections: *The Routledge Handbook of Literature and Space*, ed. by Robert T. Tally Jr (London: Routledge, 2017), and *Spatial Literary Studies: Interdisciplinary Approaches to Space, Geography, and the Imagination*, ed. by Robert T. Tally Jr (New York: Routledge, 2020).
24. Frank Lestringant, *L'Atelier du cosmographe: Ou l'image du monde à la Renaissance* (Paris: Albin Michel, 1991); Tom Conley, *The Self-Made Map: Cartographic Writing in Early Modern France* (Minneapolis: University of Minnesota Press, 1996); Phillip John Usher, *Errance et cohérence: Essai sur la littérature transfrontalière à la Renaissance* (Paris: Garnier, 2010); Tom Conley, *An Errant Eye: Poetry and Topography in Early Modern France* (Minneapolis: University of Minnesota Press, 2011); Louisa Mackenzie, *The Poetry of Place: Lyric, Landscape, and Ideology in Renaissance France* (Toronto: University of Toronto Press, 2011); Phillip John Usher, *L'Aède et le géographe: Poésie et espace du monde à l'époque prémoderne* (Paris: Garnier, 2018); *Early Modern Visions of Space: France and Beyond*, ed. by Dorothea Heitsch and Jeremie C. Korta (Chapel Hill: University of North Carolina Press, 2021).
25. Philippe Desan, '*Locus Narrandi*: The Place of Leisure in the Renaissance', in *Early Modern Visions of Space: France and Beyond*, ed. by Dorothea Heitsch and Jeremie C. Korta (Chapel Hill: University of North Carolina Press, 2021), pp. 405–20.
26. On the definition of place and the distinction between space and place, see Tim Creswell, *Place: An Introduction* (Chichester: Wiley-Blackwell, 2015), pp. 1–17.
27. Robert T. Tally Jr, 'Spaces of the Text: Literary Studies after the Spatial Turn', in *Spatial Literary Studies: Interdisciplinary Approaches to Space, Geography, and the Imagination*, ed. by Robert T. Tally Jr (New York: Routledge, 2020), pp. 1–10 (p. 2).
28. Martin Lewis and Kären Wigen, *The Myth of Continents: A Critique of Metageography* (Berkeley: University of California Press, 1997).
29. Ayesha Ramachandran has considered how the even larger geographical concept of 'the world' was imagined as a whole in the early modern period in *The Worldmakers: Global Imagining in Early Modern Europe* (Chicago: University of Chicago Press, 2015).
30. Terence Cave, 'Epilogue: Time's Arrow', in *Pre-Histories and Afterlives: Studies in Critical Method for Terence Cave*, ed. by Anna Holland and Richard Scholar (London: Legenda, 2009), pp. 135–46 (p. 145 n. 9).
31. Rosalie Colie, *The Resources of Kind: Genre-Theory in the Renaissance*, ed. by Barbara K. Lewalski (Berkeley: University of California Press, 1973), p. 128.
32. See Terence Cave, *Pré-histoires: Textes troublés au seuil de la modernité* (Geneva: Droz, 199 9) and *Pré-histoires*, II: *Langues étrangères et troubles économique s au XVIe siècle* (Geneva: Droz, 2001).
33. Cave argues that the early modern period is particularly relevant for the method of pre-history since it is often assumed that much of what makes us today 'modern' began to emerge at this time. See *Pré-histoires*, p. 17.
34. Anna Holland and Richard Scholar, 'Introduction', in *Pre-Histories and Afterlives*, ed. by Holland and Scholar, pp. 1–14 (p. 4).

35. For Edward Said's use of the term 'imaginative geography', see *Orientalism* (London: Penguin, 1978), pp. 49–73.
36. Said, p. 54.
37. Said, p. 54.
38. On geography, see, for instance, Derek Gregory, *Geographical Imaginations* (Oxford: Blackwell, 1994); on history, Geoffrey C. Gunn, *Imagined Geographies: The Maritime Silk Roads in World History, 100–1800* (Hong Kong: Hong Kong University Press, 2021).
39. *Isocrates*, trans. by George Norlin and Larue Van Hook, 3 vols (London: Heinemann, 1928–1945), II, trans. by George Norlin (1929), p. 401.
40. Said, p. 57.
41. Dipesh Chakrabarty, *Provincializing Europe: Postcolonial Thought and Historical Difference* (Princeton: Princeton University Press, 2007), p. 27.
42. Numa Broc, *La Géographie de la Renaissance (1420–1620)* (Paris: Bibliothèque Nationale, 1980), p. 209. Jean-Marc Besse has outlined the emergence in the sixteenth-century of the concept of a universally habitable globe in *Les Grandeurs de la Terre: Aspects du savoir géographique à la Renaissance* (Lyon: ENS Éditions, 2003).
43. For an account of the importance of Ptolemy in the geographical thought of the Renaissance see Broc, pp. 9–19.
44. Dainotto, p. 41.
45. Walter Mignolo, *The Darker Side of the Renaissance: Literacy: Territoriality, and Colonization* (Ann Arbor: University of Michigan Press, 1995).
46. Wintle, p. 29.
47. Montaigne, *Les Essais*, p. 973; De la vanité' ('Of Vanity'), *Essais*, III.9.
48. George Hoffmann, *Reforming French Culture: Satire, Spiritual Alienation, and Connection to Strangers* (Oxford: Oxford University Press, 2017), p. 123.
49. For an overview of historians' approaches to spatiality see Sebastian Conrad, *What is Global History?* (Princeton: Princeton University Press, 2016), pp. 115–40.
50. Conrad, p. 118.
51. Usher's *Errance et cohérence* underscores the roles of movement in shaping concepts of space and place.
52. It has been argued that there is a need to expand and diversify the range of sources used to study the history of the concept of Europe: Nicolas Detering, Clementina Marsico and Isabella Walser-Bürgler, 'Contesting Europe: Comparative Perspectives on Early Modern Discourses on Europe, 1400–1800 – an Introduction', in *Contesting Europe: Comparative Perspectives on Early Modern Discourses on Europe, 1400-1800*, ed. by Nicolas Detering, Clementina Marsico and Isabella Walser-Bürgler (Leiden: Brill, 2020), pp. 1–10 (pp. 2–5).

Chapter 1

Bird's-Eye Views

Chapter 45 of Rabelais' *Quart Livre* (*Fourth Book*) opens with a brief description of the once prosperous, now depleted island of the Papefigues: 'Au lendemain matin rencontrasmes l'isle des Papefigues. Lesquelz jadis estoient riches et libres, et les nommoit on Guaillardetz, pour lors estoient paouvres, mal heureux, et subjectz aux Papimanes' ('The following morning we came to the island of the Papefigues, who long ago had been rich and free and called the Guaillardetz, whereas now they were poor, miserable and subject to the Papimanes').[1] There is said to have been 'une pestilence tant horrible que pour la moitié et plus, le pays estoit resté desert, et les terres sans possesseurs' (p. 643; 'such a terrible plague that over half the land had been abandoned and left untilled'). The technique, used throughout the *Quart Livre*, of offering a picture of a particular area resembles geographical writing of the sixteenth century.[2] In 1544, eight years before the appearance of the *Quart Livre*, *La Cosmographie de Pierre Apian* (*The Cosmography of Peter Apian*) was published. This was a French translation of Gemma Frisius's edition of Peter Apian's Latin *Cosmographia* (*Cosmography*) which was first published in 1529.[3] In this work, Apian describes Europe as a sort of paradise:

> La terre excessivement fertille ha attrempance naturelle, et le ciel assez bening, non pas a postposer a aulcune aultre, d'abondance de toutes sortes de grain, vin, et arbres: mais a comparoir aulx meilleures regions, beacoup plus excellente de vertu des peuples et nations que Asie et Africque. Elle est la plus excellente et belle, et ryche, et plus ornee des villes, chasteaulx, et villaiges, toutesfois la moindre des aultres parties de la terre.[4]

> The exceedingly fertile land is naturally temperate and the climate is moderate enough for an abundance of all sorts of grain, wine and trees. The better regions, not to esteem any the less, show it to be much more excellent in the virtue of its peoples and nations than Asia and Africa. It is the most excellent and beautiful and rich, and the most decorated with towns, castles and villages, even though it is the smallest of the different parts of the world.

With a beautiful landscape and a wonderful moderate climate, the Europe represented here is in the literary tradition of *locus amoenus*.[5] It is far removed from Rabelais' isle of the wretched Papefigues. Both passages feature the adjective 'riches'/'ryche' ('rich') but, whether of people or place, for one the richness is in the present tense, whereas for the other it has gone, a memory confined to the past. Both of these texts are concerned with geography; both provide a descriptive overview of a given space; and both of these extracts, by making reference in their invocations of place to the inhabitants, link a geographical site with a community of people who live there. However, the two texts represent different approaches to geographical writing.

Apian's *Cosmographie* marshals contemporary developments in cartography and astronomy to present 'une description universelle du monde' (fol. 3^r; 'a universal description of the world'), giving the reader the illusion of a bird's-eye view looking down at the whole world. Cosmography, the word having derived from Pliny, is closely linked to geography through the title of the first Latin translation of Claudius Ptolemy's *Geographia*, namely *Cosmographia*. The genre was popular throughout the 1500s until it suffered a marked decline towards the end of the century.[6] Cosmographers had differing emphases. Apian's reflects the more mathematical and astronomical strain of cosmography, which followed Ptolemy's text in listing the lines of latitude and longitude of regions, towns and geographical features such as mountains and rivers. Although he included a map of the world and a brief description of the 'quatre parties' (fol. 1^v; 'four parts') of the world, 'Europe, Affricque, Asie, et America [*sic*]' (fol. 2^v; 'Europe, Africa, Asia and America'), his work was much less descriptive than that of Sebastian Münster.[7] Münster's German-language *Cosmographia* was first published in 1544 with detailed descriptions of the people, history, flora and fauna of all known regions of the world, and helped to popularise the descriptive approach to cosmography. He went far beyond the level of continental description to provide detail on the constituent parts of each continent, devoting three of the six books to the countries of Europe. These descriptions were accompanied by numerous woodcut maps. An expanded Latin edition was published in 1550, and the work became a bestseller with thirty-five editions in five languages by 1628.[8] The first French translation was released in 1552, the same year as the *Quart Livre*. Apian's had been the first cosmography to appear in the French vernacular and was reprinted in several editions after 1544, and it is very likely to have been read by Rabelais.[9]

Unlike these cosmographies, Rabelais' comic tale does not set about the task of describing the real world. Nonetheless, the *Quart Livre*, structured as a sea voyage to a fictional world that is depicted in some detail, is at its heart geographical. It is an imaginary, or fictive, geography in which the fictional narrative operates within a fictional geographical framework.[10] This does not mean, though, that the *Quart Livre* bears no relation to the referential world. In the opening chapters, for instance, reference is made to both the fabled North-West Passage connecting the Atlantic Ocean to the Pacific (p. 539) and to Canada (p. 540). Like the cosmographies of Apian and Münster, then, Rabelais' text is part of a wider reflection, prevalent from the middle of the century, which took stock of the globe following the voyages of discovery. It is my contention that in the *Quart Livre* Rabelais recalls the language and features of contemporary geographical writing in order to problematise its meanings and to unsettle the geographical knowledge it produces, thereby promoting doubt where cosmographies offer certainty.[11] In effect, Rabelais' imaginary geography acts as a creative engagement with the imagined geographies, the perceptions of space, that are constructed within the cosmographical genre. Therefore, an analysis of his literary text offers insight into the historical understanding of geography, specifically how geographical ideas were received and responded to.

This chapter focuses on the representations of Europe in the *Quart Livre* and the cosmographies of Apian and Münster. Reading Rabelais alongside these two works highlights how cosmographical writing disciplines and normalises the world, forcing a rigid image of Europe upon the reader. Through the medium of fiction Rabelais is able to offer a different way of seeing the world, and to explore not only the present, but also the potential futures of Europe. We shall begin by considering the imaginary geography of the *Quart Livre*, before comparing Rabelais' book with the cosmographies of Apian and Münster along three lines: first, how the two texts delimit space; second, their uses of the word 'Europe'; and third, the images of depletion and abundance in the places they describe. The cosmographies illustrate an approach to geography with which Rabelais would have been familiar.[12] They, like all works of geography, 'present their interlocutors, their listeners, or their general public with choices that cannot be made, thus diminishing their powers of judgement or response', as Tom Conley has written.[13] Through his more indirect, uncertain, speculative and reflective way of engaging with the meaning of Europe in the *Quart Livre*, we see Rabelais reclaiming his power of response and reimagining the imagined geography of the continent.

Rabelais' Imaginary Geography

What is the world described in Rabelais' *Quart Livre*? Where is it? Frank Lestringant argues that what begins as a voyage to the west, marked by references to Canada and the North-West Passage (but no other specific references to the New World), actually comes to resemble a journey around the Mediterranean.[14] He labels the *Quart Livre* as a 'fiction en archipel' (an 'archipelagic fiction') and reads it as a fictional example of the *isolario* genre, a book of maps and descriptions of islands which originated as a guide for travellers in the Mediterranean.[15] Mireille Huchon has highlighted the influence of the *Orphic Argonautica*, suggesting that the Pantagruelists travel in the opposite direction to the Argonauts after securing the Golden Fleece, who, in the *Orphic Argonautica*, travel the River Tanais northwards to the Arctic Ocean and then return to Crete via the Straits of Gibraltar and the Mediterranean.[16] In effect, the Argonauts trace an outline around Europe. By reflecting this voyage, Huchon suggests, the Pantagruelists glorify the French monarchy, Henri II having been depicted as the pilot of the Argonauts on the triumphal arch for his 1549 entry into Paris.[17]

The question of the geography of the *Quart Livre* sits within debates about the text's narrative structure and degrees of transparency and ambiguity in the whole Rabelaisian oeuvre. In labelling the text an 'archipelagic fiction', Lestringant argues that the *Quart Livre* has a loose narrative coherence as emphasis is placed on topographical descriptions of individual islands at the expense of a global and unified perspective.[18] His reading followed a line of inquiry initiated by Terence Cave's *The Cornucopian Text*, which encouraged a hermeneutics of ambiguity, highlighting the role of narrative fragmentation and plurivocality in a constant deferral of meaning.[19] On the other hand, Michael Screech's allegorical readings argued for a more unequivocal Evangelical Humanist agenda in Rabelais' work and have encouraged scholars to see a clear structure in the *Quart Livre*.[20] Edwin Duval, for instance, has insisted on a 'coherent epic design' focused on the theme of *caritas*, embodied in the character of Pantagruel and defined against the *anticaritas* manifested in each island.[21]

I argue that the incoherence of the world of the *Quart Livre* is in itself significant and meaningful. This approach to the work has been influenced by attempts to bridge the gap between contentions of transparency and ambiguity through locating meaning in the discontinuities of Rabelais' writing, which oblige readers to participate actively in the construction of meaning.[22] The plurality of the *Quart Livre* enacts the plurality of the chaotic and divided world described. Attempts to find meaning, or the absence of meaning, in the text have relied on sequential readings of the work. Rather than interpreting the islands sequentially as they appear in the text, it would be more fruitful to understand them simultaneously. As chaotic as the world of the *Quart Livre* can seem, it is an interconnected world where characters travel between islands.[23] It is not only the Pantagruelists who move from island to island; the Papimanes and Bringuenarilles are described as journeying back and forth. Note the temporal marker 'jadis' ('long ago') used in the first quotation included in this chapter: that island and the many others that are similarly described with such a marker are explicitly presented as having a past before the arrival of the Pantagruelists and thus, presumably, a future. That is to say, within the fictional world of the text, the islands of the *Quart Livre* exist independently of the main characters.[24] It is a fractured yet nonetheless coherent world.

By describing more than one place, the *Quart Livre* offers a fictional cosmography. It should therefore be read in the same way as Lestringant reads André Thevet's *Les Singularitez de la France antarctique* (1557): that is, as a literary hybrid which offers an account of a voyage that, describing a wide range of places, reads like a cosmography, even though it does not describe the whole world.[25] The incompleteness of the *Quart Livre* makes Rabelais' imaginary geography consciously no more than suggestive; it does not purport to deal with the complexities of the whole world. Instead, its focus is on issues facing France and France's relations with neighbouring countries in Europe. The world of the *Quart Livre* is not, unlike Thomas More's Utopia, an imaginary location in the New World. It is not incommensurable otherness that the heroes meet when they land on each island, but sameness seen as through a distorting mirror, like the islanders of Ennasin who 'ressemblent aux Poictevins rouges, exceptez que tous homes, femmes, et petitz enfans ont le nez en figure d'un as de treuffles' (p. 556; 'resemble red-faced Poitevins, except that all men, women and children have a nose shaped like an ace of clubs').[26] Where the recognisable differences are matters of belief and practice, Rabelais is raising contemporary problems. In this way, the world of the *Quart Livre* is an alternative Old World, not a new and separate world.[27] This imaginary geography, occupying a liminal space between reality and imagination, invites reflection and interpretation. When read geographically, Rabelais' exaggerated portrayal of aspects of his culture, of extremists who cannot be reconciled with one another, has implications for the conception of boundaries and divisions in society, as this chapter will show.

Drawing Boundaries

A major concern in cosmographical writing is the delimitation of geographical space. The boundaries drawn within Apian's *Cosmographie* privilege the unity and coherence of Europe, distinguishing it from the other three parts of the world as follows: 'Du coste d'occident [Europe] est terminee de l'oceane Atlantique. Devers Septentrion de l'oceane Britannicque et Germanicque grande, de la partie opposite est enclose de la mer Mediterraine. Devers Orient a le fleuve Tanais' (fol. 30ᵛ; 'Europe ends at the western coast at the Atlantic Ocean; towards the north at the North Sea, with the opposite side enclosed by the Mediterranean Sea; towards the east at the river Tanais'). With no obvious spatial marker – unlike the seas to the north, south and west – the eastern frontier of the continent is more of a cultural construct. Here it is presented, as it had conventionally been since the time of the ancient Greeks, as the 'fleuve Tanais' ('river Tanais'), the modern-day Don River, which flows through what is now the Russian Federation. The frontier was regarded as having a deep historical consistency and consequently remained unchanged in the collective imaginary, in spite of political developments such as the Ottoman advance into the space conceptualised as Europe. Indeed, the boundary is not only insisted upon in writing but also visually emphasised in the map of the world, the sole map in the *Cosmographie*. Here, the division between Europe and Asia is exaggerated, the Tanais widened, so that in the map the two continents are barely connected, sharing only what looks like a slender corridor of land. Far from a mere vehicle for the diffusion of information, this map, like all maps, has the power to shape the viewer's perception. Whether consciously or unconsciously, by selecting specific information to include and presenting a certain abstraction of the landscape, cartographers discipline the world, determining what knowledge about it is made available.[28] The knowledge constructed in Apian's *Cosmographie* by the text and the accompanying map is that of Europe as a delimited unity. Internal boundaries are not represented. Instead, the towns and cities of the continent are listed alphabetically alongside their respective coordinates of latitude and longitude. Countries are not located precisely in space. Instead, it is the four continents that act as the organising principle of the text.

Countries and regions have a prominent role in the structure of Münster's more descriptive *Cosmographia*, and these are grouped together according to the continents. Europe and its constituent countries are described first, then Asia and finally Africa. Unlike Apian, Münster does not use the word 'America' or refer to America as a fourth continent, instead referring to 'novae illae insulae nostro aevo in Oceano inventae, quas novum appellant orbem' ('those new islands in the Ocean discovered in our age, which are called the new world').[29] Like Apian, though, he includes a map of the world; this exaggerates Europe's separation from Asia and is said to show 'quomodo natura rei tres praecipuae eius partes, Europa, Africa et Asia ad invicem discriminentur' ('how the three main parts of it, Europe, Africa and Asia, are naturally distinguished from one another'). A map of each continent is included, as well as maps of individual countries, which serve to reinforce the geographical borders between places that structure a huge text of 1,233 pages.

Rabelais uses the medium of fiction to rethink the boundaries of the world. He gives geographical form to the issues he raises, shaping boundaries according to cultural and ideological divisions in an imaginative drama of delimitation. Take the lands of the Papefigues and of the Papimanes: the latter, as their name suggests, are obsessed with the pope, whereas the former are characterised by one man who 'feist la figue' ('signed the fig') at a portrait of the pope, which is a rude hand gesture and a 'signe de contempnement et derision manifeste' (p. 642; 'sign of clear contempt and derision'). These opposing religious ideas form the basis of two separate communities inhabiting two separate islands. They would be familiar to readers as representing opposing religious communities in France and Europe more widely, given that the confessional divides of the Reformation did not align with the political boundaries of countries and led to conflicts within and outside France. The island form in the *Quart Livre* stands as a metaphor for the communities living there: their frontiers are fixed, inelastic; the islands are cut off from one another, isolated, separated by the waters between them, and, in the case of the Papimanes and the Papefigues, hostile to one another. As the Pantagruelists journey through the sea of islands, they create for the reader a vision of a reimagined, fractured world, one that is composed of disparate and seemingly irreconcilable communities. The borders between the islands are not ones that can be seen on a map but are rather the edges of religious, political and cultural ideas.

What the characters of the *Quart Livre* travel through, then, as they sail from island to island is a set of ideas about the potential futures of the continent, for each island constitutes a different image of what Europe might become. Though the *Quart Livre* is written in French and France is a reference point throughout, the narrative's concerns are wider and include France's foreign relations. Chapter 53, for instance, is about the transfer of gold from France to Rome. The Papimanes represent a satirical vision of unchecked extremist Catholicism, whether in France or elsewhere in Christian Europe. The use of the island form to explore such political issues would have been familiar to readers of More's *Utopia*, a connection to the *Quart Livre* which is strengthened by the travellers' first port of call at Medamothi, 'nowhere' in Greek, a name alluding to More's famous no-place of 1516.[30] The mode of thinking in Rabelais' work is not utopian, however. The Pantagruelists sail beyond Medamothi, beyond nowhere, so that the rest of the narrative takes place *somewhere*, namely, in a reimagined Europe. By moving beyond Medamothi, Rabelais indicates that his book is a different way of thinking about community: the world of the *Quart Livre* does not represent the ideal that Utopia does.

The fictionality of the *Quart Livre* is therefore a way of thinking through the problems and challenges facing society. The boundaries that Rabelais constructs challenge the geographical knowledge presented in cosmographical writing. His conceptual redrawing of the map of Europe indicates that cosmography – a method of delimiting space and organising knowledge – may not be the best way to represent society and human experience or to explore problems. The fictional form is a marker of his intellectual uncertainties and a style which both allows him to try out ideas non-dogmatically and to encourage his readers to think about the political issue of boundaries. In what follows, I argue that Rabelais' uses of geographical discourse within a fictional framework alert the reader to doubt the assertions of cosmographers and the knowledge they produce.[31]

The Uses of the Word 'Europe'

The word 'Europe' appears infrequently in Rabelais' oeuvre, twice in the *Tiers Livre* and not at all in either *Pantagruel* or *Gargantua*. The sole instance of the word 'Europe' in the *Quart Livre* occurs in chapter 5 when the Pantagruelists happen upon a boat of merchants heading in the opposite direction, one of whom, Dindenault, insults Panurge immediately upon seeing him, branding him a cuckold. Panurge counters with a jibe about the merchant's nose. Dindenault then launches into praise of his wife and an invective against Panurge in a paragraph (as marked in the 1552 edition of the text):

> Ouy vrayement, respondit le marchant, je le suys [marié]: et ne vouldrois ne l'estre pour toutes les lunettes d'Europe: non pour toutes les beziles d'Afrique. Car j'ay une des plus belles, plus advenentes, plus honestes, plus prudes femmes en mariage, qui soit en tout le pays de Xantonge: et n'en desplaise aux aultres. Je luy porte de mon voyage une belle et de unze poulsées longue branche de Coural rouge, pour ses estrenes. Qu'en as-tu à faire?

Dequoy te meslez tu? Qui es tu? Dont es tu? O Lunettier de l'Antichrist, responds si tu es de Dieu. (p. 549)

Yes indeed,' replied the merchant, 'I am married and would not have it otherwise for all the glasses in Europe, nor for all the spectacles in Africa. Because I have one of the most beautiful, most comely, most honourable and most proper wives in all the land of Saintonge; no offence to the others. I'm bringing home from my voyage a lovely eleven-inch red coral stump as a present for her. What's that got to do with you? Why are you meddling in such matters? Who are you? Where do you come from? You goggle-man of the Antichrist, answer me if you belong to God.'

In this bawdy passage there is a close emphasis on place. The very questions Dindenault poses – 'Qui es tu?' ('Who are you?') and 'Dont es tu?' ('Where do you come from?') – interrogate the nature of Panurge's identity and origin. It is within this context that the word 'Europe' is situated, deployed alongside other markers of place within a semantic field of geography. Yet at the same time it is undermined as a potential point of origin, or homeland, since it is used with hyperbole as an abstract concept, in the same manner as the word 'Africa', to designate a huge area, one unknown to the personal experience of the merchant. He is on safer ground with his use of the province of Saintonge to underline the qualities of his wife. It is used in a much more concrete fashion, born of a sense of direct involvement with the region. The term 'Europe' is empty of meaning beyond a spatial designation of a large expanse.

The tone of the passage offers an indirect reflection on the state of both nationhood and Europe. Dindenault's use of 'Antichrist' alludes to the religious strife of the Reformation which saw confessional groups accuse their enemies of heresy and which divided people in France and across the continent. Panurge and Dindenault may be kinsmen, both coming from France and speaking the same language, but their whole interaction is deeply antagonistic from the start. Given that Panurge speaks French, Dindenault presumably knows he comes from France, yet he still asks him where he is from, indicating that a more localised identity carries more significance. Like Europe, France may be too big a conceptual entity to be personally meaningful. Those questions about Panurge's identity that Dindenault poses, 'Qui es tu?' and 'Dont es tu?', are similar to those Pantagruel asks Panurge when they meet for the first time in *Pantagruel* (1532), although the mood is warm rather than hostile:

Doncques dist Pantagruel, racomptez nous quel est vostre nom, et dont vous venez. Car par foy je vous ay ja prins en amour si grand que si vous condescendez à mon vouloir, vous ne bougerez jamais de ma compaignie, et vous et moy ferons un nouveau pair d'amitié telle que feut entre Enée et Achates. (p. 249)

> So, said Pantagruel, tell us your name and where you are from. For by my faith I'm taken with so great an affection for you that if you grant my wish, you'll never move from my side, and you and I shall make a new paragon of friendship resembling that of Aeneas and Achates.

In this way, the *Quart Livre* is much more pessimistic about community and social relations than the earlier *Pantagruel*. The sole instance of the word 'Europe' in the *Quart Livre* may be used only as a marker of vastness, but its appearance is haunted by the spectre of contemporary conflict that is raised when the word appears.

In contrast, the word 'Europe' in Apian's *Cosmographie* is endowed with positive sentiment, as we saw above in the description of the fecundity of the continent. The term does have a spatial designation, one that is precisely defined, but it goes further than the *Quart Livre* by inscribing further meaning into the delimited space. The people of that land are said to be 'beaucop plus excellente de vertu des peuples et nations que Asie et Africque' (fol. 30^v; 'much more excellent in the virtue of its people and nations than Asia and Africa'), the strengths described relative to Asia and Africa, the comparison rendering Europe better than, not equal to, other continents. Europe, then, equates to superiority. Europe's landscape too is hailed as 'plus ornee des villes, chasteaulx, et villaiges' (fol. 30^v; 'the most decorated with towns, castles and villages'), the verb 'orner' here connoting artifice and beauty. A positive affective response to the settlements of Europe is thus written into Apian's *Cosmographie*. Likewise in Münster's *Cosmographia* the word 'Europe' denotes superiority vis-à-vis the rest of the world in terms of its people and environment. Münster writes:

> Est itaque Europa regio reliquis orbis partibus minor, sed populosissima, fertilissima atque cultissima [...] Nam in Europa non inveniuntur tam vastae solitudines, tam steriles arenae et tam ingens calor omnia exurens ut in Africa. Nullus est locus aut regio in Europa tam abiecta, in qua homines sibi non fecerint mansiones, et ubi vitae necessaria non commode sibi parare queant. (p. 40)

> So Europe is a smaller area of the world than the other parts, but the most populous, the most fertile and the most cultivated [...] For in Europe there are not found wastelands so empty, deserts so barren and heat so powerful as to burn everything as there are in Africa. There is no place or region in Europe so abandoned, in which people do not build homes for themselves, and in which they cannot conveniently acquire the necessities of life for themselves.

The terms by which Münster judges the different continents parallel those of Apian. Europe has a greater degree of civility: its fertility has enabled the development of agriculture and human life to flourish.

In both cosmographies the superiority of Europe is emphasised by the descriptions of the savagery – the lack of civility – in the rest of the world. Like Münster, Apian comments on the aridity of Africa, noting that there are regions 'ou qu'il ne pluyt aulcunement' ('where it doesn't rain at all') and others where there are 'quasi nulz hommes, mais plus demisauvaiges' (fol. 31ᵛ; 'almost no people, but more half-savages'). Asia, while acknowledged as 'fertille, et tempree' (fol. 31ᵛ; 'fertile and temperate'), is said to have a diversity that is not credited to Europe and to be home to 'diverses et merveilleuses facons de gens' (fol. 31ᵛ; 'diverse and marvellous forms of people'), some of whom 'mengent chair humaine' (fol. 32ʳ; 'eat human flesh'). Both Münster and Apian include the claim that cannibalism took place in the New World.[32] Apian writes: 'En ceste les habitans vont quasi tout nudz, sont Antropophages, c'est a dire, mengeans hommes, trescruelz' (fol. 32ʳ; 'Here the inhabitants go about almost completely naked, are Anthropophages, that is, maneaters, very cruel'). Here all the people of the New World are conflated into one particular type, the cannibal, and are condemned for their cruelty. Conflation and generalisation are the strategies deployed to paint a picture of Europe as a geographical area exceeding the other continents in terms of the qualities of the people and the place. Although one of Frisius's original additions to the translation is to note that Peru is 'ornee merveilleusement de fleuves, montaignes, et bois, vous la diries ung paradis terrestre' (fol. 32ᵛ; 'marvellously decorated with rivers, mountains and woods so that you would call it a terrestrial paradise'), the overall negative view of America is retained in the text. Frisius goes on to stress that the people of Peru 'ne cognoissent pas Jesu Christ' ('do not know Jesus Christ') and so 'on doibt labourer a tout engin, payne, et diligence' ('we must work with all craft, necessity and speed') to rectify this (fol. 32ᵛ). In other words, the world can be organised into a cultural hierarchy based on levels of civility with Europe at the summit.[33]

The differing geographies of Rabelais on the one hand and Apian and Münster on the other indicate that 'Europe' is a word whose meaning was contested. The cultural and political charge it carries in the cosmographies is lacking in Rabelais' work. The fact that the term is used only once in the *Quart Livre* may entail a dismissal of the kinds of ideas denoted by the word as used by Apian, Münster and others. Indeed, the work frequently warns its readers against the effacement of complexity and nuance, of which Apian's definition of the continent can be considered an example. In the Papimanes scene we see how words are sites of conflict: 'Dieu' ('God') is a locus of disagreement about religious interpretation between the Pantagruelists and the Papimanes; the Papimane bishop Homenaz interrupts Rhizotome's narration to challenge his use of the word, asking 'du quel Dieu entendez vous?' (p. 662; 'which God do you mean?') as he recognises a god in heaven and the pope as God on earth, whereas for the Pantagruelists there can only be one God and so the word holds different meaning for them. We turn now to consider how the different fictional islands created by Rabelais offer a reflection on the referential world.

Images of Depletion: The Old World in Time

In spite of the almost complete absence of the word 'Europe', the Christian world beyond the boundaries of France is a concern in the *Quart Livre*. It is the recognisability of the world of the text that allows for a creative and critical engagement with the culture and society of the Old World of Europe. Rabelais uses the medium of fictional geography as a form of inquiry which explores, and encourages the reader to reflect on, the world in a manner that conventional geographical writing does not. This kind of speculative thinking is enhanced by the episodic structure of Rabelais' text, since the various island communities open up various perspectives on the world. Each time the characters set foot on land they see the world from a different position; the world looks different from the island of the Papefigues from how it does from the island of the Papimanes. Often an island is described as having suffered a loss, as for example in the quotation with which this chapter opened. The adverb 'jadis' adds a temporal dimension to Rabelais' geographical description, drawing the reader's attention to change that is invariably of a negative nature. This section features close readings of the images of change and depletion within three scenes in the *Quart Livre*: the Papefigues, the island of Ruach and the island of the Macraeons. These episodes problematise notions that other thinkers use to define Europe – unity, Christianity, the classical heritage – and they reveal uncertainties about conflict, finance, decline and subjugation that are effaced in cosmographical writing.

The Papefigues chapters of the *Quart Livre* (45–47) are invariably paired with those concerning the Papimanes (chapters 48–54), since the mutual hostility between the two groups of islanders resulted in the devastation of the Guaillardetz. The Pantagruelists land on the isle of the Papefigues, where they see the ruined land and hear that it was caused by the Papimane invasion, a response to a rude gesture towards the papal portrait by one of the Guaillardetz. The group then travel to the island of the pope-worshipping Papimanes, where they witness their idolatry. The scenes tend to be understood within the context of

Henri II's conflict with the papacy, and most commentators agree with Screech, following Raymond Lebègue, that the episode represents the massacre of the Vaudois Protestants in 1545.[34] For this study, the identity of the Papefigues is not under question. Indeed, it is the fictionality of the Papefigues, the lack of specificity as to whom they might represent, which allows Rabelais' method of inquiry. The Papefigues occupy three temporal phases at once: they can stand for past events, such as the Vaudois massacre; they can communicate present fears (in 1552) about violent intolerance; and they can warn about what the future might look like. In adopting geographical discourse to express anxieties about religious conflicts, Rabelais undermines the idyllic view of Europe epitomised in Apian's *Cosmographie*, insisting upon violence and loss.

The opening description of the island of the Papefigues establishes the dismal mood of the place: 'jadis estoient riches et libres, et les nommoit on Guaillardetz, pour lors estoient paouvres, mal heureux, et subjectz aux Papimanes' (p. 642; 'long ago they had been rich and free and called the Guaillardetz, whereas now they were poor, miserable and subject to the Papimanes'). Where once they were free, the people are now subject to the Papimanes; where once they were rich, now they are poor, economic resources having been transferred to the occupying power. The motivation for the attack is said to have been ideological rather than economic: the Papimanes wage war on religious grounds, avenging the insulting gesture made by one of the Guaillardetz towards the portrait of the pope. The injustice of the invasion is expressed by the emphasis on the singularity of the provocative act, 'L'un d'eulx [...] feist la figue' (p. 642; 'One of them [...] signed the fig'), which contrasts with the response of the Papimanes who 'se mirent *tous* en armes, surprindrent, saccaigerent, et ruinerent *toute* l'isle des Guaillardetz' (p. 642, my emphasis; '*all* took up arms and surprised, pillaged and ruined *the whole* island of the Guaillardetz'). All of them paying for the actions of one, the Guaillardetz '[f]eurent faicts esclaves et tributaires et leurs feut imposé nom de Papefigues' (p. 643; 'were made slaves and tributaries, and the name Papefigues was imposed on them').

The scene has echoes of the contemporary discovery and conquest of the New World. The religious imperatives of the victorious army, the depletion of the occupied territory, the enslavement of the conquered peoples and the renaming of them by the Papimanes all call to mind the Spanish and Portuguese exploits in America and the unsuccessful endeavours of the French in Canada, not least because the *Quart Livre* in some respects resembles an account of a voyage to the west. However, the Papefigues are not a simple proxy for New World peoples since they are, like the Papimanes, Christians of a sort. Thus, Rabelais reimagines the dynamics of overseas conquest as the domination of one Christian confession by another. The point is made explicit and given a national dimension in chapter 53, entitled 'Comment par la vertus des Decretales est l'or subtilement tiré de France en Rome' ('How by virtue of the Decretals gold is subtly extracted from France into Rome'), in which it is said that more than four hundred thousand ducats are taken from France to Rome each year (p. 662). A parallel is thereby created between the island of the Papefigues and the kingdom of France which depicts France as a tributary of Rome, signalling an anxiety about French nationhood and relations with the papacy. Of 'nos derniers Papes' ('our last popes'), Panurge says, 'tout l'empire Christian estant en paix et silence, eulx seulz guerre faire felonne et trescruelle' (p. 655; 'all the Christian world being in peace and quiet, they alone waged pitiless and most cruel wars'), thereby damning the pope as a warmonger who would destroy the Christian commonwealth.

The switch in terms of representation from the pope as the head of Christendom to the pope as the head of an exploitative foreign power gives the spiritual considerations of the *Quart Livre* a national, political and economic edge. There was, of course, the precedent of the Church of England breaking with Rome. The French crown's relations with the papacy hit a low during the Gallican Crisis of 1551, when Henri II withdrew French cardinals and diplomats from the Vatican and considered establishing an independent Gallican church.[35] In drawing on these themes, Rabelais offers a pessimistic view of the Old World, one far removed from the *locus amoenus* of Apian's description of Europe. That said, the temporal marker 'jadis' confines the idyll to the past only for the Papefigues, not for the Papimanes. The contrast between the two groups is brought out at the start of chapter 48 when the Pantagruelists travel from one island to the other: 'Laissans l'isle desolée des Papefigues navigasmes par un jour en sereneité et tout plaisir, quand à nostre veue se offrit la benoiste isle des Papimanes' (p. 649; 'Leaving the desolated island of the Papefigues we sailed for a day in serenity and great delight until the blessed island of the Papimanes came into our sights'). Although the adjective 'benoiste' ('blessed') is used ironically, it serves additionally to flag that the Papimanes have not suffered economic depletion as their religious enemies have. The unity seen in Apian's strict delimitation of Europe is not matched in the divided world of the *Quart Livre*. Rabelais presents Christian communities whose political enemies are fellow Christians and who are not united by religion but divided by economic exploitation.

Yet the Christian world as it is found in the *Quart Livre* is not only fractured but also reduced. Homenaz compresses Christianity into his own pope-worshipping doctrine which considers the papal decretals sacred: he declares, 'qui est ce (en conscience) qui a estably, confirmé, authorisé ces belles religions, des quelles en tout endroictz voyez la Christianté ornée, decorée, illustrée, comme est le firmament de ses claires estoilles? Dives Decretales' (p. 664; 'what was it (on your conscience) that established, ratified and authorised those great religious houses that you see everywhere gracing, adorning and dignifying Christendom, like the shining stars in the sky? The most holy Decretals'). His term of reference is 'Christendom' and it is praised for its religious orders, the glories of which are attributed to the decretals, that is, papal decrees. The Papimanes' invasion of the island of the Papefigues was an attempt to impose their narrow pope-worshipping definition of Christianity on another community. Whereas contemporary travel accounts frame the voyages they describe as missions to spread Christianity, the movement of the Papimanes does not expand Christendom but rather contracts it, depleting one confessional grouping at the expense of another.

The image of a fractured and compressed Christendom communicates anxieties about the future of Rabelais' world. Homenaz is not content with the destruction of the Guaillardetz and preaches violent intolerance of other denominations: 'O lors paix obstinée infringible en l'Univers: cessation de guerres, pilleries, anguaries, briguanderies, assassinemens: exceptez contre les Hereticques, et rebelles mauldictz' (pp. 657–58; 'Then there will be constant inviolable peace in the universe: an end to wars, pillaging, drudgery, robbing, killing – except for the heretics and accursed rebels'). The temporal marker 'lors' ('then') indicates that the bishop of the Papimanes is here offering a blueprint for the future. Of Homenaz's vision of Christianity Duval has written: 'His utopia is a community not of tolerant inclusion but of terrorist exclusion and fratricide, a unity based not on the transcendence of differences but on the elimination of all difference.'[36]

Looking at the reimagined Old World of the *Quart Livre*, the reader encounters an interpretation of the state of Christendom in the middle of the sixteenth century. The antagonism of the Papimanes and the Papefigues allows the reader to view the fictional world from three different positions. From the island of the Papefigues it seems to be a much more limited and dangerous world than it did previously. The view from the isle of the Papimanes is more confident yet paranoid at the same time, plagued by the spectre of religious enemies to be crushed. By moving through this world, the Pantagruelists provide a third, cosmographical, perspective: to them it is a Christian world, fractured by different confessional and national groupings. The diverse company that travels with Pantagruel provides a model of a pluralistic community whose members stay together in spite of disagreements.[37] Homenaz's outlook, by contrast, is much more reduced; his religious belief is an exclusionary vision of the future. In this way, the Papefigues embody the fear that religious intolerance will continue to harden and that diversity will be violently quashed. The comedy of the *Quart Livre* balances the gloom, offering a humorous way of thinking about people's worries. The reader laughs at the ludicrous Homenaz and, in doing so, dismisses his extremist attitude and gets some catharsis for the very real fears about the future of Christendom that a mid-sixteenth-century reader would have had.

Elsewhere in the *Quart Livre* an image of depletion is used to explore the relationship of the classical past to the present day. Following a storm, the Pantagruelists land on an island whose aged inhabitants live among the ruins of antiquity and speak Ionic Greek. The old Macrobe's belief that the storm was caused by the death of a 'hero' provokes a discussion of this subject which progresses through an account of the death of Guillaume du Bellay, Rabelais' protector, to Pantagruel's interpretation of Plutarch's account of the death of Pan. Of the Macraeons episode it is the discourse around the death of heroes, and the Pan story in particular, that has received the most critical attention.[38] My focus here is on the significance of the topographical descriptions of the island. They function to raise contemporary political and financial concerns, and to meditate on the relevance of the classical past to the present and the future.

Like the Papefigues, the Macraeons dwell on an impoverished island, long past its best. The vocabulary of Rabelais makes explicit the link between the two: the isle of the Macraeons was 'jadis riche, frequente, opulente, marchande, populeuse et subjecte au dominateur de Bretaigne. Maintenant par laps de temps et sus la declination du monde, paouvre et deserte' (p. 599; 'long ago rich, frequented, wealthy, mercantile, populous and subject to the ruler of Britain. Now, over the course of time and upon the waning of the world, poor and abandoned'). Note once again the word 'jadis', which appears in the description of the island of the Papefigues, and note the further stress placed on change and time by the phrase 'par laps de temps' ('over the course of time'). Other lexical items ensure a parallel between the islands of the Macraeons and that of the Papefigues: the Papefigues are now 'paouvres' ('poor'), and their once-rich island has become deserted. The difference lies in the cause and speed of decline. The Papefigues, as we saw, had fallen victim to an invasion, whereas there is no such single and sudden factor in the degeneration of the island of the Macraeons but rather a slow and natural process ('par laps de temps'). Ruins of the past stand as a testament to the formerly lively culture of the Macraeons:

> par la forest umbrageuse et deserte descouvrit plusieurs vieulx temples ruinez, plusieurs obelisces, Pyramides, monumens, et sepulchres antiques, avecques inscriptions et epitaphes divers. Les uns en letres Hieroglyphicques, les aultres en languaige Ionicque, les aultres en langue Arabicque, Agarene, Sclavonicque, et aultres. (p. 598)
>
> discovered in the shady and deserted forest were several old, ruined temples, several obelisks, pyramids, monuments and ancient tombs with various inscriptions and epitaphs, some in hieroglyphics, others in the Ionic language, others in Arabic, Hagarene, Slavonic and other languages.

With pyramids, hieroglyphics and ancient inscriptions, the emphasis here is firmly on the classical world. Yet all of these constructions are associated with death, thereby signalling the end of antiquity.[39] Thus, even though this vision of the classical past includes a rich diversity of civilisations, from the Arabic to the Slavonic, there is no hope for the future of the island. The ruins are ruins, not the symbols of a renascent classical culture and not the seeds of growth of something new.

The theme of depletion is expanded during the Macraeons episode to incorporate the referential world directly. As the characters discuss the death of 'heroes', Pantagruel says of 'ces ames nobles et insignes' ('these noble and distinguished souls'):

> sus l'heure de leur discession, communement adviennent par les isles et continent grands troublemens en l'air, tenebres, fouldres, gresles: en terre concussions, tremblemens, estonnemens: en mer fortunal et tempeste, avecques lamentations des peuples, mutations des religions, transpors des Royaulmes, et eversions des Republicques. (p. 600)
>
> upon the hour of their decease, great disturbances in the heavens – darkness, thunder and hail – commonly befall the islands and mainland; with tremors, earthquakes and agitations on land, a storm and tempest at sea, and lamentations by the people, changes of religion, removals of kings and overthrows of republics.

Here, as in other instances of change, there is a temporal marker, 'sus l'heure' ('upon the hour'). Epistemon cites Guillaume du Bellay, the seigneur de Langey, as one such example of a death that caused such devastating consequences: 'lequel vivant, France estoit en telle felicité, que tout le monde avoit sus elle envie, tout le monde se y rallioit, tout le monde la redoubtoit. Soubdain aprés son trespas elle a esté en mespris de tout le monde bien longuement' (p. 600; 'while alive, France was in such prosperity that the whole world envied her, the whole world made peace with her, the whole world feared her. Soon after his death, and for so long now, the whole world has despised her'). A marker of time, 'Soubdain', is used once again here to emphasise change. Langey, a diplomat associated with the policy of religious toleration and moderation at the court of François I, died in 1543. His time on earth is made to coincide with the collective time of the destiny of France.[40] The image presented of the country is one of sudden decline, of a once-flourishing community now suffering – a motif found throughout the *Quart Livre*. The repetition of 'monde' ('world') places emphasis on the shift in France's relation to the rest of the world from an object of awe to an object of scorn. This view of the world is not the static, atemporal unity of the Europe represented in the cosmographical descriptions of Apian and Münster. France has a particular place, yet it is subject to transience: past glories have not lasted forever; just one person can alter the destiny of the country. In the *Quart Livre*, then, the concerns of the past and the present fold into anxieties about the future.

The concern of Apian's *Cosmographie*, by contrast, is firmly with the present. The presence of antiquity in the text is limited to a brief account of the continent's mythological name: 'Europe (la premiere partie du monde) est appellee de la fille de Agenor Roy des Pheniciens, laquelle en Asie aymee de Juppiter fut transportee en Crete' (fol. 30ᵛ; 'Europe (the first part of the world) is named after the Phoenician king Agenor's daughter, who, loved by Jupiter, was taken from Asia to Crete'). That said, both Apian and Münster rely on ancient sources, Ptolemy most of all, to underpin their cosmographical projects.[41] Rabelais' dialogue with the ancient world, and with the question of time and change, is much more complex. While depletion can occur suddenly or quickly, the *Quart Livre* offers little hope that it can be reversed. The classical world as it is presented in the isle of the Macraeons is far removed from the Renaissance dream of the restoration of antiquity. It paints a picture of a formerly lively classical culture reduced to one sparsely populated island, antiquity not reborn, but dwindled, dying, preserved only in fossilised form. The Pantagruelists turn their back on it, quite literally, by sailing away. As Christian unity disintegrates, it is not possible to retreat to the classical heritage as a utopian, unifying ideal. Those in the Old World need to search for a new vision, a new narrative to understand themselves. This is precisely what the voyagers do, sailing away towards more islands and more questions about the past, the present and the future.

Further images of depletion are to be found on the island of Ruach (chapters 43 and 44), where the inhabitants live on wind alone, an existence made difficult by the annual visit of the giant Bringuenarilles to devour their windmills. The reader first hears of Bringuenarilles in chapter 17 when Pantagruel's company land at the islands of Thohu and Bohu to be told of a giant who recently died from choking on a knob of butter. The Ruachites are generally considered within the context of the theme of moderation introduced in the prologue to the *Quart Livre*; they are monomaniacs, not moderate at all.[42] Bringuenarilles is often regarded as introducing the theme of death, which then predominates throughout the following scenes (the storm and the narration of the death of Guillaume du Bellay), since the tale of the giant triggers the narrator to offer a catalogue of bizarre deaths.[43] Here we will focus on life, on the giant's impact on the living world of Rabelais' text, and consider Bringuenarilles and Ruach together. Jeanneret has considered the two as antagonists in a 'guerre des ventres' ('war of stomachs') that links the islands and offers some structure to the journey, but their 'guerre' is about more than food; it is about economics more widely, a competition for resources responsible for the images of depletion on the isle of Ruach.[44] The scenes open up additional perspectives on the nature of conflict, dramatising non-ideological clashes and struggles within an island community, in an altogether pessimistic view of the future.

The vocabulary used to describe the isle of Ruach links this episode to those others in the *Quart Livre* that depict depleted communities. For the islanders, the arrival of Bringuenarilles is said to be 'une annuelle calamité bien grande et dommaigeable' ('a harmful and mighty annual calamity') which provokes 'grande misere' (pp. 640–41; 'great misery'). The words 'calamité' and 'misere' are both used also in relation to the Papefigues. Thus, the impact of the movement of Bringuenarilles to Ruach parallels that of the Papimanes to the island of the Papefigues. The peculiarities of the two scenes are, however, as notable as the similarities. The hardship on Ruach comes about because the giant goes there 'par le conseil de ses medicins' (p. 641; 'on the advice of his doctors'), since windmills, which he needs to survive, are in short supply where he lives (p. 578). Unlike the Papimanes, Bringuenarilles does not travel in order to subjugate a people; he leaves once he has eaten his fill, wishing to satisfy his appetite, not to impose his values. The windmill-eating giant and the Ruachites are not ideological enemies, but conflict emerges between them because of their needs and the resulting competition for resources. In this 'war of stomachs' the islanders, for self-defence, have filled their windmills with chickens so as to harm the insides of Bringuenarilles (p. 641), an act of violent conflict to which they were driven by economic desperation.

In addition to the conflicts between rival communities, these scenes draw attention to tensions within islands. Bringuenarilles must cause problems for those with whom he lives on the island of Thohu: 'le grand geant avoit toutes les paelles, paellons, chauldrons, coquasses, lichefretes, et marmites du pays avallé, en faulte de moulins à vent, des quelz ordinairement il se paissoit' (p 578; 'the great giant had swallowed all the shovels, skillets, cauldrons, kettles, pans and pots in the land on account of the scarcity of windmills, with which he ordinarily contented himself'). The adjective 'toutes' ('all') is the critical word in this quotation, indicating that there are no more pots at all remaining on the isles and thereby raising the question of how the inhabitants will be able to cook.[45]

In Ruach, too, there is competition for resources; during the short time they are there the Pantagruelists see and hear about such conflicts. It is an island of unequal wealth distribution: 'Le peuple commun pour soy alimenter use de esvantoirs de plumes, de papier, de toille, scelon leur faculté, et puissance. Les riches vivent de moulins à vent' (p. 638; 'The common people feed themselves with fans made from feathers, paper or cloth, depending on their means and abilities. The rich live on windmills'). Inequality breeds tensions on Ruach as the poor take from the rich: one man beats his valet and a page boy for having stolen from him (pp. 638–69), and a bag of wind is pilfered from the king (p. 639). Wind is, as Duval points out, the source of all contention on Ruach.[46] Yet when the islander who gives the account of Bringuenarilles's annual windmill-eating pilgrimage ends with, 'Voyez là nostre malheur' (p. 641; 'Behold in that our misfortune'), we must treat the possessive adjective with some scepticism. Windmills are a sign of luxury: 'Quand ilz [les riches] font quelque festin ou banquet, on dresse les tables soubs un ou deux moulins à vent' (p. 638; 'When the rich have a feast or banquet, they have their tables erected under one or two windmills'). In other words, the rich of Ruach have a different relationship with windmills from the poor; they will be affected differently by Bringuenarilles. Whereas the speaker's utterance, 'nostre' ('our'), aimed to articulate a united island, it actually represents one partial viewpoint, that of the rich of Ruach. In speaking thus, he eradicates alternative ideas, collapsing the views of the wider community into one perspective. Just as resources can be controlled by particular individuals, so too can the definitions of words. The Ruachite whose ostensibly expansive 'nostre' obscures a partisan perspective is the same one who provides the reader with the image of depletion, of 'calamité' and 'misere'. This demonstration of a weakness of topographic description – the partiality of the author – is bound up in the *Quart Livre*'s play with geographical discourse. It can only undermine the confidence the reader can have in the veracity of accounts such as Apian's *Cosmographie*, a text that describes Europe as 'riche' and does not, like the *Quart Livre*, reflect on the inequalities of the haves and the have-nots. It asks, in a more comic way than chapter 53's consideration of the extraction of money from France to Rome, who holds wealth and how it is distributed.

The topographic description of the isle of Ruach offers an image of depletion with a different focus from others in the *Quart Livre*. The central concern is economic anxiety, with threats to the wellbeing of the island coming from outside and inside. Bringuenarilles, the external threat, provides another means of thinking about the nature of community and a different angle of vision on the conflict. The individual scenes focusing on these enemies are not juxtaposed, contrary to the Papefigues and Papimanes chapters, so the antagonistic relations between the two appear to be contingent, not linked to a clash of values. However, the lack of ideology in the conflict is not a sign of hope. While the death of the windmill-eating giant offers respite, there remains strife between the islanders. Economic struggles between, and within, communities seem to be an unavoidable feature of the world of the *Quart Livre*. This reimagined Old World is a place of inevitable conflicts, arising from disputes over resources as well as ideas.

These disputes over resources tie into the ideas of empire discussed above in the context of the Papefigues and the Papimanes. Both of the paired episodes (Ruach and Bringuenarilles, and the Papefigues and the Papimanes) depict economic expansion from the viewpoint of those undertaking the expansion, Bringuenarilles and the Papimanes, and also from the perspective of those at whose expense this expansion is taking place. Expansion, Rabelais demonstrates, leads to depletion in terms of destruction of habitats and extraction of resources. Thus, the expansion of the world actually contracts the world. Rabelais was writing at a time when capitalism was beginning to develop, when commerce and financial markets took on more significance, and when long-distance trade was becoming more important and commodities from the New World, especially precious metals, were flooding markets in the Old World.[47] Inflation had become a concern by the 1540s and was only to get worse in the second half of the sixteenth century as price levels continued to rise.[48] The *Quart Livre* offers the twenty-first-century reader an insight into the human experience and, in particular, the social anxiety of the economic troubles of the Renaissance.

Conclusion

The ways in which religious and economic conflicts are presented in the *Quart Livre* suggest a lack of hope for the future, a fear that clashes between communities will be unavoidable. Accordingly, the text exhibits the sentiment that a unified Christendom is either on the point of extinction or has already disappeared, and crucially it does not articulate any sense of an alternative unifying vision. The comedy of the text, however, does provide some catharsis and hope that warlike violence need not prevail; the comical healing of the Andouilles, who represent Protestants opposed to the concept of Lent, by the application of mustard (p. 636) offers a less pessimistic outlook than the scenes examined in this chapter. In representing fears of a potentially nightmarish future, though, Rabelais borrows from the form, style and vocabulary of cosmographies and travel accounts. Cosmographies offer a bird's-eye view of what Europe as a whole looks like. Rabelais too offers a bird's-eye view as each island offers a view from a different vantage point.[49] His geographical imagination, however, is very different from that shared by Apian and Münster. Where those writers each offer one overt idea of what Europe means, Rabelais provides several competing visions of what the future could look like. The imagined geography of Europe constructed in the cosmographies is one of unity, in contrast to Rabelais' world of imaginary communities where the dominant frame is fragmentation along national, confessional and economic lines.

These effects are created by the contrasting forms of the texts. Cosmographical writing is a method of organising and explaining the world which gives coherence and closed form to the continent Europe. It allows Apian and Münster to impose one meaning on the term 'Europe'. The fiction of the *Quart Livre* is a method of thinking which depicts a series of communities recognisable as distortions of communities in the Old World. It allows Rabelais to challenge rigid geographical definitions and to give his readers material with which to think about what 'Europe' signifies. His focus is on the human and social dimension, thereby suggesting that the world cannot be divided as neatly as it is in the cosmographies. Rabelais is not dogmatic and his work opens up a space for doubt, encouraging reflection on geographical issues. By mixing fiction with reality, he points the reader towards certain ideas and problems, rather than making direct assertions. Different groups of chapters make points about the Old World in different ways. They offer different versions of Europe, each operating with its own temporal mechanisms; they do not all have the same dynamic, referring to the past, to the present and to situations that might come about. The unfinished nature of the Pantagruelists' journey invites the readers to think of other island communities that might constitute the Old World.

The image at the close of the *Quart Livre* of Pantagruel and his company sailing away is itself a reflection on the potential futures of the Old World. In leaving the sea of islands behind them, they reject the visions of community that were offered at each landing. The text is reaching out towards something new, without knowing what that something new is or will be. The Pantagruelists themselves are one of the potential futures. They represent a community that is not held together primarily by hostile opposition towards outsiders. Instead, they are a diverse group of characters, united by friendship and laughter, who disagree but stay together.[50] They do not identify simply with the dominant national or confessional trends of the day; Panurge is hostile to his fellow Frenchman Dindenault, for example. In this way, the Pantagruelists express a Europe that might be, a pluralistic and tolerant Europe. Only pluralism and tolerance, it seems, can offer an adequate response to national, confessional and other communitarian concerns.

Of course, the word 'Europe' makes just one appearance in the *Quart Livre*. What I have shown in this chapter is how a nexus of words and associations that Apian and Münster linked to the term 'Europe' – 'belle', 'riche' and 'fertile' – was deployed in Rabelais' text. Examining this vocabulary and its related ideas within the context of the *Quart Livre* as a whole has demonstrated how Rabelais engaged creatively and critically with the geographical discourse of his day. Where the word 'Europe' as it was used by Apian and Münster denoted unity and superiority, in the *Quart Livre* it indicates the sense of a vast area. The notion of unity is rejected in Rabelais' fictional work. It is rejected through the adoption of terms from geographical writing and the plotting of them temporally, not spatially. Apian uses this vocabulary in a spatial manner: Europe is 'riche' and the rest of the world is not. Rabelais, on the contrary, adds a temporal dimension to depict places that used to be 'riche'. In doing so, he highlights the limitations of contemporary geographical writing, namely the simplifying present-tense description of a world that is changing and facing an uncertain future.

Notes

1. Rabelais, *Œuvres complètes*, ed. by Mireille Huchon (Paris: Gallimard, 1994), p. 642. Further references to this edition are given in parentheses after quotations in the text.
2. Paul J. Smith detects the style of contemporary geographical writing in Rabelais' use of temporal markers – 'Au lendemain matin', for example – and his descriptions of exotic animals, and regards the *Quart Livre* as a parody or a pastiche of contemporary *récits de voyage*, especially that of Jacques Cartier (*Voyage et écriture: Étude sur le 'Quart Livre' de Rabelais*, Études Rabelaisiennes, 19 (Geneva: Droz, 1987), p. 40). For Michael

Heath, the descriptions of the islands recall the style of cosmographies (*Rabelais* (Tempe: Arizona Center for Medieval and Renaissance Studies, 1996), p. 97).

3. For a study of Apian's *Cosmographie*, see Tom Conley, *An Errant Eye: Poetry and Topography in Early Modern France* (Minneapolis: University of Minnesota Press, 2011), pp. 53–80.
4. *La Cosmographie de Pierre Apian, libvre tresutile, traictant de toutes les regions & pays du monde par artifice astronomicque, nouvellement traduict de Latin en François. Et par Gemma Frison mathematicien & docteur en medicine de Louvain corrige* (Antwerp: Gregoire Bonte, 1544), fol. 30^v. Further references to this edition are given in parentheses after quotations in the text.
5. For more on the *locus amoenus* topos and the literary depiction of the idealised landscape more generally, see Ernst Robert Curtius, *European Literature and the Latin Middle Ages*, trans. by Willard R. Trask (London: Routledge & Kegan Paul, 1953), pp. 183–202.
6. Frank Lestringant, 'Le Déclin d'un savoir: La crise de la cosmographie à la fin de la Renaissance', *Annales: histoire, sciences sociales*, 46 (1991), 239–60 (pp. 240, 255–56).
7. Adam Mosley provides a good account of approaches to cosmography through an examination of how different cosmographers understood their practice. See 'The Cosmographer's Role in the Sixteenth Century: A Preliminary Study', *Archives internationales d'histoire des sciences*, 59 (2009), 424–39.
8. For a detailed study of Münster's *Cosmographia* see Matthew McLean, *The 'Cosmographia' of Sebastian Münster: Describing the World in the Reformation* (Aldershot: Ashgate, 2007). On the editions of the text see Gerald Strauss, 'A Sixteenth-Century Encyclopedia: Sebastian Münster's *Cosmography* and its Editions', in *From the Renaissance to the Counter-Reformation: Essays in Honour of Garrett Mattingly*, ed. by Charles Carter (London: Jonathan Cape, 1966), pp. 145–63.
9. Frank Lestringant suggests that Rabelais made use of Apian's *Cosmographie* when writing the earlier *Tiers Livre*: 'Rabelais and Travel Literature', in *A Companion to François Rabelais*, ed. by Bernd Renner (Leiden: Brill, 2021), pp. 185–215 (p. 192).
10. From Frank Lestringant's 'une géographie imaginaire' in 'L'Insulaire de Rabelais ou la fiction en archipel (pour une lecture topographique du *Quart Livre*)', in *Rabelais en son demi-millénaire: Actes du colloque international de Tours (24–29 septembre 1984)*, Études Rabelaisiennes, 21, ed. by Jean Céard and Jean-Claude Margolin (Geneva: Droz, 1988), pp. 249–74 (p. 256). The phrase should be distinguished from 'imagined geography'.
11. This approach to the text differs from that of Tom Conley, who analysed Rabelais' *Pantagruel* and *Gargantua* as examples of what he calls 'cartographic literature', that is, writing which engages in plotting space within printed discourse. He shows how Rabelais' books are productively influenced by contemporary works of cartography, especially those of Oronce Finé, whereas this study will argue that the *Quart Livre* works largely against, not with, geographical writing. See Tom Conley, *The Self-*

Made Map: Cartographic Writing in Early Modern France (Minneapolis: University of Minnesota Press, 1996).
12. A study of the geographical texts with which Rabelais is likely to have been familiar is James William Romer, 'François Rabelais and the New World: A Study of Geography and Navigation in Rabelais's Romance' (unpublished doctoral thesis, University of North Carolina, 1977).
13. Conley, *The Self-Made Map*, p. 15.
14. Lestringant, 'L'Insulaire de Rabelais', pp. 249–74.
15. For more on archipelagic fiction, see Frank Lestringant's *Bribes d'îles: La littérature en archipel de Benedetto Bordone à Nicolas Bouvier* (Paris: Garnier, 2020).
16. In Huchon's Pléiade edition of Rabelais: '*Quart Livre*: Notice', in Rabelais, *Œuvres complètes*, pp. 1456–76.
17. In Rabelais, *Œuvres complètes*, p. 1464.
18. Lestringant, 'L'Insulaire de Rabelais', p. 274.
19. Terence Cave, *The Cornucopian Text: Problems of Writing in the French Renaissance* (Oxford: Oxford University Press, 1979). See Michel Jeanneret, *Le Défi des signes: Rabelais et la crise de l'interprétation à la Renaissance* (Orléans: Paradigme, 1994), and Floyd Gray, *Rabelais et le comique du discontinu* (Paris: Champion, 1994).
20. M. A. Screech, *Rabelais* (London: Duckworth, 1979).
21. Edwin Duval, *The Design of Rabelais's 'Quart Livre de Pantagruel'* (Geneva: Droz, 1998), especially pp. 15–22, 65–69 and 81–107. See also Guy Demerson, *Rabelais* (Paris: Balland, 1986). Demerson detects a symmetrical structure centred on the condemnation of evil.
22. See André Tournon, *'En sens agile': Les acrobaties de l'esprit selon Rabelais* (Paris: Champion, 1995); Nicolas Le Cadet, *L'Évangelisme fictionnel: Les 'Livres rabelaisiens', le 'Cymbalum mundi', 'L'Heptaméron' (1532–1552)* (Paris: Garnier, 2010); David Quint, *Origin and Originality in Renaissance Literature: Versions of the Source* (New Haven, CT: Yale University Press, 1983), pp. 170–206.
23. Paul J. Smith noted that the *Quart Livre* has a coherence of composition since the islands are linked to each other, even if those connections tend to be conflictual: *Voyage et écriture*, p. 128.
24. For an alternative view see Emmanuelle Lacore-Martin, *Figures de l'histoire et du temps dans l'œuvre de Rabelais*, Études Rabelaisiennes, 51 (Geneva: Droz, 2011). She argues that once an island has been left by the Pantagruelists it never reappears in the text and 'se fige ainsi dans le texte' (p. 78; 'so is frozen in the text').
25. Frank Lestringant, 'Le Récit de voyage et la question des genres: L'exemple des *Singularitez de la France antarctique d'André Thevet* (1557)', in *D'encre de Brésil: Jean de Léry, écrivain*, ed. by Frank Lestringant and Marie-Christine Gomez-Géraud (Orléans: Paradigme, 1999), pp. 93–108. Lestringant argues that the *Quart Livre* should be considered a topography because of the ostensibly unfinished nature of the text, which ends before the journey is complete: 'L'Insulaire de Rabelais', p. 257.
26. Margaret Broom Harp has written that 'in each [island] Rabelais exaggerates an aspect of his own culture and presents it as a guiding principle': *The Portrayal of Community in Rabelais's 'Quart Livre'* (New York: Peter Lang,

1997), p. 80. Lestringant categorises the islands as heterotopias where each represents a satirical deviation from the norm: 'Paysages anthropomorphes à la Renaissance', in *Nature et paysages: L'émergence d'une nouvelle subjectivité à la Renaissance*, ed. by Dominique de Courcelles (Paris: École des Chartes, 2006), pp. 261–79.

27. Usher's reading of the *Quart Livre* alongside Jacques Cartier's *Relations* highlights Rabelais' strategy of making comparisons between the islands and Europe: Phillip John Usher, *Errance et cohérence: Essai sur la littérature transfrontalière à la Renaissance* (Paris: Garnier, 2010), pp. 59–92.
28. See J. B. Harley, 'Deconstructing the Map', *Cartographica*, 26 (1989), 1–20. Harley argues that cartography is a discourse in the Foucauldian sense of a system of rules governing the representation of knowledge.
29. Sebastian Münster, *Cosmographiae universalis libri* VI (Basle, 1550). This quotation appears on the unpaginated map of the world which is included in the volume. Further references to this edition are given in parentheses after quotations in the text.
30. The first vernacular French translation of *Utopia* appeared in 1550. It was known in France prior to that date through Latin editions. See *Thomas More's 'Utopia' in Early Modern Europe: Paratexts and Contexts*, ed. by Terence Cave (Manchester: Manchester University Press, 2008), pp. 14–31, 67–86.
31. Wes Williams argues that the Rabelaisian text is a quest not for knowledge but for 'reflexive understanding' about what we think and why we come to think that: *Monsters and their Meanings in Early Modern Culture: Mighty Magic* (Oxford: Oxford University Press, 2011), p. 69.
32. For a study of how Amerindians were represented in Münster's *Cosmographia* see Surekha Davies, 'America and Amerindians in Sebastian Münster's *Cosmographiae universalis libri* VI (1550)', *Renaissance Studies*, 25.3 (2011), 351–73.
33. For examples of other geographical and travel writings that comment on the civility, or lack thereof, of the peoples of the world, see Olive Patricia Dickason, *The Myth of the Savage: And the Beginnings of French Colonialism in the Americas* (Edmonton: University of Alberta Press, 1997).
34. Screech, *Rabelais*, pp. 401–10. Gérard Defaux considers the whole of the *Quart Livre* to be a parody of Rome and the papacy: *Rabelais agonistès: Du rieur au prophète. Études sur 'Pantagruel', 'Gargantua' et 'Le Quart Livre'*, Études Rabelaisiennes, 32 (Geneva: Droz, 1997), pp. 507–13. For other commentaries on the scenes, see Jerome Schwartz, *Irony and Ideology in Rabelais: Structures of Subversion* (Cambridge: Cambridge University Press, 1990); Duval, *The Design of Rabelais's "Quart Livre de Pantagruel"*; Frank-Rutger Hausmann, 'Comment doit-on lire l'épisode de "L'isle des Papefigues" (*Quart Livre*, 45–47)?', in *Rabelais en son demi-millénaire: Actes du colloque international de Tours (24–29 septembre 1984)*, ed. by Jean Céard and Jean-Claude Margolin, Études Rabelaisiennes, 21 (Geneva: Droz, 1988), pp. 121–29. Where Screech finds the Papefigues worthy of sympathy, both Duval and Hausmann suggest they deserve some blame for their plight. Marie-Luce Demonet has challenged the identification of the Papefigues with the Vaudois Protestants, suggesting they might represent

Jews: 'Raves, Rabbis et Raboulière: la persecution des Papefigues (Rabelais, *Quart Livre*, chapitre XLV)', in *Questions de littérature: Béroul, Rabelais, La Fontaine, Saint-Simon, Maupassant, Lagarce*, ed. by Jean-Michel Gouvard (Bordeaux: Presses Universitaires de Bordeaux, 2011), pp. 33–59.

35. Rabelais' position in the Gallican Crisis is thoroughly covered by Richard Cooper, 'Rabelais, Jean Du Bellay et la crise gallicane', in *Rabelais pour le XXIe siècle*, ed. by Michel Simonin, Études Rabelaisiennes, 33 (Geneva: Droz, 1998), pp. 299–325.
36. Duval, *The Design of Rabelais's 'Quart Livre de Pantagruel'*, p. 74.
37. On this point see Quint, *Origin and Originality*, pp. 194–206.
38. Many commentators have followed M. A. Screech, who regards the scene as an attempt on the part of Rabelais at syncretism of classical culture with Christian belief: 'The Death of Pan and the Death of Heroes in the *Fourth Book* of Rabelais: A Study in Syncretism', *Bibliothèque d'humanisme et Renaissance*, 17 (1955), 36–55. Duval, on the other hand, argues that Pantagruel is less concerned with theology than with behaving kindly towards his host in seeking common ground between them: *The Design of Rabelais's 'Quart Livre de Pantagruel'*, p. 101. More recent accounts of this episode have stressed the importance of ambiguity. Nicolas Le Cadet, for example, rejects the notion of syncretism in favour of *transitus* from Hellenism to Christianity. Borrowing from Guillaume Budé's *De transitu hellenismi ad christianismum*, he outlines two ways of conceptualising the passage from pagan wisdom to Christian wisdom which are especially relevant to the Macraeons scene: first, the transition to Christianity represents a break with antiquity, the values of the two being incompatible, and, second, the cultural resources of the classical world are put to the service of Christianity. Of the two, Le Cadet asserts, Rabelais does not favour one, preferring to keep ambiguous the interpretation of the *transitus*. See 'L'Ile des Macraeons, ou les ambiguïtés du *transitus* rabelaisien (*Quart Livre*, ch. XXV à XXVIII)', *Réforme, humanisme, Renaissance*, 61 (2005), 51–72.
39. Le Cadet, 'L'Ile des Macraeons', pp. 66–67.
40. Lacore-Martin, p. 223.
41. On Münster's sources, see McLean, pp. 233–39.
42. See Heath, *Rabelais*, p. 67.
43. For Schwartz (p. 174) the 'trivial' death of Bringuenarilles frames the cosmic importance of Langey's. André Tournon treats the chapter more seriously, judging it to deal with one unimaginable aspect of death, its natural absurdity, while the death of du Bellay treats a second, its supernatural mystery: 'Nargues, Zargues et le concept de trépas', *Réforme, humanisme, Renaissance*, 64 (2007), 111–23 (p. 123).
44. Jeanneret, *Le Défi des signes*, p. 159.
45. Heath has noted a similar problem: with all the windmills gone, how will the people survive without flour?: *Rabelais*, p. 101.
46. Duval, *The Design of Rabelais's 'Quart Livre de Pantagruel'*, pp. 72–73.
47. See Robert DuPlessis, *Transitions to Capitalism in Early Modern Europe* (Cambridge: Cambridge University Press, 1997); Jotham Parsons, *Making Money in Sixteenth-Century France: Currency, Culture, and the State* (Ithaca, NY: Cornell University Press, 2014).
48. Parsons, pp. 107–08.

49. In contrast, Lestringant argues that the *Quart Livre* 'abandons the bird's eye view for the surface perspective' as earth is viewed 'from just above the waterline, from island to island': 'Rabelais and Travel Literature', p. 203. I suggest that in the *Quart Livre*, as in Renaissance cosmographies, it is the compilation of surface perspectives that constructs a bird's-eye view.
50. Quint, *Origin and Originality*, p. 195.

Chapter 2

Views from Brazil

France came to the exploration and conquest of the New World of the Americas after Portugal and Spain. Jacques Cartier was sponsored by François I to lead three journeys to North America between 1534 and 1542. Admiral Nicolas de Villegaignon led an expedition to Brazil in 1555, with the intention of establishing a colony in what is now Rio de Janeiro. And in 1564 there was an attempt to found a colony in Florida by René Goulaine de Laudonnière. While the French eventually found long-term success in Canada, it was arguably Brazil that had the biggest impact on the French imagination in the second half of the sixteenth century. The failure of the colony of *France antarctique* ('Antarctic France') in Brazil was the subject of a confessional blame game, with Catholics and Protestants each accusing the other group of responsibility. One of those propagandists, the Calvinist Jean de Léry features in Chapter 5. The present chapter examines representations of Europe in two works on Brazil that largely avoid confessional disputation, André Thevet's account of his journey to South America, *Les Singularitez de la France antarctique* (*The Singularities of Antarctic France*), and Montaigne's essay 'Des cannibales' ('Of Cannibals'). Thevet constructs an imagined geography of Europe which legitimises France as a conquering, imperial nation alongside Spain and Portugal. In 'Des cannibales' Montaigne, who had read Thevet's *Singularitez*, offers a productive response to this idea of Europe. In his only essay to feature the term 'Europe', Montaigne interrogates the network of vocabulary related to the word as it is used by Thevet. Aware of the power of words, Montaigne declares, in a now much-celebrated maxim, 'chacun appelle barbarie ce qui n'est pas de son usage' ('everyone one calls barbarism that which is unfamiliar').[1] Often read as an early modern expression of cultural relativism, 'Des cannibales' is as much concerned with the world closer to home as it is with Brazil.[2] Yet, unlike *Les Singularitez*, it resists constructing rigid boundaries and leaves the reader uncertain of the imagined geographies of the Old World of Europe.

André Thevet's *Les Singularitez de la France antarctique*: A Europe of Imperial Nations

André Thevet was the chaplain of Admiral Nicolas de Villegaignon's expedition to South America which led to the foundation of the colony of *France antarctique* in present-day Rio de Janeiro. They set out from Le Havre in July 1555 and landed on 15 November 1555. Thevet was there for only ten weeks before illness forced him to leave for France at the end of January 1556. His notes, embellished by the Hellenist and doctor Mathurin Héret, were published in 1557 as *Les Singularitez de la France antarctique*.[3] The work is hybrid in form.[4] It is structured as the account of a journey to Brazil and back again but has little narration of the actual voyage, focusing primarily on descriptions of the flora, fauna and peoples of Brazil. It also includes descriptions of parts of Africa and the Americas that he did not visit on the voyage, as well as an account of the Amazons as if they were not mythological.[5] The book was published before the short-lived colony was destroyed by the Portuguese. Thevet wrote again of *France antarctique* in his 1575 *Cosmographie universelle*, in which he blamed the Calvinist party for the failure of the colony, although it had arrived after his exit. Consequently, it has been suggested that, unlike the later account, *Les Singularitez* is largely apolitical.[6] Nonetheless, the detailed descriptions of Brazil in *Les Singularitez* do indicate that there are natural resources that can be exploited, as well as people ripe for evangelisation.[7] Moreover, the overall political framework of the travel account serves to promote the superiority of Europe over the rest of the world and thereby justify overseas empire-building. In this section, I argue that in *Les Singularitez* Thevet represents Europe in a way that advances French imperial ambitions.

Although Thevet was official cosmographer to the French king and wrote in French for, it can be assumed, a predominantly Francophone audience, the word 'Europe' appears more frequently than the word 'France' in *Les Singularitez*. The importance of the imagined geography of Europe to Thevet's work is underlined by the use of the word when recounting the voyage's turn towards home: 'Il fut question pour notre conduite commencer à compter nos degrés depuis là jusques en notre Europe' (p. 341; 'It was a matter for our navigator to start to measure the degrees from there to our Europe'). Later, 'pour atteindre notre Europe' (p. 363; 'to reach our Europe') is the phrase he uses to describe the goal of the final journey. This is a meaningful choice since other geographical reference points are found in the text: the Canary Islands are said to be 'îles distantes de l'équinoxial de vingt-sept degrés et de notre France de cinq cents lieues' (p. 58; 'islands situated twenty-seven degrees from the equator and 500 leagues from our France'). A narrative of travel like *Les Singularitez* involves positions of origin and destination, and often a return to the point of origin. Thevet conceptualises his point of return not as France or a particular region, but as Europe. In doing so, the geographical term is invested with emotive meaning, taking on the connotations of home.

The perceptions of the continent that are articulated in *Les Singularitez* focus around the notion that Europe is superior to the rest of the world. Like others who wrote about the New World, Thevet's descriptions offer an image against which a conception of Europe is constructed through contrast.[8] Deploying a commonplace of writing about America, he lists the characteristics regarded as lacking in the native inhabitants: 'Elle a été et est habitée pour le jourd'hui, outre les chrétiens qui depuis Améric Vespuce l'habitent, de gens merveilleusement étranges et sauvages, sans foi, sans loi, sans religion, sans civilité aucune' (p. 162; 'America has been and is inhabited today – apart from the Christians who have lived there since the time of Amerigo Vespucci – by people incredibly strange and savage, without faith, without law, without religion, without any civility'). Thevet uses the opposing notions of civility and savagery to compare the Christians of Europe with the peoples of the New World.[9] While *Les Singularitez* is broadly typical of writing about the voyages of discovery, there are two notable features. The first is the form: the adaption of the travel account structure to include descriptions of places not visited gives greater emphasis to the superiority of Europe since the continent is depicted as superior not only to Brazil, but also to most of Africa and the Americas. The second is the frequency of the word 'Europe'.

Thevet takes the early modern idea that reducing nature to order marked out humankind from the animal world and applies this to Europe's past:

> Et même en toute notre Europe, avant que l'on commençât à cultiver la terre, à planter et semer diversité de fruits, les hommes se contentaient seulement de ce que la terre produisait de son naturel; ayant pour breuvage de belle eau claire; pour vêtements quelques écorces de bois, feuillages et quelques peaux. (p. 404)

> And even in all of our Europe before they started to plough the land, to plant and sow a range of plants, men were content with only what the earth produced in its natural course, having to drink clean, fresh water, and having clothes made from some bark, foliage and animal hides.

The 'toute' here suggests a homogeneous continent, unified by a set of cultural practices that evolved from the cultivation of the earth, such as the wearing of certain types of clothing. This historical dimension adds the notion of development over time to the imagined geography of Europe. The Amerindians of Brazil, portrayed as living in a state of nature, resemble the people of Europe far back in time. This view presents Europe as a marker of progress and maps other parts of the world according to different degrees of inferiority, that is, how developed their cultural practices are.[10]

The representation of the progress and superiority of Europe in *Les Singularitez* is used to justify empire-building by the Spanish and Portuguese and, by extension, underscore French imperial ambitions. The righteousness of the developing empires in the Americas is the dominant political thread of the text. This is emphasised by the inclusion of places other than Brazil. The first appearance of the word 'sauvage' in *Les Singularitez* is in chapter 5, in which it refers to the original inhabitants of the Canary Islands before the Castilian conquest resulted in the cultivation of the land and the introduction of Christianity (pp. 71–72).[11] This scene, with its justification for the actions of the Spanish, frames the cultural encounters that are described later in the narrative. Thevet makes similar use of the Spanish conquest of Mexico:

> Les habitants du jourd'hui jadis cruels et inhumains, par succession de temps ont changé si bien de mœurs et de condition, qu'au lieu d'être barbares et cruels, sont à présent humains et gracieux, en sorte qu'ils ont laissé toutes anciennes incivilités, inhumanités et mauvaises coutumes; comme de s'entretuer l'un l'autre, manger chairs humaines, avoir compagnie à la première femme qu'ils trouvaient, sans avoir aucun égard au sang et parentage, et autres semblables vices et imperfections. (p. 362)

> The inhabitants of today, formerly cruel and inhuman, have over time changed their laws and manners so well that instead of being barbarous and cruel they are now human and gentle, and thus they have abandoned all their former incivilities, inhumanities and depraved customs, such as killing one another, eating human flesh, having the company of the first woman they find with no regard for blood or kinship, and other similar vices and weaknesses.

This extract is taken almost word for word from the 1539 French translation of Boemus's 1520 *Omnium gentium mores*, a text that spurred Renaissance interest in cultural customs.[12] Thevet uses it to frame the meanings of Europe and the Americas. No mention of the New World is made in Boemus's work, which weaves a narrative of humanity's rise from savagery to civility following the Flood. Thevet transplants this account from its original context to the Americas in order to provide an interpretation and justification of the Spanish conquest.[13] Thevet stresses that as well as improving the morals of the native inhabitants, the Spanish have made a positive mark on the built environment of the New World, writing that in Peru 'à présent y trouverez villes, châteaux, cités, bourgades, maisons, villes épiscopales, républiques, et toute autre manière de vivre que vous jugeriez être une autre Europe' (p. 349; 'you will now find there large towns, castles, cities, small towns, houses, bishoprics, republics, and all other ways of living that you would deem it to be another Europe'). Peru is represented not as a new Spain, but as a new Europe, which serves both to position Europe as a central notion in Thevet's ideology of empire and to include France. Whereas some French writers, like Montaigne and Jean de Léry, were critical of the actions of the Spanish and Portuguese in the Americas, Thevet is laudatory, presenting them as models for France to follow and justifying the French colony of *France antarctique*. The development of empires in the New World was not without controversy, not least because of the bloodshed it involved, and Thevet was writing against the backdrop of intellectual disputes about the treatment of indigenous Americans, such as the Valladolid debate (1550–51) between Bartolomé de Las Casas and Juan Ginés de Sepúlveda.[14] To this end, Thevet largely conceals the atrocities committed in the New World. On the rare occasions when he does not ignore the violence of conquest, he reverses the perspective to focus attention on generating sympathy for the Europeans in America, reminding his readers of the cruelties of the Amerindians: 'Or ne faut penser telles découvertures avoir été faites sans grande effusion de sang humain, spécialement des pauvres chrétiens qui ont exposé leur vie, sans avoir égard à la cruauté et inhumanité de ces peuples, bref, ni difficulté quelconque' (p. 328; 'Now it must not be thought that such discoveries have been made without great spilling of human blood, especially of the poor Christians who have exposed their life without regard for the cruelty and inhumanity of those peoples, nor, to be brief, for any difficulty whatsoever'). In this way, Thevet pre-empts concerns his readers may have about the violence of empire-building.

The word 'Europe' as it is used in *Les Singularitez* masks differences between the French, Spanish and Portuguese. It creates between them a cultural equivalence, which serves the ambitions of French nationhood by suggesting that France is on a parity with the two countries which have had much earlier and greater success in conquering land overseas. Thevet highlights Christianity as a defining feature of the continent: 'En quoi ne pouvons assez louer et reconnaître notre Dieu, lequel par singulière affection, sur toutes les autres parties du monde, aurait uniquement favorisé à notre Europe' (pp. 380–81; 'How can we sufficiently praise and acknowledge our God who, by His singular affection, has uniquely favoured our Europe over all the other parts of the world'). This is not to say that Thevet effaces nationality, and indeed he writes of 'les Portugais' ('the Portuguese') and 'les Espagnols' ('the Spanish') in the New World, but he does refer more often to 'chrétiens' ('Christians'). He emphasises the unity of Europe and Christendom, largely ignoring the context of the Reformation. He makes just one reference to growing religious heterodoxy, judging the Amerindian 'ignorance' of God to be more 'tolérable' than the beliefs of 'les damnables athéistes de notre temps' (p. 198; 'the damnable atheists of our time').[15] His references to 'notre religion' belie the reality of religious controversy in Europe and the brewing tensions that would erupt in civil wars in France from 1562. Similarly, Thevet ignores the tensions between the countries competing to expand into the New World, although there is arguably a confessional dimension to this since both the Spanish and Portuguese shared Thevet's Catholic faith. In his writing, 'Europe' is an important word for effacing political and cultural differences, thereby aligning France with Spain and Portugal and promoting French imperial ambitions.

In addition to contemporary empires, France is also linked with the ancient Romans. This is not surprising as the theoretical underpinnings of the European empires in the Americas owed a great debt to the ancient world, with sixteenth-century thinkers borrowing Roman political models, ideas and language to understand the nature and the legitimacy of the developing empires in the New World.[16] Thevet uses Aeneas and the Trojans as an imperial motif to articulate French aspirations in Brazil. He describes his arrival in the New World as akin to Aeneas' landing in Italy:

> Après que par la divine clémence, avec tant de travaux communs et ordinaires à si longue navigation, fûmes parvenus en terre ferme, non si tôt que notre vouloir et espérance le désirait, qui fut le dixième jour de novembre, au lieu de se reposer, ne fut question, sinon de découvrir et chercher lieux propres à faire sièges nouveaux, autant étonnés comme les Troyens arrivant en Italie. (p. 150)

> Thanks to divine mercy, we reached firm ground after so many of the common and usual pains of such a long navigation, no sooner than we had hoped and wanted, on the tenth day of November. We were not concerned with resting but with searching for and discovering new places to make our own, being as astonished as the Trojans arriving in Italy.

With this allusion to the *Aeneid*, Thevet represents the landing of the French mission to Brazil as the foundational moment of a future great empire.[17] Mythical past exploits fold into the present, reinforcing the validity of the small colony of *France antarctique*, encapsulating a hope for its success. Elsewhere, Thevet connects the word 'Europe', which is so important in his thinking, to the ancient Romans: 'Nous voyons en notre Europe combien les Romains, au commencement voulant amplifier leur Empire [. . .] ont épandu de sang, tant d'eux que de leurs ennemis' (p. 328; 'We see in our Europe how far the Romans, from the outset wanting to expand their empire [. . .] have spilled blood, as much of their own as of their enemies'). This comment continues Thevet's defence of violence in the New World, discussed above, but also offers an imagined geography of Europe with a stable genealogy reaching back to the Romans. In doing so, Thevet presents a link between the past and the present that justifies contemporary empire-building by polities in Europe as parallel to ancient practice.

In summary, *Les Singularitez* is an overtly ideological work. As well as fashioning its author as an authority on geography and foreign cultures, the imagined voyage on which it takes the reader through Africa and the Americas promotes overseas expansion by European powers. Within Thevet's political thinking, Europe is a key concept. It is construed as the opposite of savagery, signifying Christianity, civility, cultivation and progress. It is from the vantage point of Brazil that an imagined geography of Europe's superiority is constructed. The rest of the world looks more like Brazil than like Europe. As a part of Europe, France shares that superiority and is therefore well placed to follow Spain and Portugal in developing an empire in the New World. Indeed, further conquest is actively encouraged, given the supposed benefits that the culture of Europe brings.[18] In this way, the conception of Europe in *Les Singularitez* is one that supports national ambitions. It is an idea that is in harmony, not conflict, with French nationhood.

Montaigne's 'Des cannibales': An Uncertain View across the Atlantic

One of Montaigne's sources for 'Des cannibales', the chapter of the *Essais* in which he writes about the Tupi of Brazil, was Thevet's *Les Singularitez*. Yet while the term 'Europe' plays a significant role in Thevet's work, it does not in 'Des cannibales', making just one appearance. Where Thevet compares Brazil with Europe, Montaigne compares Brazil with 'nous', without specifying exactly to what the 'nous' refers, whether it be the people of Europe, Christendom, France or any other entity. Nonetheless, the instance of the word 'Europe' in 'Des cannibales' is its sole appearance in the whole of Montaigne's voluminous *Essais*. In that sense, its use is inherently meaningful and worthy of examination. Moreover, as a Renaissance humanist, Montaigne has been regarded as a cosmopolitan figure with an international outlook and, therefore, an interest in the idea of Europe.[19] Philippe Desan has argued that Montaigne viewed himself as a citizen of the world who regarded Europe as 'un seul espace' ('a single space'); and Claude-Gilbert Dubois has suggested that Montaigne had a symbolic conception of a Europe of travel and circulation of people and ideas.[20] Such interpretations might reveal more about a modern tendency to associate Europe with internationalism and cosmopolitanism (and thus downplay the presumed exclusion of non-Europeans) than they do about Montaigne's understanding of a concept designated by a word he used only once in his published work.[21]

Accordingly, this section analyses the word in context, considering Montaigne as a reader of Thevet. I argue that Montaigne unsettles the imagined geography of Europe constructed in *Les Singularitez*. When Montaigne travels to Brazil in his imagination and looks back at Europe, what he sees is different from what Thevet sees. Where the latter offers his readers a confident vision of a superior Europe, Montaigne enacts a much more uncertain reading of the terrain, critiquing the vocabulary that underpins Thevet's conception of Europe in such a way as to cast doubt on the possibility of constructing a fixed perception of geography.

In 'Des cannibales' Montaigne is critical of contemporary geographical writing. As he never travelled to Brazil, reading was one of the two means he had of acquiring information about the country, the other being talking with those who knew about it.[22] He claims to have spoken through an interpreter to a native of Brazil in Rouen (p. 214), but he particularly values what a man who had lived there for ten or twelve years has told him (p. 203): 'je me contente de cette information, sans m'enquerir de ce que les cosmographes en disent' (p. 205; 'I am content with this information, without inquiring what the cosmographers say about it'). Yet 'Des cannibales' offers a critique of written accounts of life in the Americas which makes it clear that Montaigne is familiar with what cosmographers, geographers and travellers have written in spite of his assertion to the contrary. In fact, there is a clear allusion to Thevet in his criticism of New World writing when he takes aim at cosmographers for embellishing their ethnographic descriptions with information beyond their direct experience: 'pour avoir cet avantage sur nous d'avoir veu la Palestine, ils veulent jouir de ce privilege de nous conter nouvelles de tout le demeurant du monde' (p. 205; 'since they have the advantage over us of having seen Palestine, they want to enjoy that privilege of telling us tales about all the rest of the world').[23] Not only did Thevet hold the title of 'cosmographe du Roy' (cosmographer to the King), he had also visited Palestine and written a *Cosmographie de Levant* (1554) before using his trip to Brazil to produce a description of Africa and the Americas in his *Singularitez de la France antarctique* and then publishing a description of the whole world, the *Cosmographie universelle* in 1575.[24] Moreover, Montaigne's reference to 'France antarctique' (p. 203), rather than 'Brésil', invokes Thevet's *récit de voyage*; by contrast, Jean de Léry, whose account of his journey to the New World was published before 'Des cannibales', prefers the term 'Brésil'. Montaigne juxtaposes his dismissal of cosmographical writing with a comment on the (mis)use of language: 'il n'y a rien de barbare et de sauvage en cette nation, à ce qu'on m'en a rapporté, sinon que chacun appelle barbarie ce qui n'est pas de son usage' (p. 205; 'there is nothing barbarous or savage about that people, according to what I have been told, except that everyone calls barbarous that which is unfamiliar'). With this juxtaposition Montaigne positions his critique of cosmography as a problem of language. Similarly, the particular terms whose usage he challenges, 'barbare' and 'sauvage', are those that are commonly deployed by Thevet and other travel and cosmographical writers. The problem with geographical writing was flagged before the direct attack on cosmographers: the course of 'ma riviere de Dordoigne' ('my river, the Dordogne') has visibly altered in Montaigne's lifetime, and his brother's area has 'perdu quatre lieuës de terre' (p. 204; 'lost four leagues of land') to the sea.[25] If the world is physically changing then must not the language used to describe the world, and the categories for understanding it, change too?[26] Cosmography is a static genre aiming to fix the world on the page and is therefore unable to reflect a world in flux that is visibly changing. With his sceptical attitude towards cosmography, Montaigne's comments suggest the application of Pyrrhonism to geographical knowledge claims.[27]

It is just prior to the expression of these doubts about geographical discourse that the word 'Europe' appears. Since this word denotes a geographical entity, its presence is striking and must be understood within the context of the critical attitude that follows. Montaigne first mentions 'cet autre monde qui a esté descouvert en nostre siecle' (p. 203; 'that other world which has been discovered in our century') before discussing the mythical island of Atlantis, describing how its kings 's'estoyent estendus dans la terre ferme si avant qu'ils tenoyent de la largeur d'Afrique jusques en Ægypte, et de la longueur de l'Europe jusques en la Toscane' (p. 203; 'extended on to the mainland so far that they possessed the breadth of Africa up to Egypt, and the length of Europe up to Tuscany'). The term 'Europe' is used here in its purely spatial sense, devoid of the cultural connotations of superiority that predominate in Thevet's *Singularitez*. Nonetheless, the word is placed in a comparable discursive context; 'Des cannibales', like *Les Singularitez*, is ostensibly about Brazil and the Tupi while commenting on other matters. Montaigne's text further recalls New World travel writing by noting that the kings of Atlantis 'entreprindrent d'enjamber jusques sur l'Asie, et subjuguer toutes les nations qui bordent la mer Mediterranée jusques au golfe de la mer Majour' (p. 203; 'undertook to encroach into Asia and subdue all the nations that border the Mediterranean Sea up to the gulf of the Black Sea'), thereby raising the issue of conquest and imperial expansion in a clear parallel with the contemporary world. However, in spite of Montaigne's deliberate evocation of similar contextual ground to Thevet's *Singularitez*, the signification of the word 'Europe' in 'Des cannibales' is different. Given that the term is restricted to a neutral spatial designation in an essay that is concerned with the New World and the Old and that provides explicit criticism of geographical writing, it behoves readers to question the meaning of Europe. The style of Montaigne's personal essay contrasts with that of travel accounts in that it offers a space for doubt, in place of the certainty of geographical discourse.[28]

Montaigne expresses doubt about Thevet's conception of Europe by scrutinising the vocabulary that constructs the imagined geography of the continent in *Les Singularitez*. Much of 'Des cannibales' focuses on the terms that for Thevet define what Europe is not, 'sauvage' and 'barbare', destabilising their semantic content by continually shifting the way in which the terms are used.[29] First, 'barbare' is stripped of its negative connotations and said to refer to nothing more than difference (p. 205). The term 'sauvage' is then valorised as meaning wild or natural (p. 205). Montaigne's next move is to reinstate the negative meaning of the word 'barbare', declaring the Tupi to be barbarous, since they practise anthropophagy, yet less barbarous than 'nous' ('us'; pp. 209–10). Then, the Brazilians are said to be not 'sauvage', as they are braver in war than 'nous' (p. 212). Finally, they are no longer regarded as 'barbare' given the artfulness of their music (p. 213).[30] These shifts serve to interrogate the language and ideas of travel writing, leaving the reader on unstable ground.[31] The effect is not to establish alternative definitions of the terms, but rather to think through the uses, meanings and consequences of them, creating a process of reconsideration of the ideas and beliefs associated with these terms, which casts doubt on how they are used in texts by other writers. Furthermore, the shifting meanings expose the malleable nature of words, staging the manipulation of language that takes place to uphold a fixed viewpoint. In this case, Montaigne alters the arguments that he makes about the notions of savagery and barbarism in order to support the position that he sticks to throughout 'Des cannibales', namely that the Amerindians of

Brazil are more praiseworthy than the people of Europe, regardless of whether they are savage, barbarous or neither.[32] This technique, which makes use of the very terms that were crucial to Thevet in articulating a conception of Europe, exposes how the assumptions of geographical writing rest on words that are polyvalent and are used rhetorically with the intention of advancing a particular viewpoint.

While 'Des cannibales' challenges the imagined geography of Europe articulated in *Les Singularitez*, it does not offer a clear alternative conception of the continent, presenting instead a vision of a changing world that cannot be fixed in language. Given the focus on the words 'sauvage' and 'barbare' and the prevalence of the term 'Europe' in Thevet's *Singularitez*, it is striking that 'Europe' makes only one appearance in 'Des cannibales'. That it is used in a restricted spatial sense and then not used again in an essay that compares the Old World and the New indicates a dismissal, on the part of Montaigne, of the value and utility of the term. Where Thevet writes from the position of 'nostre Europe', Montaigne's use of spatial deixis is deliberately unclear. He refers throughout 'Des cannibales' to a plural subject, constituted by the pronoun 'nous' ('we') and the possessive adjective 'nostre/nos' ('our'), but the referent is unstable and constantly shifting. The collective subject refers to the Old World in general ('Ils [. . .] se font le poil beaucoup plus nettement que nous', p. 208; 'they cut their hair much more cleanly than us'), countries that have expanded into the New World ('Les loix naturelles leur commandent encores, fort peu abastardies par les nostres', p. 206; 'Natural laws still govern them, only a little bastardised by ours'), and France more specifically ('nos ancestres, estans assiegez par Cæsar en la ville de Alexia', p. 209; 'our ancestors, being besieged by Caesar in the town of Alesia'). Signifiers in 'Des cannibales' struggle to pin down the respective referent as it is forever in motion.[33] With its shifting referents, the 'nous' allows for strategic ambiguity by Montaigne, whereas spatial terms like 'Europe' are static and cannot adequately reflect a fluid sense of collective identity.[34]

France in particular is resisted as a stable reference point in 'Des cannibales'. The words 'France' and 'French' are absent from the essay, whereas 'l'Italie' (p. 203; 'Italy') and 'les Portuguois' (p. 209; 'the Portuguese') are mentioned. It is notable that when describing the Brazilians in Rouen, Montaigne avoids referring to 'nostre Roy' ('our King'), which would anchor France as the deictic centre of his remark, preferring instead to avoid deixis and use the definite article: 'le feu Roy Charles neufiesme' (p. 213; 'the late King Charles the Ninth') and again 'Le Roy' (p. 213; 'the King'). This presents a striking contrast with Montaigne's practice in other chapters of the *Essais*, in which, for instance, he refers to 'nostre Roy Charles huictieme' (p. 144; 'our King Charles the Eighth': Du pedantisme' ('Of Pedantry'), *Essais*, I.25) and 'nostre Roy Henry second' ('p. 294; 'our King Henry the Second': 'Des destries' ('Of War Horses'), *Essais*, I.48). Indeed, there is an attempt to place the narrative 'je' of 'Des cannibales' as impartial and unattached to a specific place with comments such as 'nous n'avons autre mire de la verité et de la raison que l'exemple et idée des opinions et usances du païs où nous sommes' (p. 205; 'we have no other criterion of truth or reason than the example and idea of opinions and customs of the country where we are'). Montaigne avoids referring to 'our country', which might be interpreted as France or a region of France, and, though writing in French, instead addresses himself to a potentially wider readership. Certainly, when contemplating Brazil, Montaigne grasps at a collective identity that is larger than France alone. The refusal, or inability, to name this community reveals that Montaigne is struggling to understand the nature of a changing world and to find the vocabulary to articulate the experience.

The use of the unstable 'nous' also offers a challenge to the notion of imagined geography. Contrary to Thevet's *Singularitez*, which confidently articulates a clear idea of Europe and its cultural meanings, 'Des cannibales' asks whether it is even possible to imagine geography beyond our personal experience. The singular possessive adjective in 'ma riviere de Dordoigne' lends the authority of observation to Montaigne's comment on this geographical feature. It emphasises that an experiential geography is preferable to the abstract geography offered by Thevet and other writers. In articulating a first-person voice, the essay form privileges the personal experience of space, eschewing the synthesis and generalisation favoured in *Les Singularitez*. Montaigne is happy to ground the first-person singular possessive adjective in a specific place (by the Dordogne), but unprepared to situate a plural, collective subject. The 'nous' floats, unnamed, unlocated. The 'nous' shifts and fragments. Thus Montaigne's engagement with the collective subject in 'Des cannibales' is different from his consideration in his later essay on the New World, 'Des coches'. Timothy Hampton argues that in 'Des coches' there is an attempt to construct a collective French identity in relation to the Spanish, to whom he feels a shared cultural connection although he condemns their behaviour towards the inhabitants of the New World.[35] By contrast, 'Des cannibales' does not envision a national identity. France, like Europe, seems an abstract geographical entity.

Besides, given the Wars of Religion, is it possible to speak of a coherent nation? Montaigne's reassessment of the supposed savagery and barbarism prompts a comparison with the French civil wars:

jugeans bien de leurs fautes, nous soyons si aveuglez aux nostres. Je pense qu'il y a plus de barbarie à manger un homme vivant qu'à le manger mort, à deschirer, par tourmens et par geénes, un corps encore plein de sentiment, le faire rostir par le menu, le faire mordre et meurtrir aux chiens et aux pourceaux (comme nous l'avons, non seulement leu, mais veu de fresche memoire, non entre des ennemis anciens, mais entre des voisins et concitoyens, et, qui pis est, sous pretexte de pieté et de religion), que de le rostir et manger apres qu'il est trespassé. (p. 209)

judging rightly their faults, we are so blind to ours. I think there is more barbarity in eating a living man than in eating him dead; in tearing apart, by torture and rack, a body still full of feeling; in roasting him piecemeal; in having him bitten and bruised by dogs and pigs (as we have not only read about but seen in recent memory, not among ancient enemies, but among neighbours and fellow citizens, and what is worse, under the pretext of piety and religion) than in roasting and eating him after he has died.

The terminology of community – 'voisins et concitoyens' – is governed by the indefinite article 'des', rather than a possessive adjective, and so at this moment in which Montaigne alludes to the Wars of Religion, he does not align himself with any particular group, Catholic or Protestant.[36] He does not here use religious conflict to articulate a confessional identity or a unifying national identity. The writer and his readers ('nous') are positioned as spectators of the civil wars, and what they see is one community of 'concitoyens' that has been fractured into a series of neighbouring warring communities. Once again, the value of the slippery way in which Montaigne uses the 'nous' is evident. How can geography be used as a stable marker of collective identity when people from the same place turn against each other? The collective cannot be mapped geographically. The 'nous' cannot be fixed in space. In this way, the shifts in the referent of the 'nous' throughout 'Des cannibales' dramatise the fracturing and fluctuating of identities in a period of religious and civil upheaval.

By and large, 'Des cannibales' is concerned with scrutinising two words that were used by Thevet to represent Europe in contradistinction, 'sauvage' and barbare'. In this way, Montaigne positions his essay relative to geographical writing as a reassessment of the terms that underlie the cultural values expressed in travel and cosmographical literature. Over and above the claims of such writing, Montaigne champions a personal and experiential understanding of geography, unmoored from large and abstract geographical entities like countries and continents. In place of collective identities attached to these abstract places, Montaigne destabilises the plural subject, revealing on his part communitarian impulses that fluctuate as to who and what they embrace. To convey these shifts, he uses plural subject markers ('nous', 'nostre', 'nos') without a fixed point of reference. In *Les Singularitez* Thevet writes about Brazil and offers his readers a clear view of Europe. In 'Des cannibales' Montaigne writes about Brazil and offers his readers an uncertain view which arguably raises more questions than answers and certainly casts doubt on claims to knowledge about Europe, as reflected in Thevet's confident and frequent use of the term.

Conclusion

This chapter has traced how Montaigne reads, interprets and rewrites Thevet's discourse on Brazil, Europe and France. Thevet's Europe is a culture of superiority which presupposes a right of conquest over the inferior world beyond its boundaries. Spain and Portugal, unlike France, had by 1557 achieved significant inroads in the Americas; framing its endeavours as glories for 'nostre Europe' allows Thevet to support the then germinating French colony in Brazil. He does not position Spain and Portugal as rivals of France, but rather positions France as their equal. There is arguably a confessional dimension here, with the Catholic Thevet supporting the expansion of Catholic Spain and Portugal. Montaigne wrote after the failure of the French missions to Brazil, Florida and Canada, at the height of the French religious wars. He, contrary to Thevet, is a pessimistic interpreter of his society, a society he reflects on at great length but never names as Europe or even France. 'Des cannibales' is a personal essay, and for Montaigne self-definition is personal. He offers no clear term for group self-definition. In *Les Singularitez* group definition is paramount; Thevet is attached to Christianity, to Europe and to France. When Montaigne uses the word 'Europe' on the only occasion in the *Essais* it is with its spatial signification and nothing more. His rejection of the term entails a rejection of what it had come to signify in geographical writing: cultural superiority and an impulse to conquest.

In another essay on the New World, 'Des coches', Montaigne writes: '[i]l n'y a rien de seul et de rare eu esgard à nature, ouy bien eu esgard à nostre cognoissance, qui est un miserable fondement de nos regles et qui nous represente volontiers une tres-fauce image des choses' (p. 908; 'there is nothing singular or rare as regards nature; whereas, yes, there really is as regards our knowledge, which is a miserable foundation for our rules and which readily represents to us a very false image of things'). While travel accounts and other forms of geographical writing purport to deepen human understanding and knowledge, Montaigne is sceptical of their ability to represent truth. He uses the flexible form of the personal essay to unsettle the vocabulary that underpins imagined geographies. 'Europe' is a word which itself offers 'a very false image of things'. How can the term 'Europe' adequately reflect and explain a changing world? With its changing referents, the shifting 'nous' in 'Des cannibales' is both part of the problem of a world in flux and the answer. The unmoored 'nous' dramatises the very sense of unfixed, moving boundaries. There can be no place in which to ground a stable collective identity in a period of civil war and religious conflict. The challenge of articulating this cannot be met by forcing a static word, a static definition, on an unstable and abstract concept, as Thevet does with Europe.

Notes

1. Michel de Montaigne, *Les Essais*, ed. by Pierre Villey and V. L. Saulnier (Paris: Presses Universitaires de France, 2004), p. 205. All references are to this edition. Further references to this edition are given in parentheses after quotations in the text.
2. On Montaigne's engagement with the Old World in 'Des cannibales', see, for example, David Quint, 'A Reconsideration of Montaigne's *Des cannibales*', *Modern Language Quarterly*, 51 (1990), 459–90; and Celso Martins Azar Filho, 'Nouveau monde, homme nouveau', *Montaigne Studies*, 22 (2010), 71–84.
3. For an account of Thevet's voyage and return to France, see Frank Lestringant, *André Thevet: Cosmographe des derniers Valois* (Geneva: Droz, 1991), pp. 89–104; pp. 100–04 detail Héret's role in the publication of *Les Singularitez*.
4. For a study of the form of *Les Singularitez*, see Frank Lestringant, 'Le Récit de voyage et la question des genres: L'exemple des *Singularitez de la France antarctique d'André Thevet* (1557)', in *D'encre de Brésil: Jean de Léry, écrivain*, ed. by Frank Lestringant and Marie-Christine Gomez-Géraud (Orléans: Paradigme, 1999), pp. 93–108.
5. André Thevet, *Le Brésil d'André Thevet: Les singularités de la France antarctique*, ed. by Frank Lestringant (Paris: Chandeigne, 2011). Further references to this edition are given in parentheses after quotations in the text. The description of the Amazons can be found at pp. 312–23. Thevet's ethnographic descriptions of Brazil have been praised, nonetheless; see Olive Patricia Dickason, *The Myth of the Savage: And the Beginnings of French Colonialism in the Americas* (Edmonton: University of Alberta Press, 1997), p. 177.
6. Tom Conley, 'Thevet Revisits Guanabara', *Hispanic American Historical Review*, 80 (2000), 753–81.
7. Nicholas Canny, 'A Protestant or Catholic Atlantic World? Confessional Divisions and the Writing of Natural History', *Proceedings of the British Academy*, 181 (2012), 83–121 (p. 91).
8. See Jean-Claude Margolin, 'L'Europe dans le miroir du nouveau monde', in *La Conscience européenne au XVe et au XVIe siècle: Actes du colloque*

international organisé à l'École Normale Supérieure de Jeunes Filles (30 septembre – 3 octobre 1980) (Paris: École Normale Supérieure de Jeunes Filles, 1982), pp. 235–64. Anthony Pagden writes, 'all European cultures [. . .] require the presence of something against which they can represent themselves, invariably to their own advantage' (*European Encounters with the New World: From Renaissance to Romanticism* (New Haven, CT: Yale University Press, 1993), pp. 183–84).

9. See Olive Dickason's wide-ranging study of the term 'savage', *The Myth of the Savage*, especially pp. 63–91.
10. Frank Lestringant (*L'Atelier du cosmographe: Ou l'image du monde à la Renaissance* (Paris: Albin Michel, 1991), p. 94) suggests that, for Thevet, Brazil is a means of measuring the progress of Europe, but it would be just as accurate to argue that Europe is a means of measuring the progress of the rest of the world.
11. Dickason has argued (p. xiii) that the classification of Amerindians as savages allowed Europeans to create the ideology which made possible the establishment of overseas empires.
12. 'En somme les mortelz par succession de temps changerent si bien de conditions qu'en lieu d'estre Barbares et cruelz ilz furent humains et gracieulx deulx mesmes, et se reiglerent en sorte qu'ilz delaisserent toutes anciennes incivilitez et inhumanitez: comme de s'entretuer l'ung l'aultre, de manger chairs humaines, et prendre la compaignie de la premiere rencontree, sans aucune discretion de sang ou parentage, et au tres semblables vices, et imperfections.' Johann Boemus, 'Prologue au lecteur' in *Recueil de diverses histoires touchant les situations de toutes regions & pays contenuz es trois parties du monde, avec les particulieres mœurs, loix, & ceremonies de toutes nations & peuples y habitans* (Paris: Galliot de Pré, 1539).
13. Inga Clendinnen has argued that the conquest of Mexico acted as a paradigm for understanding European encounters with organised societies in the New World: 'Cortés, Signs, and the Conquest of Mexico', in *The Transmission of Culture in Early Modern Europe*, ed. by Anthony Grafton and Ann Blair (Philadelphia: University of Pennsylvania Press, 1990), pp. 87–130.
14. For an account of the Valladolid debate and its background and aftermath, see Lewis Hanke, *All Mankind is One: A Study of the Disputation between Bartolomé de Las Casas and Juan Ginés de Sepúlveda in 1550 on the Intellectual and Religious Capacity of the American Indians* (DeKalb: Northern Illinois University Press, 1974). Other accounts can be found in Anthony Pagden, *The Fall of Natural Man: The American Indian and the Origins of Comparative Ethnology* (Cambridge: Cambridge University Press, 1987), pp. 109–45; and David A. Lupher, *Romans in a New World: Classical Models in Sixteenth-Century Spanish America* (Ann Arbor: University of Michigan Press, 2003), pp. 103–49.
15. The meaning of the word 'atheists' was not the same as today, used as it was by writers to mean whatever they wanted it to mean, often to condemn any ideas regarded as unorthodox, not only disbelief in God. For a discussion of the meanings of atheism in the sixteenth century, see Denis J.-J. Robichaud, 'Renaissance and Reformation', in *The Oxford Handbook of Atheism*, ed. by Stephen Bullivant and Michael Ruse (Oxford: Oxford University Press, 2013), pp. 179–94.

16. See Anthony Pagden, *Lords of All the World: Ideologies of Empire in Spain, Britain and France c.1500–c.1800* (New Haven, CT: Yale University Press, 1998), pp. 11–28, and Lupher.
17. On the uses of Virgil in *Les Singularitez*, see Phillip John Usher, 'L'Intertexte virgilien dans les *Singularités de la France antarctique* (1557) d'André Thevet', in *La Renaissance au grand large: Mélanges en l'honneur de Frank Lestringant*, ed. by Véronique Ferrer, Olivier Millet and Alexandre Tarrête (Geneva: Droz, 2019), pp. 119–28.
18. Frank Lestringant, 'Le Récit de voyage et la question des genres', p. 98. Thevet represents Europe as a culture which should be expanded to outsiders. Earlier models of cultural identity did likewise: Roman conceptions of *civitas* conceived Roman citizenship as a civilisation for exportation, and Christianity entailed an obligation to extend the faith; see Pagden, *Lords of All the World*, pp. 22–24, 30–31.
19. Testament to this are the 1992 colloquium in Bordeaux entitled 'Montaigne et l'Europe' and the volume of essays that arose from the event, *Montaigne et l'Europe: Actes du colloque international de Bordeaux (1992)*, ed. by Claude-Gilbert Dubois (Mont-de-Marsan: Éditions InterUniversitaires, 1992).
20. Philippe Desan, 'Être Français à la Renaissance: L'expérience de Montaigne', in *Montaigne et l'Europe: Actes du colloque international de Bordeaux (1992)*, ed. by Claude-Gilbert Dubois (Mont-de-Marsan: Éditions InterUniversitaires, 1992), pp. 47–59 (p. 58); Claude-Gilbert Dubois, *Essais sur Montaigne: La régulation de l'imaginaire éthique et politique* (Caen: Paradigme, 1992), p. 133.
21. In relation to the question of Montaigne's idea of Europe, Michel Peronnet cautions against using the term 'Europe' anachronistically: 'Montaigne et l'Europe?', in *Montaigne et l'Europe: Actes du colloque international de Bordeaux (1992)*, ed. by Claude-Gilbert Dubois (Mont-de-Marsan: Éditions InterUniversitaires, 1992), pp. 61–71 (p. 70). Claude Blum suggests an intermediary position between that of Desan and Dubois on the one hand and Peronnet on the other, noting that there is no concept of European consciousness in Montaigne's work, but arguing that there are elements of what will later become essential to European consciousness: 'Des *Essais* au *Journal de voyage*: Espace humain et conscience européenne à la fin du XVIe siècle', in *La Conscience européenne au XVe et au XVIe siècle: Actes du colloque international organisé à l'École Normale Supérieure de Jeunes Filles (30 septembre – 3 octobre 1980)* (Paris: École Normale Supérieure de Jeunes Filles, 1982), pp. 23–33.
22. For a consideration of which geographical writers Montaigne was familiar with, see Gérard Defaux, 'Un cannibale en haut de chausses: Montaigne, la différence et la logique de l'identité', *Modern Language Notes*, 97 (1982), 919–57 (p. 937). See also Philip Ford, *The Montaigne Library of Gilbert de Botton at Cambridge University Library* (Cambridge: Cambridge University Library, 2008).
23. Defaux, 'Un cannibale en haut de chausses', p. 938.
24. These two works of Thevet's are examined in Chapter 4 of the present book.
25. Colin Dickson argues that this 1588 addition to the original chapter helps to clarify the meaning of 'Des cannibales' by emphasising the 'unknowability

of the world': 'Geographic Imagination in the *Essais* and Geomorphism in Montaigne Criticism', in *Geo/graphies: Mapping the Imagination in French and Francophone Literature and Film*, ed. by Freeman G. Henry, French Literature Series, 30 (Amsterdam: Rodopi, 2003), pp. 29–40 (p. 33).

26. Ayesha Ramachandran suggests that the central theme of 'Des cannibales' is 'the epistemological problem of knowing and narrating the world, a process that depends on hearsay, mediation, embroidered narratives, and the imaginative conjuring of faraway places'. See *The Worldmakers: Global Imagining in Early Modern Europe* (Chicago: University of Chicago Press, 2015), p. 84.

27. Frank Lestringant, 'Cosmographes', in *Dictionnaire de Michel de Montaigne*, ed. by Philippe Desan (Paris: Garnier, 2007), pp. 256–58 (p. 257).

28. In that sense, 'Des cannibales' is, as Defaux has indicated, a reflexive essay encouraging readers to exercise their judgement: 'Un cannibale en haut de chausses', p. 935. More generally, it has been demonstrated that Montaigne's *Essais* are experiments in thinking that use the essay form to think about issues rather than to present readers with a specific viewpoint; see Terence Cave, *How to Read Montaigne* (London: Granta, 2007), and Richard Scholar, *Montaigne and the Art of Free-Thinking* (Oxford: Peter Lang, 2010).

29. Edwin Duval has traced at length Montaigne's play with the meaning of these two words in 'Lessons of the New World: Design and Meaning in Montaigne's "Des cannibales" (I:31) and "Des coches" (III:6)', *Yale French Studies*, 64 (1983), 95–112. See also Paul J. Smith's study of barbarism in 'Des cannibales' in which he argues that Montaigne wants his reader to consider the term's meaning: 'Naked Indians, Trousered Gauls: Montaigne on Barbarism', in *Barbarism Revisited: New Perspectives on an Old Concept*, ed. by Maria Boletsi and Christian Moser (Leiden: Brill, 2015), pp. 105–22. For a reading of 'Des cannibales' that situates barbarism in relation to its meanings in antiquity, see François Hartog, 'Barbarians: From the Ancient to the New World', in *Barbarism Revisited: New Perspectives on an Old Concept*, ed. by Maria Boletsi and Christian Moser (Leiden: Brill, 2015), pp. 31–44. For a study of the term 'cannibale' in this context, see John O'Brien, '"Le Propre de l'homme": Reading Montaigne's "Des cannibales" in Context', *Forum for Modern Language Studies*, 53 (2017), 220–34.

30. André Tournon has identified three different values in the concept of barbarism: one is pejorative, another is praiseworthy (of the simplicity of primitive life), and the final is neutral (a marker of different cultural customs): *La Glose et l'essai* (Paris: Champion, 2000), p. 217.

31. Duval argues that these shifts of perspective illustrate a point made by Montaigne in the 'Apologie de Raimond Sebond' (II.12): 'nous, et nostre jugement, et toutes choses mortelles, vont coulant et roulant sans cesse' (p. 601; 'we, our judgement and all mortal things are flowing and rolling continually'). See 'Lessons of the New World', p. 104. Similarly, Tournon has suggested that the chapter is structured like a methodical inquiry, assessing the common view against the utopian counter-opinion (*La Glose et l'essai*, p. 221).

32. Duval noted that Montaigne's view of the Tupi remains positive throughout 'Des cannibales' ('Lessons of the New World', p. 102). An alternative view is offered by Quint ('A Reconsideration of Montaigne's *Des cannibales*'), who emphasises Montaigne's critique of Brazilian cruelty and cautions against an idealistic reading of 'Des cannibales'. Even if Quint's argument is accepted, the point still stands that the Brazilians are represented positively in comparison to the peoples of the Old World.
33. The strained relationship between language and the referential world, between appearance and reality, is at the heart of Jean Starobinski's study *Montaigne en mouvement* (Paris: Gallimard, 1993).
34. Marcus Keller has noted the indeterminate 'nous' in another essay of Montaigne's that considers the New World, 'Des coches', arguing that it raises questions about the existence of collective identities: 'France, Europe, and the Orient in the *Essays*: Montaigne's Dialectics', in *The Dialectics of Orientalism in Early Modern Europe*, ed. by Marcus Keller and Javier Irigoyen-García (London: Palgrave Macmillan, 2018), pp. 121–36.
35. Timothy Hampton, *Literature and Nation in the Sixteenth Century: Inventing Renaissance France* (Ithaca, NY: Cornell University Press, 2001), pp. 195–226. An alternative reading is provided by Keller in 'France, Europe, and the Orient in the *Essays*', where he argues that the fluid 'nous' generates uncertainty about community and identity.
36. George Hoffmann interprets 'Des cannibales' as a sceptical engagement with the Catholic Mass, alluding to contemporary Protestant attacks on Catholics as cannibalistic god-eaters ('Anatomy of the Mass: Montaigne's "Cannibals"', *PMLA*, 117 (2002), 207–21). Lestringant, on the other hand, considers Montaigne to be less polemical and more reflective in his reflections on the Eucharistic debate (*Une sainte horreur, ou le voyage en Eucharistie: XVIe–XVIIIe siècle* (Paris: Presses Universitaires de France, 1996), p. 247).

Chapter 3

Views from Constantinople

In a preface to *La Franciade* (*The Franciad*) published posthumously, Pierre de Ronsard, the most famous poet of the French Renaissance, wrote of '[le] Seigneur Turc occupant par armes la meilleure partie de l'Europe, [...] reduisant la Chrestienté, de si vaste et grande qu'elle estoit' ('the Turkish Lord occupying by arms the worthiest part of Europe, [...] reducing Christendom, so vast and great that it was').[1] This concern with Europe, Christendom and the Ottoman Empire in the poet's epic on the founding of France demonstrates how the claims of nationhood played out on a wider international scale. It also shows how the word 'Europe' was used in relation to the Ottoman Empire, with the military power of the Turks representing a territorial threat. The capture of Constantinople in 1453 had ushered in an era of Ottoman expansion across the Bosporus westwards into Europe. The anti-Islamic rhetoric galvanised by this danger is considered to have played a crucial role in the development of the idea of Europe.[2] Indeed, it has been argued that a specifically European (as opposed to Christian) identity was born of resistance to Ottoman expansion.[3]

However, an imagined geography of a Christian Europe facing a Muslim east overlooks the complexities of the interactions between Christians and Ottomans. Relations between east and west were not solely hostile and combative, and there was an array of both positive and negative views about the Turks in the Renaissance.[4] Over the last twenty-five years much light has been shed on the social, cultural, economic, intellectual and political developments of the period that depended upon the movement of people, ideas, skills and goods between the Ottoman Empire and Christian Europe.[5] The impact of this has been to 're-orient' our understanding of the Renaissance, revealing how cultural exchange made borders more porous than has been assumed.[6] Yet there has not been a reassessment of how interactions between the east and the west shaped thinking about Europe.[7] That many Frenchmen who travelled to the Ottoman Empire held positive views about the culture and society they found there has been attested in scholarship on the subject, but this has not made its mark on studies of the idea of Europe.[8]

Accordingly, this chapter re-orients the role of the Ottoman Empire in shaping Renaissance ideas of Europe. In examining the Ottoman Empire as a central theme of discourses about Europe, we shall first consider the poetry of Ronsard, who never visited the Ottoman Empire and draws on the image of the Turk as a threatening other, before turning to the political tracts of a man who crossed cultural boundaries, the diplomat and scholar François Savary de Brèves, who was French ambassador to Constantinople and later to Rome. The analysis focuses on how their understandings of the Ottoman Empire shape their conceptions of Europe and how their thinking about the Ottomans relates to their wider thought. For both Ronsard and Savary de Brèves, nationhood is central. We shall see that the two writers display a variety of concerns and depict a variety of interactions between east and west – economic, cultural, political and ideological – which offer different ideas of Europe. And while the notion of confrontation – of Europe versus the Ottoman Empire, of Christendom versus the Muslim world – is elaborated differently by Ronsard and Savary de Brèves, what they share is a concern with the place of France in relation to Europe, Christendom and the Ottoman Empire.[9] The comparison of Ronsard's literary work with the non-literary writings of Savary de Brèves indicates the coexistence of different attitudes about the Ottoman Empire and its relationship to France and Christian Europe. The more flexible and pragmatic view presented by Savary de Brèves points towards an acceptance of the Ottoman Empire as a legitimate political entity, while Ronsard's reliance on a Christian-Muslim binary underscores the continuing significance of religious identity in shaping cultural perceptions of geography.[10]

Pierre de Ronsard and the Place of France in Europe

Ronsard was the unofficial leader of the Pléiade group of poets, whose aims Joachim du Bellay described as the enrichment of the French language by imitation of Greek and Latin authors for the glorification of the French nation.[11] As such, Ronsard is an important figure in sixteenth-century constructions of nationhood.[12] Within his poetic works the word 'Europe' appears on eighty-two occasions.[13] By contrast, the term 'Chrestienté' ('Christendom') occurs only three times.

This less frequent usage can no doubt be explained by the demands of verse – 'Europe' offering greater flexibility than 'Chrestienté' – and a humanist preference for a word of classical origin over one of medieval Latin.[14] Yet the number of appearances of 'Europe' (it is within the 1,000 most frequently used words in his verse) also suggests that the idea of Europe occupies a certain importance within Ronsard's poetic vision. By situating the word in relation to images of the Turk, Ronsard, as we shall see, develops an idea of Europe which links the discourses of Ottoman expansion, the classical past and French nationhood.

Ronsard adopts the trope of the Ottoman Empire as a threat to Europe. Following the 1565 siege of Malta, where Suleiman the Magnificent's forces failed to capture the island from the Knights Hospitaller, Ronsard wrote of the Ottoman menace in a poem addressed to Charles IX:

> Comme Alexandre, aurez l'ame animée
> Du chaud desir de conduire une armée
> Outre l'Europe, et d'assauts vehemens
> Oster le Sceptre aux puissans Ottomans,
> Qui sous leurs mains par armes ont saisie
> Tout le meilleur d'Europe et de l'Asie,
> Lesquels hardis d'hommes et de vaisseaux
> Ont d'avirons ja couvertes les eaux
> Qu'on voit flotter dessus la mer Tyrrhene:
> Ont ja campé leurs soldars sur l'arene
> De la Sicile et de Calabre, afin
> Que nostre loy par le Turc prenne fin. (II, p. 47)

> Like Alexander, you will have your soul motivated by the fervent desire to drive an army beyond Europe and, with fierce attacks, to remove the Sceptre from the powerful Ottomans who by arms have laid hands on all the best of Europe and of Asia, who with many men and many vessels have already covered with their oars the waters flowing upon the Tyrrhenian Sea: already their soldiers have pitched camp on the sand of Sicily and of Calabria in order for the Turk to bring our law to an end.

The continent is here defined in opposition to the Ottomans and is held together culturally by 'nostre loy', the Christian faith. The image of the Ottomans camped on the Italian peninsula plays on a fear of proximity, of penetration ever further westward that threatens the whole of Europe. It is a rhetorical move that effaces the fact that while the Habsburgs were expending resources in wars against the Ottomans, France had a military alliance with the Ottoman Empire that had been established since the reign of François I.[15] The image of 'le barbare Turc' (II, p. 39; 'the barbarous Turk') advancing into Europe was common in Renaissance thought and is used in this poem to spur a counterattack. Ronsard reminds the king of a popular prophecy:

C'est qu'un grand Roy de France doit un jour,
En les dontant et chassant du sejour
Que Constantin esleut pour sa demeure,
Rompre leur Sceptre, et d'une foy meilleure
Gaigner les cœurs des peuples Asiens,
De Circoncis en faire des Chrestiens,
François d'habits, de mœurs, et de langage. (II, p. 48)

> It is that a great King of France must one day, by overcoming them and chasing them from the place Constantine elected for his abode, break their Sceptre and, with a worthier faith, win the hearts of the Asian peoples, making the Circumcised into Christians, French in habits, manners and language.

In the sixteenth century, the promotion of a crusade against the Ottoman Empire was often an appeal for warring Christian princes to unite against a common enemy.[16] This is not the case here as Ronsard figures the French king as the head of a crusade to capture Constantinople, drawing on the prophecy that a second Charlemagne would come to defeat the Turks, which had been useful political rhetoric for the French monarchy since the fourteenth century.[17]

Thus, Ronsard's representation of a clash between Europe and the Ottoman Empire serves to emphasise French ambition and glory by mapping it onto a larger geographical and political canvas. The juxtaposition of 'Chrestiens' and 'François' in the previous quotation invests Charles IX with the significance of the spiritual leadership of Christendom and rejects an alliance of Christian powers in favour of spreading the religion alongside the customs and language of the French. Moreover, Ronsard's references to Alexander the Great and the Roman Emperor Constantine depict France as the heir to Greco-Roman antiquity through the figure of Charles IX, who will emulate the feats of Alexander and Constantine by advancing militarily beyond Europe to Asia. In his doing so, Greece – 'Mere des Arts, des Philosophes mere' ('Mother of Arts, of Philosophers mother') – will be freed from 'servitude / Sous ce Grand Turc, qui presque de l'esprit / Du people Grec a chassé Jesus-Christ' ('servitude under the Great Turk who has almost from the spirit of the Greek people driven away Jesus Christ'; II, p. 49). Christianity and classical antiquity, then, are both important to Ronsard's conception of Europe, and it is these values that Ronsard claims for France.

The references to Greece in Ronsard's poetry highlight the fact that the military threat posed to Europe by the Ottoman Empire is as much cultural as it is political. Greece's present situation as part of the Ottoman Empire and its cultural significance are used to articulate France's role within Europe. In the 'Discours ou dialogue entre les Muses deslogées, et Ronsard' ('Discourse or Dialogue between the Homeless Muses and Ronsard') the poet dramatises an encounter between himself and the Muses who have been exiled from Greece by the Turkish advance. They tell Ronsard that:

> Nous eusmes autrefois des habits precieux,
> Mais le barbare Turc de tout victorieux,
> Ayant vaincu l'Asie et l'Afrique, et d'Europe
> La meilleure partie, a chassé nostre trope
> De la Grece natale, et fuyant ses prisons
> Errons, comme tu vois, sans biens et sans maisons,
> Où le pied nous conduit, pour voir si sans excuses
> Les peuples et les Rois auront pitié des Muses. (II, p. 39)

> We had in times past precious habits, but the barbarous Turk, victorious over all, having vanquished Asia and Africa and the better part of Europe, has chased our company from our native Greece, and fleeing his prisons we wander, as you see, without possessions and without homes, wherever our feet drive us, to see if, without pretext to refuse, peoples and Kings will have pity on the Muses.

Goddesses of the arts and sciences, the Muses represent intellectual culture. The supposed barbarity of the Turks means that civilisation can no longer flourish in its cradle, Greece. Thus the shabbily dressed Muses make their way towards France:

> Nous avons ouy dire
> Que le Prince qui tient maintenant vostre Empire,
> Et qui d'un double sceptre honore sa grandeur,
> Est dessus tous les Roys des lettres amateur,
> Caresse les sçavans, et des livres fait conte,
> Estimant l'ignorance estre une grande honte:
> Dy luy de nostre part qu'il luy plaise changer
> En mieux nostre fortune, et nous donne à loger. (II, pp. 40–41)

> We have heard it said that the Prince who now holds your Empire, and whose greatness is honoured by a double sceptre, is above all Kings a lover of learning, who cherishes the wise and esteems books, considering ignorance to be a great shame. Ask him on our behalf if it would please him to change our fortune for the better and afford us a lodging.

The double sceptre refers to Henri III, who was King of Poland before inheriting the crown of France. The westward migration of the Muses away from Greece represents the *translatio studii* to Henri's kingdom, where a culture of 'lettres', 'sçavans' and 'livres' can now thrive thanks to the king's patronage.[18] The image of the Muses fleeing the Ottomans invests Europe with literary and humanistic associations; their destination situates France as the centre of contemporary culture and learning.[19]

In emphasising France's role in Europe, Ronsard draws on the idea of universal monarchy. The conflicts that erupted across the continent as a result of the Reformation made the notion of a world leader who could ensure order and stability an attractive prospect.[20] The threat of the Turks was often raised in relation to warring Christians, forming as it did an urgent appeal to make peace. Ronsard himself lamented 'La pauvre Europe' ('poor Europe') at war with itself, vulnerable to the great Turk, in 'Les Isles fortunees' ('The Blessed Isles') of 1553 (II, p. 780). Although linked with desires for peace and unity, the idea of universal monarchy became a vehicle for patriotism as it begged the question of who would fulfil the role. Not surprisingly, competing claims to leadership of the continent and the whole world were a feature of the rivalry between the Habsburgs and the French Valois. The status of Charlemagne as King of the Franks and the first Holy Roman Emperor provided legitimacy to the French monarch's claims. In *Le Troisiesme Livre des odes* (*The Third Book of Odes*, 1555) Ronsard published a series of poems in which he depicts a future universal monarchy, the whole world divided between the three eldest male children of Henri II. He opens the third ode of the volume by asking 'Que pourroy-je, moy François, / Mieux celebrer que la France' ('What could I, my François, better celebrate than France') and goes on to imagine Europe united under one monarch, Henri's heir, François:

> Tu penseras en ton cœur
> D'acquerir l'Europe encore,
> Et de te faire veinqueur
> Des Gades jusqu'au Bosphore. (I, p. 734)
>
> You will still think in your heart of acquiring Europe and making yourself conqueror from Cadiz to the Bosporus.

It is because of Europe's superiority to the other continents that the eldest son is urged to conquer it. Ronsard articulates that superiority in terms of the cultivation of people and land, as was commonly found across other written genres:

> Mais tu as Roy plus heureux
> Choisi les terres fertiles,
> Pleines d'hommes valeureux,
> Pleines de ports et de villes. (I, p. 738)
>
> But you most happy King have chosen the fertile lands, full of valorous men, full of ports and of towns.

Ronsard includes a classical parallel to explain and to glorify François's future exploits, claiming that, after bringing the continent as far as Greece under his control, François will return to Paris 'Ainsi qu'à Rome

Cesar / Triomphant d'une victoire' (I, p. 735; 'Like Caesar to Rome, triumphant with victory'). Ronsard here adopts the topos of *translatio imperii*, a companion to *translatio studii*. It is a vision of Europe remade in the image of a dominant power. Ronsard positions France as the political and cultural heir of antiquity, of Rome as the universal monarchy, and in doing so he transforms a limited national model of community into a potentially limitless imperial model.

Nevertheless, as Ronsard was a court poet, his literary output was subject to shifting royal policy and he adapted his representations of Europe and of France in accordance with changing priorities. In 1559 the treaty of Cateau-Cambrésis brought an end to the Habsburg–Valois Wars. During the negotiations Ronsard published his 'Exhortation pour la paix' ('Exhortation for Peace'), which urged peace between France and Spain.[21] The spectre of the Ottoman Empire and the territorial threat it poses to Europe – 'le Turc n'est / Si eslongné d'ici [. . .] ils ont (sans coups ruer) en Europe passé' (II, p. 808; 'the Turk is not so far away from here [. . .] they have (without inflicting great blows) passed into Europe') – provide the background to the appeal for a crusade: 'Chassez les Sarrasins hors de la saincte Terre' (II, p. 809; 'chase the Saracens out of the Holy Land'). Ronsard diverges from the sixteenth-century trend in positing Constantinople, rather than Jerusalem, as the object of crusade.[22] This contrasts with his later reference to removing the Ottomans from Constantinople, which we saw above. This underlines that in the 'Exhortation pour la paix' the focus is very much on Christianity. It opens with a direct appeal to religious sentiment: 'Non, ne combatez pas, vivez en amitié, / Chrestiens, changez vostre ire avecques la pitié' (II, p. 807; 'No, don't fight, live in friendship, Christians, transform your anger with pity'). Fears of a common enemy in Europe are evoked to support the poet's argument, but the primary appeal is to the Christian identity that was shared by the combatants and binds them in a relationship of kinship: 'ne trempez vos dars dans le sang de vos freres' (II, p. 807; 'don't soak your spears with the blood of your brothers'). In this context, the idea of Europe carries less emotional value than references to Christianity, although the two are of course very closely associated with one another. Europe is the political theatre in which the Habsburg–Valois Wars have played out and which continues to be threatened by the Ottomans. Where elsewhere Ronsard imagines the achievement of unity in Europe through universal monarchy, here peace and stability are guaranteed through the political and military cooperation of different nations united by Christianity.

This adaptability of the concept of Europe – its potential to be used in different ways to appeal to changing political circumstances – is reflected in variants that Ronsard introduced as he revised his poems for republication. When Ronsard first published the 'Discours à G. Des-Autels' ('Discourse to Guillaume Desautels') in 1560, he wrote of 'le temps orageux qui par l'Europe court' (II, p. 1011; 'the stormy weather which ravages Europe'), changing this to 'le temps orageux qui par la France court' (II, p. 1581; 'the stormy weather which ravages France') in 1562 when the massacre of Vassy prompted the outbreak of the first of France's religious civil wars.[23] The edit marks a change in the angle of Ronsard's vision. A comment initially on religious division across the continent gives way to a focalisation on the crisis in France. This shift in emphasis centres nationhood at the expense of thinking about the consequences of the Reformation for Europe as a whole. Ronsard returns to the broader geographical view of religious conflict in his 1565 'Bergerie' ('Pastoral'), writing, 'nos Princes seigneurs de diverses contrées [. . .] Ont effroyé les loups' ('our lord Princes from different countries [. . .] have frightened the wolves'), the 'loups' referring to Protestants (II, pp. 144, 1346). But in 1578, during a lull in the fighting in France, this was altered to strike a less combative tone: 'nos Princes [. . .] Ont défendu l'Europe' (II, p. 144; 'our Princes [. . .] have defended Europe'). The new image is of rulers working together for common defence. There is an ambiguity here as to whether they are defending their realms from heresy or from the Ottomans, but the mood has unmistakeably shifted as a result of the usage of the term 'Europe'. This is a Europe of diversity, of cooperation between rulers, rather than a Europe united under a universal monarch. The imperial associations of the term 'Europe' are absent. Indeed, the word in this context serves a neutral purpose, being less divisive than an allusion to Christendom. In changing the meaning of the line of poetry, the adoption of the word 'Europe' indicates the flexibility, or malleability, of the term, its potential to be deployed – rhetorically and politically – in different contexts and for different purposes.

In spite of the shifting and contingent nature of the ideas and emphases in Ronsard's poetry, the imagined geography of Europe in his work is shaped in relation to both France and the Ottoman Empire. His poetry is situated within the tradition of anti-Ottoman discourse, and his use of the trope of the Turk as a threatening other allows Ronsard to project his different arguments. In the 'Exhortation pour la paix' the Ottomans function as a warning to advocate peace between France and Spain. Elsewhere they are used by Ronsard as an opportunity to assert French pride, to imagine a successful French crusade against Constantinople. He pictures a Europe of peace and of a coalition against the Ottoman Empire, and he pictures a Europe under French rule. In this way, the meanings of the term 'Europe' in his poetry fluctuate. He uses Europe as a political idea and as a cultural idea, emphasising especially the continuation, or rebirth, of classical civilisation. The dominant thread is the figure of the French king.[24] Whether as a political actor seeking peace with its neighbours or as a Christian imperial power seeking to dominate the whole world, the French nation is central to the poetic uses of the word 'Europe' in Ronsard's oeuvre.

François Savary de Brèves and the Franco-Ottoman Alliance

Ronsard's cultural take on the Turks ignores France's economic and political relations with the Ottoman Empire. François I's rivalry with the Habsburg Charles V led him to inaugurate diplomatic, trading and military relations with the Ottoman sultan Suleiman.[25] This was not an alliance on paper only; French and Ottoman troops cooperated to launch joint attacks against Habsburg forces. This policy was continued after François's death, with the Ottoman Empire and France capturing Corsica together in 1553. Even after the 1559 Peace of Cateau-Cambrésis between France and Spain, ambassadors continued to be sent to the Sublime Porte in Constantinople. The world of sixteenth-century diplomacy was pragmatic, and France was not the only power to make diplomatic overtures to the Ottomans. Nonetheless, the alliance generated an array of opinions, positive and negative. The Huguenot soldier François de La Noue condemned it in his 1587 *Discours politiques et militaires* as having 'contamin[é]' 'l'integrité chrestienne' ('defiled Christian integrity').[26] Others such as Jean de Monluc, an ambassador to Venice, argued that the alliance was in the interests of Christendom.[27] François Savary de Brèves, French ambassador to Constantinople from 1592 to 1605, published two discourses, one describing how to conduct a crusade to overthrow the Ottoman Empire and the other arguing that the Franco-Ottoman alliance was beneficial for Christendom.

Savary de Brèves negotiated a renewal in 1604 of the Franco-Ottoman treaty with Ahmed I, which increased France's commercial interests and afforded protection to pilgrims to the Holy Land and to churches in Ottoman lands. He had initially travelled to Constantinople in 1585 when his uncle had been appointed ambassador. During his two decades in the Ottoman Empire he acquired proficiency in the language and, unlike other diplomats at the Sublime Porte, did not require an interpreter. From 1608 to 1614 he served as ambassador in Rome, where he established an Arabic printing press, the Typographia Savariana, becoming the first person to publish Ottoman texts in Europe. Returning to France, he brought his press with him, and in 1615 he published the 1604 treaty in a bilingual French and Turkish edition.[28] Later his two ostensibly contradictory discourses concerning the Ottoman Empire were published alongside one another: the *Discours abrégé des asseurez moyens d'aneantir & ruiner la monarchie des Princes Ottomans* (*Abridged Discourse on the Assured Means to Weaken and Ruin the Monarchy of the Ottoman Princes*) and the *Discours sur l'alliance qu'a le Roy avec le grand Seigneur, & de l'utilité qu'elle apporte à la Chrestienté* (*Discourse on the Alliance that the King Has with the Great Lord and on the Utility that it Brings to Christendom*).[29] This section will examine the division between east and west in Savary de Brèves's writings on the Ottoman Empire, assessing his usage of the terms 'Europe' and 'Chrestienté'. I argue that while Savary de Brèves, keen to promote the circulation of goods and people, considers the boundaries between Europe/Christendom and the Ottoman Empire to be porous, he makes use of the idea of Europe/Christendom and the Ottoman Empire as antithetical and clashing cultures in order to argue his political points and promote French national interests.

The *Discours abrégé*, which precedes the *Discours sur l'alliance* in the published editions of these works, opens with the image of powerful Ottomans ruling in Europe.[30] Savary de Brèves writes: 'Ils se sont rendus seigneurs souverains d'une partie de l'Europe, de l'Asie, et de tout plein de pays de l'Afrique' ('They made themselves the sovereign lords of a part of Europe, of Asia and of many countries of Africa').[31] He warns that the Ottoman Empire could expand further, suggesting that the sultan could easily 'ruiner le Royaume de Sicile' (p. 11; 'ruin the Kingdom of Sicily'). According to Savary de Brèves, 'le repos de l'Europe' ('the peace of Europe') is assured only since the sultans 'ont negligé les moyens de mal-faire aux Princes de l'Europe' ('have neglected the means of doing ill to the Princes of Europe') as they are busy warring with the Persians (p. 12). These uses of the word 'Europe' indicate that the Ottomans are considered to represent more of a political and territorial threat than a spiritual challenge. Indeed, Savary de Brèves offers a mild portrait of the Ottoman treatment towards conquered peoples: 'on leur laisse la possession de leurs biens, et l'exercice de leur Religion' ('they leave them in the possession of their goods and the practice of their religion'; p. 8). Strikingly, he does not label the Ottomans 'barbares' in either the *Discours abrégé* or the *Discours sur l'alliance*. Nevertheless, integral to the *Discours abrégé* is the assumption of the desirability of the destruction of the Ottoman Empire, which 'a ravallé la grandeur et la gloire de la Chrestienté' (p. 46; 'has debased the grandeur and the glory of

Christendom'). 'Chrestienté', for Savary de Brèves, carries cultural and ideological signification, whereas 'Europe' is more of a political term. Both words are emotive and have spatial meaning. 'Chrestienté' appeals to cultural identity; 'Europe' appeals to fears of a political enemy with expansionist aims. Indeed, Savary de Brèves wants to stress the Ottoman Empire's 'espouventable puissance, afin que ceux qui prendront la peine de lire [. . .] cognoissent le pouvoir qu'elle a de mal-faire à l'Europe [. . .] [et] qu'elle n'est pas aisée à battre, n'y à vaincre' (p. 14; 'fearful strength in order that those who take the trouble to read [. . .] understand the power that it has to do ill to Europe [. . .] [and] that it would not be easy to beat, nor to vanquish'). That said, Savary de Brèves does assure his readers that the Ottomans could be defeated by a naval attack 'si la puissance Chrestienne se vouloit unir' (p. 32; 'if the Christian force had the will to unite').

Whom does Savary de Brèves include within the contentious label 'Chrestienne'? His plan for crusade involves both the Catholic and the Protestant powers of the continent. In outlining the forces that he recommends attack Constantinople, he includes the navies of Spain, France, Venice and the pope, as well as those of Protestant England and the Dutch Provinces (pp. 34–35). He estimates that the Ottoman Empire could not be defeated without a unified force:

> L'execution de ceste proposition, est une œuvre de Dieu; s'il n'y met sa puissante main, et n'inspire nos Princes tant de l'une que de l'autre creance, il est impossible que les hommes y trouvent un acheminement. D'autre part, il se faudroit despouiller de toute sorte de mesfiance, n'entrer point en dispute sur la différence des Religions, n'estre point sur la démarche de la precedence, les uns avec les autres, ains seulement penser à battre ce puissant enemy. (p. 46)

> The execution of this proposition is a work of God; if he does not turn his powerful hand to it and inspire our Princes of both beliefs, it is impossible that men will find a way. Moreover, it would be necessary to throw off all manner of mistrust and not to enter into dispute on the difference of Religions, nor to take steps to establish precedence over one another, but rather to think only of beating this powerful enemy.

Savary de Brèves does not present a plan that is designed to unite the various powers of Christendom as one. A union of Catholic and Protestant states is the means by which the goal of destroying the Ottoman Empire could be achieved, not the desired end in itself.[32] Nor would unity emerge as a beneficial side effect:

> Il seroit aussi necessaire, si ce dessein estoit aggrée desdits Princes, qui en faciliteroient la conqueste, par l'effort de leurs armes; qu'il se fist un project du partage, afin que (Dieu permettant la victoire) l'on évitast les debats qui pourroient, pour ce regard, arriver entre eux. (p. 47)

It would also be necessary, if this design is agreed by the said Princes who will facilitate the conquest by the endeavour of their arms, for them to fashion a plan for dividing the gains in order that (God permitting victory) they avoid the disputes that could, in this respect, arrive between them.

The plan which Savary de Brèves outlines is therefore not one that dissolves differences. While to be successful the attack must be a collective endeavour, the good of the collective is important insofar as it advances the interests of the individual political units. Although their rulers have a different faith ('creance') from one another, they are nonetheless 'nos Princes', having more in common with each other than with the Ottomans. The 'nos' which incorporates the different states articulates a diverse yet shared Christianity. Indeed, the acceptance of diversity is crucial to the plan; Savary de Brèves suggests that Orthodox Christians within the current boundaries of the Ottoman Empire will join the campaign: 'Chrestiens sujects du Grand Seigneur [. . .] se revolteroient à la faveur de nostre armée' (p. 36; 'Christians subject to the Great Lord would rebel in support of our army'); 'bien qu'ils [les Grecs] n'ayment pas nostre creance [. . .] infailliblement ils se revolteroient et prendroient les armes contre luy [le Turc]' (pp. 37–38; 'although the Greeks do not like our faith [. . .] they would without fail rebel and take arms against the Turk').[33] The Orthodox Church can be hostile to 'nostre creance' and at the same time part of a universal and varied Christianity. In short, Savary de Brèves's crusade plan is a matter of political expediency, rather than ideological purity. The central argument of the *Discours abrégé* is that a union of Christians would have the potential to capture Constantinople, but there is no sweeping rhetoric to advance the cause of crusade.

Savary de Brèves's defence of French diplomatic relations with the Ottomans, the *Discours sur l'alliance*, appeals to the idea of Christendom to argue for the utility of the Franco-Ottoman alliance. Savary de Brèves downplays French political concerns, insisting that '[nos Roys] ne conservent pas ceste amitié, pour leur interest particulier, ny celuy de leurs sujets, mais encore pour le bien universel de la Chrestienté' (p. 5; 'our Kings do not maintain this friendship for their particular interest, nor that of their subjects, but for the common benefit of Christendom'). He stresses that the pact's commercial advantages benefit 'all of Europe', not only France: 'les marchands François, et ceux qui veulent arborer nostre estendart, en [des richesses de l'Asie] charge leurs vaisseaux, et les distribuent ainsi par toute l'Europe' (p. 5; 'French merchants, and those who wish to fly our ensign, load their vessels with the riches of Asia and therefore distribute them to all of Europe'). The words 'Chrestienté' and 'Europe' are used here as synonyms, both articulating a broad collectivity. Savary de Brèves is following the emerging trend for recognising the Ottoman Empire as a political unit rather than a religious foe.[34] Religious rhetoric is deployed, though, in order to justify political action. Savary de Brèves highlights the alliance's benefits for all Christians, such as the possibility for pilgrims 'de toutes nations' ('of all nations') to visit holy sites in security (p. 9) and the permission for monasteries to operate in Constantinople (p. 6). The language of Christianity has an emotive pull, which Savary de Brèves relies on to support his argument: 'Quel contentement de voir au milieu de l'Estat des infidelles, florir le nom Chrestien?' (p. 8; 'What satisfaction to see the name Christian flourish in the centre of the State of the infidels?').

What we see in Savary de Brèves's treatise, then, is an interest in cooperation with the Ottoman Empire and a preoccupation with the fluidity and movement that cooperation both requires and makes possible. His *Discours sur l'alliance* champions the circulation of people and goods and defends the treaty, which allows 'toutes sortes de nations Chrestiennes, de trafiquer' (p. 5; 'all manner of Christian nations to trade'). Cultural transfers and exchanges break down an imagined geography of opposition and hostility between the Christian and Muslim worlds. To Savary de Brèves, the border between the Ottoman Empire and Christendom is not a hostile, fixed frontier but a malleable contact zone. From the viewpoint of someone who travels between cultures, the world does not appear to be divided into neat binaries. The fixed geographical conception of Europe runs counter to Savary de Brèves's fluid understanding of culture and community. Boundaries are less about geography than about cultural identity, and these boundaries move with people and communities as they travel. Transfers of people and goods between the west and the Ottoman Empire do not undo the fragmentation of Christianity. Although Savary de Brèves appeals to a wide idea of Christendom, the concerns of the Catholic Church are important in his thinking: 'la conservation du nom Chrestien, et de la Religion Catholique, Apostolique et Romaine, dans leur pays, sera jugée tres-importante' (p. 5; 'the preservation of the name Christian and of the Catholic, Apostolic and Roman Religion in their country will be deemed very important'). Like the *Discours abrégé*, the *Discours sur l'alliance* is not interested in overcoming confessional difference. For Savary de Brèves, Christendom is a useful emotional idea in promoting a diplomatic initiative that serves the interests of France and, by extension, the religion of the French state.

French interests are central to the *Discours sur l'alliance*, even though Savary de Brèves plays down their significance with his rhetorical appeal to Christendom. He acknowledges the national rivalries that led François I to an agreement with Suleiman: '[le Roy] injustement pressé par les entreprises sur ceste Monarchie, de Charles quint, du Roy d'Angleterre, et de la plus-part des Princes de la Chrestienté' (pp. 3–4; 'the King unjustly pressed by the encroachments upon this Monarchy by Charles V, the King of England and most of the Christian Princes'). Christendom is represented as fractured by competing political units, with France cast in the role of victim. The alliance with the Ottomans is cast as a legitimate defence, which in turn led to the guarantee of rights and privileges for the whole of Christendom, including those states that threatened France. The treaty can also help to counter any future Habsburg aggression:

> la mesme consideration qui fait naistre ceste amitié, peut convier sa Majesté, de la conserver et d'en faire estat: dautant qu'elle n'est pas asseurée d'estre tousjours en bonne intelligence avec ses voisins, et pourroit arriver par succession de temps, que les Princes de l'Empire, jaloux de sa grandeur, voudroient troubler son repos. Ce qu'avenant, il seroit fort aisé de destourner leur armes, par l'entremise du Turc, lequel en mettant une puissante armée sur pied, et envoyant du costé de Hongrie, pourroit traverser leurs desseins, et les obliger à retourner chez eux, pour défendre leur pays. (p. 9)

> the same consideration that gave rise to this friendship may invite his Majesty to preserve it and make use of it: so much so since he is not assured of being always on good terms with his neighbours, and it could happen in time that the Princes of the Empire, jealous of his greatness, desire to disturb his peace. In that case, it would be very easy to divert their arms by means of the Turk who, in setting a powerful army on the ground and sending it towards Hungary, could thwart their designs and oblige them to return home to defend their country.

Savary de Brèves is clear that for the safety of France he would not be opposed to the Ottomans advancing further into the continent. La Noue, whose crusade plan is much more earnest than Savary de Brèves's *Discours abrégé*, offered an alternative view, decrying that 'du costé de la mer nous avons ces barbares pres de nos portes, et du costé de la terre, nous les avons dedans nos portes' ('at sea with have these barbarians near our gates, and on land we have them within our gates').[35] La Noue articulates a more expansive imagined geography shaped by opposition to the 'barbares' Turks. Whereas for La Noue the Ottoman Empire is close at hand, for Savary de Brèves it is distant from France. A French perception of international relations indicates there are more serious threats. Indeed, when in 1624 Savary de Brèves sent an updated manuscript version of the *Discours sur l'alliance* to Louis XIII, he stressed the threat from the King of Spain, who sought to 'parvenir a la Monarchie Chrestienne' ('attain the Christian Monarchy', that is, govern the whole of Christendom).[36] Alongside this, Savary de Brèves sent the king another treatise, the *Discours tres important des affaires de la mer et des moyens que Dieu a donnez a vostre Majesté pour empescher les desseins qu'a le Roy Catholique de se rendre absolu Seigneur de toute l'Europe comme il fera s'il n'y est remedié* (fol. 25^r; *Very Important Discourse on the Affairs of the Sea and the Means that God has Given to your Majesty to Prevent the Designs that the Catholic King Has to Make Himself Absolute Lord of All Europe as he Will do if he is not Dealt With*) in which he claimed that French military strength was 'le seul obstacle qu'il [le Roy d'Espagne] a pour devenir absolu Seigneur de toute l'Europe' (fol. 26^v; 'the only obstacle that the King of Spain faces in becoming absolute Lord of all Europe'). To argue against unity he raised the spectre of universal monarchy, presenting Spain as a greater threat than the Ottoman Empire. His critique of Spanish hegemony appealed to the rhetoric of both Europe and Christianity, yet the object of his concern was really neither Europe nor Christendom but France.

In this section we have seen what might be termed the paradox of Europe. There was not one European idea of the Turk; rather there were, as Savary de Brèves's two texts illustrate, different conceptions of the Ottoman Empire's relationship with Europe and with France. The two treatises testify to the coexistence of two views about the Turks: they could be seen as both a political player and a religious foe. These competing stories of warfare and cooperation are not mutually exclusive. This complicates the notion of an idea of Europe, or even a European identity, shaped by opposition to the Ottomans. Running alongside, and against, the currents of ideological hostility were the realities of geopolitics, which undermined the imagined geography of Europe as the antithesis of the Muslim Ottoman Empire. As a diplomat, Savary de Brèves had to follow the shifting aims of French foreign policy and appeal as required either to a national struggle against the other dynastic states of Europe or to an anti-Ottoman union, as his two discourses make clear. Accordingly, his conception of Europe was fluid, responding to a vision of the movement of people, goods and ideas across unfixed and permeable boundaries. Nevertheless, alongside this line of thinking, he uses an idea of Europe, and an idea of Christendom, as an opposition to the Ottoman Empire in order to support the arguments he makes in the *Discours abrégé* and the *Discours sur l'alliance*. In championing positive relations with the Ottomans, Savary de Brèves found it prudent to harness negative views of them to bolster his rhetorical position.

Conclusion: Savary de Brèves in Rome

After his long residence in Constantinople, Savary de Brèves was posted to Rome, where he served as Henri IV's ambassador to the papal court. His private correspondence during this time reveals many of the same concerns that he made public in his published discourses: Christendom, national interest, the Ottoman Empire and the threats posed by other powers in Europe. In Henri IV's written instructions, dated May 1608, Savary de Brèves is ordered to speak of all the good the Franco-Ottoman alliance has done for Christians should the pope discuss his desire for crusade, and to extol peace between France and Spain for 'le bien universel de la Chrestienté' ('the common benefit of Christendom').[37] Terminology relating to Christianity is prevalent in this letter, whereas the word 'Europe' does not feature at all. When writing to the king, Savary de Brèves uses similar language, describing initiatives as 'utile à la Republique Chrestienne' (fol. 68; 'beneficial for the Christian Republic';) or for 'le bien de la Chrestienté' (fol. 69; 'the benefit of Christendom'). As well as its cultural and political signification, 'Christendom' is used as an explicitly spatial term: 'toutes les despesches qui sont escrites en France, en Espagne et autres lieux de la Chrestienté passent par ses mains' (fol. 231; 'all the dispatches that are written in France, Spain and other places in Christendom pass through his hands'). The term 'Europe' appears very infrequently in Savary de Brèves's letters, and is restricted to its spatial sense. He writes that he has told the pope of letters he has received from Constantinople, informing him of 'la resolution qu'il [le grand Seigneur] avoit prise d'armer cent galeres pour s'en servir au dommage de la Chrestienté' ('the resolution that the great Lord had taken to arm one hundred galleys and make use of them to the detriment of Christendom') on account of there 'estant en repos du costé de l'Asie, voire mesme de l'Europe' (fol. 253; 'being peace in that part of Asia, and indeed the same in Europe'). Here the word 'Europe' is used to offer a more specific geographical designation than 'Christendom'. While it is used in the context of a discussion about the Ottoman military threat, the word used to specify the target of the threat is 'Christendom'. Savary de Brèves's correspondence also reports what Pope Paul V has said to him in their private audiences. Unsurprisingly, the term 'Christendom', unlike 'Europe', is central to his rhetoric and features in his discussions of his desire to attack the Ottoman Empire: 'son but de voir la Chrestienté en repos et union, pour puis apres faire quelque grand dessein contre les ennemis de l'Eglise de Dieu' (fol. 116; 'his goal to see Christendom at peace and in union so as to then afterwards affect some grand strategy against the enemies of the Church of God'). In other words, the vocabulary referring to ideas of Europe and Christendom depends on context. At the papal court Christendom is the appropriate conceptual reference point. The word 'Christendom' dominates Savary de Brèves's everyday discourse at the Holy See, and he retains it in his letters that report his activities and conversations.

In the *Discours abrégé* Savary de Brèves could write of 'le repos de l'Europe' ('the peace of Europe'), but in Rome he complained to the pope (so he writes to Henri IV) that the Spanish do more to disturb 'le repos de la France et du reste de la Chrestienté que les heretiques' (fol. 226; 'the peace of France and the rest of Christendom than the heretics'), the reference to 'Christendom' carrying more emotional force in this context. Read together, his private diplomatic correspondence and his public political tracts demonstrate the flexibility of the functions of the words 'Europe' and 'Christendom'. Whereas in the *Discours abrégé* and the *Discours sur l'alliance* Savary de Brèves used the two words with a similar frequency, 'Chrestienté' is found much more regularly in his diplomatic letters than the term 'Europe' is. The two were potentially synonymous since both could express spatial, cultural or political meanings when an author so desired. Equally, the two were distinguishable. The words 'Europe' and 'Christendom' carried different weight in different contexts, and writers with a case to make were open to exploiting these nuances. To Ronsard, 'Europe' was preferable to 'Chrestienté' in his metrical poetry. It also allowed him to elaborate a notion which drew on the term's classical associations as well as those of religion. Savary de Brèves's work offers a different perspective. To him, without the constraints of poetic metre, both were regarded as applicable and rhetorically stirring in polemical tracts on the political subject of relations with the Ottoman Empire. However, his diplomatic correspondence reveals that within a religio-political discursive framework the word 'Europe' was a much more neutral word, lacking the emotional charge of 'Chrestienté'.

Place played an important role in shaping these differing conceptions of Europe. Savary de Brèves spent two decades of his life in Constantinople, a city which sits on the Bosporus Strait at the geographical border of Asia and Europe. His experiences there as ambassador – concerned as he was with politics and familiar with Ottoman military capabilities – framed how he wrote about the Ottoman Empire. In his discourses he presented Europe as a geopolitical unit, a political stage on which the interests of different states played out. Europe mattered insofar as movement across the boundaries of the Ottoman Empire for the purposes of trade mattered. When he moved to Rome, Europe looked different. It was more distant than when he had lived on the edge of the continent, for now he was at the centre of Christendom, or at least the centre as it was conceived by those living in Rome. Accordingly, as his diplomatic correspondence attests, Europe was further from his mind, a geographical concept of limited use. Christendom offered a meaningful political and cultural concept. Europe was significant, though, in the thinking of Ronsard, who travelled to Constantinople only in his imagination. He envisaged a French army defeating the Ottomans and restoring Europe to Christianity. Europe represented a nexus of ideas – including Christianity, classical antiquity and a civilisational clash between east and west – which Ronsard used to project a fantasy of a French empire. Greece looms large in this conception of Europe since it is unambiguously within the geographical borders of the continent, whereas Christendom's boundaries may or may not include Orthodox communities. The cultural perceptions of Europe, as represented in Ronsard's poetry, draw on both classical civilisation and Christianity.

What we have seen in this chapter is evidence for the complexity of the development of discourses on Europe and Islam during the Renaissance period. It was not the case that Europe was imagined only as the antithesis of the Ottoman Empire to the east, although that idea certainly did circulate and was used by Savary de Brèves as a political tool and by Ronsard as a literary trope. On the other hand, Savary de Brèves argued for the movement of people and goods between the Christian and Muslim worlds, for cross-cultural interaction rather than ideological hostility, for porous and shifting boundaries.[38] Just as the intellectual understanding of the Ottoman Empire was multifaceted, so too was the conception of Europe it influenced. As well as the threat, the opportunities provided by the Ottoman Empire in terms of commercial exchange also shaped thinking about Europe. There were in effect multiple imagined Europes: an economic Europe which clashed with an ideological Europe, the former privileging trade and cooperation over hostility; a cultural Europe as Christian and superior to the non-Christian world beyond; and a political Europe to which the Ottoman Empire could be either friend or foe depending on transient political objectives. These conceptions of Europe were elaborated in relation to discourses of Christendom. Since the meanings of the two terms 'Europe' and 'Christendom' overlapped, distinctions between them could be drawn, and both were evoked in the face of the Ottoman Empire's territorial and cultural challenge. A writer's choice in using one term or the other, or both interchangeably, depended upon a range of factors.

A key factor in the works of both Ronsard and Savary de Brèves was the position of France. Their discourses of Europe intertwined with discourses of French nationhood in that they used the concept of Europe in their writings to communicate something about France. This is not surprising since both men relied on the French royal court for their professional status. In his *Discours abrégé* Savary de Brèves drew on his extensive knowledge of the Ottoman Empire to argue that a crusade to Constantinople could be successful only if the Catholic and Protestant powers of the continent worked together. Given French rivalry with the Habsburgs and the continuing confessional conflicts that eventually erupted in the Thirty Years War in 1618, the plan for a united attack seems most unlikely.[39] As such, it laid the groundwork for the more earnest *Discours sur l'alliance* which justified French relations with the Ottoman Empire. In these treatises Savary de Brèves uses Europe as a political and geographical idea to promote peaceful cooperation and trade. Europe offered a useful alternative to the concept of Christendom as it allowed him to redraw boundaries so that the Turks were presented as friend of France and the Spanish as enemy. Ronsard's poetry was produced over a longer period and reflects changing political circumstances. Although he could appeal to the threat the Ottomans posed to Europe to promote peace negotiations between France and Spain, as he did in the 'Exhortation pour la paix', poetry also offered a space for fantasy. Europe, with its associations as the superior continent and home to both Greece and Rome, was used as a vehicle to project Ronsard's poetic dreams of glorifying France. Even with a state weakened by years of religious warfare, Ronsard returned in 1578 to the theme of universal monarchy, penning a panegyric to Henri III: L'Europe est trop petite, et l'Asie et l'Afrique, / Pour toy qui te verras de tout le monde Roy' (I, p. 469; 'Europe is too small, and Asia and Africa, for you who will see yourself as King of all the world'). Throughout his life Ronsard urged action against the Turks in poems addressed to successive French kings. This was less a genuine attempt to persuade the king than it was an opportunity to praise him and his people. Where Savary de Brèves had to be pragmatic in his writing, acknowledging both French royal policy and papal strategy, Ronsard was able to exploit the imaginative scope of poetry to convey a vision of the French monarch and nation. It can be seen, then, that the literary construction of the French nation was not isolated from ideas about Europe, but rather that the two discourses informed one another.

Notes

1. Pierre de Ronsard, *Œuvres complètes*, ed. by Jean Céard, Daniel Ménager and Michel Simonin, 2 vols (Paris: Gallimard, 1993), I, p. 1177. All references are to this edition; further references to it are given in parentheses after quotations in the text.
2. Denys Hay cites the fall of Constantinople and the consequent challenge posed to the continent as a factor which helped to increase the emotional content of the word 'Europe': *Europe: The Emergence of an Idea*, 2nd edn (Edinburgh: Edinburgh University Press, 1968), pp. 73, 83–87. Mustafa Soykut has argued that after the fall of Constantinople the Turks were identified as the antithesis of Europe: *Image of the 'Turk' in Italy: A History of the 'Other' in Early Modern Europe, 1453–1683* (Berlin: Klaus Schwarz, 2001). On the understanding of the Ottoman Empire in the Christian world see Frederick Quinn, *The Sum of All Heresies: The Image of Islam in Western Thought* (Oxford: Oxford University Press, 2008). On the uses of the Ottoman Empire in political thinking, see Noel Malcolm, *Useful Enemies: Islam and the Ottoman Empire in Western Political Thought, 1450–1750* (Oxford: Oxford University Press, 2019). On responses to the fall of Constantinople, see Robert Schwoebel, *The Shadow of the Crescent: The Renaissance Image of the Turk (1453–1517)* (New York: St Martin's Press, 1967).
3. Gerard Delanty, *Inventing Europe: Idea, Identity, Reality* (Basingstoke: Macmillan, 1995), p. 30; Nancy Bisaha, *Creating East and West: Renaissance Humanists and the Ottoman Turks* (Philadelphia: University of Pennsylvania Press, 2004), p. 5. Of course, Edward Said's *Orientalism* (London: Penguin, 1978) remains a seminal work in the field of east–west relations. He argues that European colonialism in the eighteenth and nineteenth centuries established a discourse of the 'Orient' which was crucial in defining Europe, and 'the west', as the superior opposite of the east. Scholarship on the history of the idea of Europe tends to suggest that the sense of European superiority predated this period and existed during the Renaissance when the continent was under threat from the Ottomans; see, for example, Bisaha, p. 6. Early modern scholars have tended to argue that orientalism as phenomenon and discourse predated the eighteenth century and was much more dynamic and less systematic than Said accounts for; see Marcus Keller, 'The Turk of Early Modern France', *L'Esprit créateur*, 53.4 (2013), 1–8 (pp. 6–7). Ina Baghdiantz McCabe traces the impact of orientalism in France to the beginning of diplomatic relations between France and the Ottoman Empire in 1526: *Orientalism in Early Modern France: Eurasian Trade, Exoticism, and the Ancien Régime* (Oxford: Berg, 2008). A broader consideration of orientalism in Europe in the early modern period can be found in *The Dialectics of Orientalism in Early Modern Europe*, ed. by Marcus Keller and Javier Irigoyen-García (London: Palgrave Macmillan, 2018).
4. Bisaha, pp. 6–9; Frank Lestringant, 'Guillaume Postel et l'"obsession turque"', in *Guillaume Postel 1581–1981: Actes du colloque d'Avranches* (Paris: Éditions de la Maisnie, 1985), pp. 265–98. France is particularly interesting in this regard since the French were never in military conflict

with the Ottoman Empire yet shared the same fears of Ottoman expansion with states that were at war with the Ottomans. On the ambivalence of the Turk in the early modern French imagination, see Keller, 'The Turk of Early Modern France'. Clarence Dana Rouillard's comprehensive work long ago demonstrated the cordial relations between France and the Ottoman Empire: *The Turk in French History, Thought, and Literature (1520–1660)* (Paris: Boivin et Companie, 1940). On French travellers to the Ottoman Empire see Frédéric Tinguely, *L'Écriture du Levant à la Renaissance: Enquête sur les voyageurs français dans l'empire de Soliman le Magnifique* (Geneva: Droz, 2000). On the representation of cross-cultural relations in French literature and culture see Pascale Barthe, *French Encounters with the Ottomans, 1510–1560* (Abingdon: Routledge, 2016).
5. Lisa Jardine's *Worldly Goods: A New History of the Renaissance* (London: Macmillan, 1996) put trade between east and west at the centre of the story of the Renaissance. And in *The Renaissance Bazaar: From the Silk Road to Michelangelo* (Oxford: Oxford University Press, 2002) Jerry Brotton explored the influence of cultural cross-fertilisation on art and learning. McCabe's *Orientalism in Early Modern France* argues that French culture and society was transformed by contact with the 'Orient'.
6. See the essays in the collection *Re-Orienting the Renaissance: Cultural Exchanges with the East*, ed. by Gerald MacLean (Basingstoke: Palgrave Macmillan, 2005).
7. Christine Isom-Verhaaren has highlighted the fact that scholars who have argued that Europe and European identity were formed by conflict between Christianity and Islam have not taken into account the fluid and pragmatic worlds of travel and diplomacy: *Allies with the Infidel: The Ottoman and French Alliance in the Sixteenth Century* (London: I. B. Tauris, 2011), pp. 10–11.
8. See Philip Mansel, 'The French Renaissance in Search of the Ottoman Empire', in *Re-Orienting the Renaissance: Cultural Exchanges with the East*, ed. by Gerald MacLean (Basingstoke: Palgrave Macmillan, 2005), pp. 96–107.
9. Phillip John Usher has argued that no one border divided France from the Ottoman Empire and that the sorts of borders that were conceived varied from writer to writer. He reads the works of several authors, Ronsard included, in dialogue with other texts which offer different viewpoints on France's cultural borders. See 'Walking East in the Renaissance', in *French Global: A New Approach to Literary History*, ed. by Christie McDonald and Susan Rubin Suleiman (New York: Columbia University Press, 2010), pp. 193–206. This chapter of the present book aims to extend Usher's work by bringing Europe/Christendom into the picture, asking what borders distinguished France, Christendom, Europe and the Ottoman Empire from one another, and how these borders interacted and overlapped.
10. Noel Malcolm has suggested that the writings of French travellers to the Ottoman Empire in the middle of the sixteenth century led to the development of a 'new paradigm' by which Ottoman society was seen as a well-governed entity; see *Useful Enemies*, pp. 131–58.
11. See Joachim du Bellay's famous *La Deffence, et illustration de la langue françoyse*, ed. by Jean-Charles Monferran (Geneva: Droz, 2001).

12. In his study of literary nation-building, Marcus Keller examines Ronsard's *Discours des misères de ce temps* and *Continuation du discours des misères de ce temps*. He argues that Ronsard figures the French people as an imaginary family, conflating Frenchness and the Catholic religion to suggest that Reformers were betraying their country. See *Figurations of France: Literary Nation-Building in Times of Crisis (1550–1650)*, pp. 41–53.
13. A. E. Creore, *A Word-Index to the Poetic Works of Ronsard*, 2 vols (Leeds: W. S. Maney, 1972), I, p. 533. Creore suggests that seventy-one of the occurrences refer to the continent and eleven to the mythical princess Europa.
14. Hay (p. 87) posits these as two reasons why the word 'Europe' was used increasingly frequently in writing during the period.
15. See Isom-Verhaaren for a full account of French relations with the Ottoman Empire. For information on Habsburg–Ottoman relations, see Andrew Hess, *The Forgotten Frontier: A History of the Sixteenth-Century Ibero-African Frontier* (Chicago: University of Chicago Press, 2011) and Phillip Williams, *Empire and Holy War in the Mediterranean: The Galley and Maritime Conflict between the Habsburgs and Ottomans* (London: I. B. Tauris, 2014).
16. On crusading rhetoric in the period, see Michael J. Heath, *Crusading Commonplaces: La Noue, Lucinge and Rhetoric against the Turks* (Geneva: Droz, 1986) and James Hankins, 'Renaissance Crusaders: Humanist Crusade Literature in the Age of Mehmed II', *Dumbarton Oaks Papers*, 49 (1995), 111–207.
17. Bisaha, p. 40.
18. On the *translatio studii* topos and the related *translatio imperii*, see Ernst Robert Curtius, *European Literature and the Latin Middle Ages*, trans. by Willard R. Trask (London: Routledge & Kegan Paul, 1953), p. 29.
19. Terence Cave reads this poem as representative of a crisis of confidence suffered by Ronsard towards the end of his career as he struggled to obtain patronage and worried that his inspiration was spent: 'Ronsard's Mythological Universe', in *Ronsard the Poet*, ed. by Terence Cave (London: Methuen, 1973), pp. 159–208 (pp. 198–99). Certainly, the Muses represent a challenge to meet the lofty ideal of the ancient world rather than straightforwardly celebrate French culture as it is. In terms of Europe, the point is that the French king above all other potential patrons is best placed to nurture the continent's cultural inheritance.
20. See Frances Yates, *Astraea: The Imperial Theme in the Sixteenth Century* (London: Routledge & Kegan Paul, 1975).
21. Francis Higman has underlined the political and personal context in which this poem was produced. It was written during a period when Ronsard was at court and had close acquaintance with royal policy. It seems that Ronsard was preparing the public for the official change in policy that led to the 1559 peace treaty. See 'Ronsard's Political and Polemical Poetry', in *Ronsard the Poet*, ed. by Terence Cave (London: Methuen, 1973), pp. 241–85 (pp. 247–48).
22. On this trend see Heath, *Crusading Commonplaces*, p. 32.
23. A useful overview of the Wars of Religion in France is Robert J. Knecht, *The French Religious Wars 1562–1598* (Oxford: Osprey, 2002).

24. Daniel Ménager's study of Ronsard's political poetry flagged the centrality of the figure of the king in the poet's work: *Ronsard: Le roi, le poète et les hommes* (Geneva: Droz, 1979). Cave has suggested that Ronsard's praise of the monarchy is not simply flattery in the hope of financial gain but reflects a genuine desire for national greatness: 'Ronsard's Mythological Universe', p. 204.
25. For an overview of Franco-Ottoman relations in the sixteenth century see Isom-Verhaaren.
26. François de La Noue, *Discours politiques et militaires*, ed. by F. E. Sutcliffe (Geneva: Droz, 1967), p. 430.
27. In a speech reported by his brother, Blaise de Monluc, *Commentaires, 1521–1576*, ed. by Paul Courteault (Paris: Gallimard, 1964), pp. 85–86.
28. Until recently, the most complete biographies of Savary de Brèves were to be found in Viorel Panaite, 'East Encounters West: French Merchants and Islamic Law in the Ottoman Mediterranean (Late-Sixteenth and Early-Seventeenth Centuries)', *IRCICA Journal: A Journal on Islamic History and Civilisation*, 1 (2013), 47–91, and Alastair Hamilton, 'François Savary de Brèves', in *Christian–Muslim Relations: A Bibliographical History*, IX: *Western and Southern Europe (1600–1700)*, ed. by David Thomas and John Chesworth (Leiden: Brill, 2017), pp. 415–22. For a fuller biography which situates Savary de Brèves's career within the world of early modern Mediterranean diplomacy, see the recent full study of his life and work by Darren M. Smith: '"Le monde est un logement d'étrangers": François Savary de Brèves (1560–1628), Diplomatic Agent in the Early Modern Mediterranean' (unpublished doctoral thesis, University of Sydney, 2022). Smith's thesis is the first full-length study of Savary de Brèves since Isabelle Petitclerc's 'François Savary de Brèves, ambassadeur de Henri IV à Constantinople (1585–1605): Diplomatie française dans l'Empire ottoman et recherche orientaliste' (unpublished doctoral thesis, Université Paris IV, 1988). For more on Savary de Brèves's scholarly work see Gérald Duverdier, 'Savary de Brèves et Ibrahim Müteferrika: Deux drogmans culturels à l'origine de l'imprimerie turque', *Bulletin du bibliophile*, 3 (1987), 322–59. His influence on other scholars has attracted some interest; see Peter N. Miller, *Peiresc's Mediterranean World* (Cambridge, MA: Harvard University Press, 2015) and Alastair Hamilton and Francis Richard, *André du Ryer and Oriental Studies in Seventeenth-Century France* (Oxford: Arcadian Library, 2004).
29. The text is undated. Gérald Duverdier argues that the publication was in 1618 when Savary de Brèves was dismissed from his post as tutor to King Louis XIII's brother: 'Les Circonstances favorables à l'apparition d'impressions orientales pour l'Europe savante', in *Le Livre et le Liban jusqu'à 1900*, ed. by C. Aboussouan (Paris: UNESCO, 1982), pp. 175–89. Darren Smith's more recent study suggests the treatises were written not long after Louis XIII attained his majority in 1618 and notes that Savary de Brèves may not have been responsible for their printing (pp. 251–55).
30. For a study of how the two discourses relate to one another see Niall Oddy, 'Crusade or Cooperation? Savary de Brèves's Treatises on the Ottoman Empire', *The Seventeenth Century*, 34 (2019), 143–57.

31. François Savary de Brèves, *Discours abrégé des asseurez moyens d'aneantir & ruiner la monarchie des Princes Ottomans* (Paris: [n.pub.], [n.d.]), p. 1. The various editions paginate the two tracts separately. For all future references to both discourses I shall use the pagination to be found in François Savary de Brèves, *Relation des voyages de Monsieur de Brèves, tant en Grèce, Terre Saincte et Ægypte, qu'aux royaumes de Tunis et Arger, ensemble un traicté faict l'an 1604 entre le Roy Henry le Grand, et l'Empereur des Turcs, et trois discours dudit sieur, le tout recueilly par le S.D.C.* (Paris: Nicolas Gasse, 1628). This volume can be found online (https://gallica.bnf.fr/ark:/12148/btv1b8608280r?rk=21459;2) and is thus the most accessible to the reader. Further references to this edition are given in parentheses after quotations in the text.
32. In this way, Savary de Brèves's view diverges from those of other thinkers on the matter: René de Lucinge's project involves suppressing Protestant groups before embarking on a crusade, whereas François de La Noue considers the attack on Constantinople to be part of a mission to reuinfy Christendom. See Heath, *Crusading Commonplaces* for a study of Lucinge's and La Noue's crusade plans.
33. The idea of Christians in the Ottoman Empire as a potential fifth column was a commonplace of Renaissance crusade writing. See Heath, *Crusading Commonplaces*, pp. 63–64.
34. Heath, *Crusading Commonplaces*, p. 21. The two tracts testify to the coexistence of the two views of the Ottomans; they could be seen as both a political unit and a religious foe.
35. La Noue, p. 439.
36. 'Mémoires politiques et diplomatiques de François Savary de Brèves', Paris, Bibliothèque Nationale de France, MS fonds français 18075, fol. 2^r. Further references to this document are given in parentheses after quotations in the text.
37. 'Copies des "letres et despesches de Monsieur François Savary de Breves, pendant son ambassade de Rome depuis l'année 1608 jusques en 1614": Lettres de François Savary de Brèves, 25 juillet 1608–24 décembre 1611', Paris, Bibliothèque Nationale de France, MS fonds cinq cents de Colbert 351, fols 1–49. Further references to this document are given in parentheses after quotations in the text.
38. His advocacy of relations with the Ottoman Empire represents, as Miller (p. 39) has put it, 'the coming predominance of commerce, rather than military conflict, as the main form of the interaction between West and East'.
39. A thorough overview of the background to the Thirty Years War can be found in part 1 of Peter Wilson, *Europe's Tragedy: A New History of the Thirty Years War* (London: Allen Lane, 2009).

Chapter 4

Views from Malta

The previous chapter examined the supposed civilisational clash between Christianity and Islam, and its attendant role in determining a conception of Europe. This chapter shifts the view from the Ottoman Empire to the Mediterranean Sea, where the paradigm of Christianity versus Islam has also served as an interpretative lens. It has been argued that where the Mediterranean was an important site of activity for the Roman Empire, it turned into a frontier between two conflicting religious cultures.[1] Counter to this, Fernand Braudel's famous *La Méditerranée et le monde méditerranéen à l'époque de Philippe II* (*The Mediterranean and the Mediterranean World in the Age of Philip II*, 1949) argued for the sea as unified by a network of connections, not as a boundary between two religions, a view that has increasingly been explored in more recent scholarship.[2] Such work has revealed the Mediterranean as a place of trade, commerce and cooperation.[3] However, France is relatively underrepresented in studies of the early modern Mediterranean, the historical development of the nation generally understood as relating little to its southern coastline.[4]

This chapter examines French writing on Europe from the perspective of the Mediterranean island of Malta, asking how reflections on Malta shaped and were shaped by an imaginary geography of Europe. Malta posed the challenge of how to interpret an island in the sea between continents, whose people were Catholic, a marker of Europeanness, yet spoke a non-European language. Following a long and varied history of occupation, from Phoenicians, Romans and Byzantines to Arabs and Normans, Malta by the sixteenth century was an outpost of the Spanish Kingdom of Sicily, with an association with Christianity stretching back to the shipwreck of the Apostle Paul on the island. Following the expulsion from Rhodes by the Ottoman Empire of the Order of St John, the Knights Hospitaller, Malta, along with the neighbouring smaller island of Gozo and the port of Tripoli, was given as a fief to the Order by

Charles V. The Ottomans attempted to take the island in 1565 but were kept at bay by the knights. Following this, Malta grew in prominence as a bulwark against the Ottoman Empire and became more integrated with wider trading and political networks.[5] In spite of Malta's increasingly important place in Christendom, most geographers mapped the island as a part of Africa.

How Malta was written about in the Renaissance, then, had implications for the imagined geography of Europe, namely how the continent's boundaries were delimited and understood. To examine this, the chapter explores two broad textual genres: cosmography and travel account. Both André Thevet's *Cosmographie universelle* (*Universal Cosmography*) of 1575 and François de Belleforest's rival *Cosmographie universelle* of the same year aim to delimit the world precisely and offer a stable conception of Europe. Yet their descriptions of specific places, as exemplified by Malta, open up different angles of vision, problematising the imagined geography of Europe. The imagined journey across the whole world on which a universal cosmography takes the reader can be contrasted with the accounts of real journeys that took place to Malta and beyond. The narration of travel in André Thevet's *Cosmographie de Levant* (*Cosmography of the Levant*, 1554), an account of places he visited rather than the whole world, and in Nicolas de Nicolay's *Les Quatre Premiers Livres des navigations et peregrinations orientales* (*The First Four Books of Oriental Navigations and Peregrinations*, 1567), decentres the cosmographical view of the world, revealing different ways of experiencing geography.[6] In these accounts, the imagined geography of Europe is much less significant than in the cosmographies. From the point of view of the traveller, national identities offer much more useful ways of understanding the world.

Malta in the Cosmographies of André Thevet and François de Belleforest

In 1575 two multi-volume folios entitled *La Cosmographie universelle* were published, one by André Thevet and one by François de Belleforest. Both took descriptive approaches to cosmographical writing, providing detailed accounts of the geography, history, customs, flora and fauna of all the regions of the world. Thevet's *Cosmographie* consists of two folio volumes, each totalling over one thousand pages.[7] The work of Belleforest is similarly huge, consisting of two volumes, bound as three, and a total of four thousand pages. It is an adaptation, rather than a translation, of Münster's *Cosmographia*, with much new material.[8]

His *Cosmographie* opens with a long section on the principles of cosmography, including explanations of celestial spheres and the earth's winds and seas (material which is present but shorter in Thevet's work), before embarking on a description of Europe that takes up the remainder of the first tome and continues into the second. Both Thevet and Belleforest eschew the lists of places with their latitudes and longitudes marked which predominate in Apian's *Cosmographie*. Where Thevet, as a seasoned traveller, insists on the authority of his eyewitness observations even though he does fabricate and incorporate the work of other authors, Belleforest is more open about his reliance on the information of others, most obviously Münster, who himself gathered his information from a wide variety of sources.[9] Both Thevet and Belleforest use the genre of cosmography to impose order on the vast space of the known world, constructing imagined geographies for the places they write about. They delimit the boundaries of Europe and invest the geographical space with cultural meanings. As the Mediterranean Sea is presented as one of the continent's borders, Thevet and Belleforest have to judge to which continent each Mediterranean island belongs. In doing so, they articulate what is most at stake in defining Europe, in distinguishing the continent from Africa and Asia. The authors' descriptions of particular lands reveal perspectives that complicate their attempts to offer a neat summary of a continent's culture and environment, as this section will show. The generalising bird's-eye perspective of Europe that both Thevet and Belleforest offer differs from the perspective of Europe as seen from Malta. I first explore the imagined geography of Europe in each cosmography before examining how the descriptions of Malta illuminate the conceptions of the continent and its relationship with Africa. I then compare Malta with Crete, a Mediterranean island whose people are followers of the Orthodox, not Latin, Church.

The four parts of the world, as they were known, of Europe, Asia, Africa and America represent the predominant organising principle of both Thevet's and Belleforest's cosmographies. Thevet's text is divided into four tomes, each one corresponding to a particular continent. His description of each place is disordered, with no clear or consistent structure to the nature of the remarks he makes, but the overarching framework is coherent, dividing the world into four parts, each of which is further subdivided into distinct *pays* (lands).[10] Belleforest's *Cosmographie universelle* follows the same model of classifying the world according to four continents. Though it differs from Thevet's in that each continent is not the subject of a separate volume, it follows Münster in using the continents as a device to order the material. Europe and its constituent *pays* are described first, before the same process is repeated for Asia, then Africa and finally America. The textual designs of both Thevet and Belleforest represent a way of imposing a structure on the world that privileges the four continents as the primary categories of organisation and classification. According to their schemas, every place in the world belongs to one of four parts.

This importance accorded to Europe, Asia, Africa and America as categories is reflected in the concern that both Thevet's and Belleforest's cosmographies exhibit with the geographical boundaries of the continents. Spatial points that mark frontiers dividing continent from continent are emphasised and grounded in a historical sense of permanence. Thevet's descriptions chart an itinerary around a continent, with his tomes on Africa and Europe both beginning at the border between the two, the Straits of Gibraltar. The section on Africa in Thevet's *Cosmographie universelle* begins thus:

> Les anciens Grecs, Mores, Arabes et Latins, ont tous d'un consentement recognu, que le destroict de Gibraltar (dict des Ethiopiens *Gebbethon*, ou *Gebel-tarif* en langue Moresque, du nom de *Tarif*, ville qui luy aboutit) estoit celuy qui separoit l'Afrique d'avec l'Europe, par et avec ces deux monts fameux.[11]

> The ancient Greeks, Moors, Arabs and Latins have all in agreement acknowledged that the strait of Gibraltar (called by the Ethiopians *Gebbethon*, or *Gebel-tarif* in the Moorish language, from the name of *Tarif*, a town near there) is that which separates Africa from Europe, by and with those two famous mountains.

The significance of the Straits of Gibraltar is that they signal the separation between Africa and Europe. This geographical division is invested with wide recognition and historical credence, thereby granting stability and authority to the notion of a limit point between the two continents. Thevet's care to stress the boundary demonstrates the increasing importance that the idea of continents was gaining throughout the sixteenth century.[12] While the discovery of the New World had destroyed the medieval conception of the world as a single ecumene surrounded by water, the reconceptualisation of the world as divided into four parts was not inevitable; for instance, in *Les Trois Mondes* Lancelot Voisin de la Popelinière offered a tripartite division of the world: the 'vieil monde' ('old world') consisting of Europe, Asia and Africa; the New World of the Americas; and the as yet unexplored 'terre Australe' ('southerly land') of the Antarctic.[13]

Belleforest is as keen as Thevet to establish the continents as the primary geographical divisions of the world. He follows Münster in inviting the reader to consult the text in tandem with a map of the world that is included in the volume:

> Afin donc que tu ayes en memoire la disposition de la terre, et des parties d'icelle, regarde la table ou figure du monde universel, et prens premierement garde à l'Europe, en laquelle nous conversons, qui est separee de l'Afrique par la mer mediterranee, et en partie aussi de l'Asie. Car ceste mer-là se retourne en Septentrion, là où elle obtient divers noms, à sçavoir, en l'extremité d'Aquilon, et est appellee Pont Euxin, ou mer majeur, où vient tomber ce beau fleuve Tanais, et separe l'Asie de l'Europe.[14]

> In order that you remember the arrangement of the earth and its parts, look at the index or image of the universal world, and firstly take heed of Europe, in which we converse, and which is separated by the Mediterranean Sea from Africa and also in part from Asia, since this sea turns towards the north, where (that is, at its northern border) it acquires various names and is called the Euxine Sea, or Major Sea [Black Sea], from where flows the beautiful river Tanais, and separates Asia from Europe.

With the instruction 'regarde' and the reference to 'memoire', Belleforest appeals to the reader's memory as a place of stability for the geographical concept of Europe. The focus is the integrity of Europe, its existence as a place that is separated from Africa and Asia by the fixed boundaries of the Tanais and the Mediterranean.

However, the idea of the Mediterranean as a border is problematic. The division of the world into four parts demands that the islands in the Mediterranean Sea are classified as within a continent, even while the emphasis on using bodies of water to represent the boundaries between continents places them on, not inside, a border. As a result, there is a certain fluidity in the geography of the Mediterranean, as Thevet acknowledges: 'Quant aux Isles, qui sont en la mer Mediterranee, quelques unes participent plus de l'Europe, que de l'Afrique et Asie. Ce qui se voit en partie par les mœurs ou langages, qui sont Grec et Italien' (II, fols 935^v–936^r; 'As for the Islands that are in the Mediterranean Sea, some of them share more with Europe than with Africa and Asia. These can be identified in part by customs and languages, which are Greek and Italian'). This notion of sharing *more* with, or adhering *more* to, Europe implies that the geographical division of the world is not as clear-cut as it is made out to be elsewhere in Thevet's cosmography. The bird's-eye view of the world that both Thevet and Belleforest offer is complicated when the angle of vision zooms in to focus on a geographical entity smaller than a continent. These complications arise since the geographical divisions of the world are not solely geographical but are in fact cultural, as Thevet makes clear. The islands to which he refers are not of Europe in the straightforward way that France and Spain are, yet they can be classified as part of Europe as they have more in common with Europe than they do with Africa or Asia.

In their cosmographies, both Thevet and Belleforest set out the cultural markers that distinguish Europe from the other parts of the world and help to determine with which continent a Mediterranean island should be classified. Like other cosmographers of the Renaissance, they both borrow from the ancient geographer Strabo's description of Europe as habitable and fecund.[15] Belleforest puts it thus:

> Europe est plus petite, que toutes les autres parties, si tu regardes les grandeurs des trois: mais pourtant elle n'est pas moindre que les autres en abondance de toutes choses: et pource qu'elle est naturellement temperee, elle a une fertilité excellente, et d'autant qu'elle a l'air plus doux et plus bening pour les froments, vins, et fruictages. Elle n'a quasi point de deserts, elle est par tout propre à estre cultivee, tous ses lieux sont ornez de belles citez, forteresses, villes et chasteaux: avec ce, les hommes naiz et nourriz en ceste partie de la terre, se trouvent beaucoup plus robustes que ceux d'Afrique et d'Asie. (I, p. 28)

> Europe is smaller than the other parts of the world, if you consider the size of the three, yet it is not lesser than the others in terms of abundance of all things because it is naturally temperate, exceedingly fertile and, as well, the air is milder and more favourable for wheats, wines and crops. It has hardly any barren land; it is everywhere suitable for cultivation; all settlements are decorated with beautiful cities, fortresses, towns and castles. What's more, the people born and raised in this part of the word are much stronger than those in Africa and Asia.

What marks out Europe from the rest of the world is the climate that allows for the ready cultivation of crops, which is regarded as the basis for human development and civilisation. The attendant consequences of climate make the peoples of Europe superior to those of Africa and Asia, as can be seen in the built environments they have created. Thevet makes the same point, describing Europe as 'plus habitee et fertille, et a des hommes plus accorts et de meilleur esprit' (II, fol. 935^r; 'more inhabited and fertile, and having people more agreeable and of better spirit'). As with Belleforest, the comparative dimension is critical; Europe is not defined with reference only to itself, but as better than the other parts of the world. Interest in the influence of climate on customs developed after the voyages of discovery and environmental theories found their way into works of politics and philosophy, as well as travel and geography.[16] Such theories attempted to explain the character and specificity of places of varying sizes from locality to country to continent. Thevet's and Belleforest's application of climate theory constructs an imagined geography of Europe that attaches cultural meaning to the spatial signifier. The cultural characteristics of the Mediterranean islands are measured against the cultural characteristics of each continent in order to determine to which one the island belongs.

Malta occupied a conceptual fault line in thinking about Europe. Both Thevet and Belleforest claim that the island is a part of Africa, while nonetheless acknowledging that this viewpoint is not settled. Thevet writes, 'ceste isle est comme une barriere entre l'Afrique et l'Europe en la mer Mediterranee, regardant d'un costé la Sicile, et d'autre la Barbarie: qui met les autheurs en doute, si elle doit tenir rang entre les isles Afriquaines' (I, fol. 24^v; 'this island is like a barrier between Africa and Europe in the Mediterranean Sea, eyeing from one side Sicily, and from the other Barbary: which puts authors in doubt about whether it should rank among the African islands'). Although the issues presented by the Mediterranean as a boundary are resolved with relative ease by categorising each island as belonging to a particular continent, Malta, being Christian and nominally part of the Kingdom of Sicily, presents a greater challenge. For Belleforest, the island's distance from Africa 'a donné occasion a plusieurs de l'estimer Europeenne' (III, pp. 1876–77; 'has given cause for many to consider it European'), one of those being Sebastian Münster. In claiming Malta to be a part of Africa, Belleforest is departing from his main source material. He refers to the Maltese language as the definitive reason why Malta should be considered African: 'L'Isle de Malthe donc estant vraiement Africane, comme encor le langage de ceux du païs le monstre, lequel raporte a celuy des Africans du temps passé' (III, pp. 1876–77; 'The island of Malta thus truly being African, as the language of those of the land demonstrates, it relating to that of Africans in times past'). Thevet likewise stresses 'son ancien langage Moresque et Africain' (II, fol. 936^r; 'its old Moorish and African language') as the grounds for his judgement.

Yet it becomes clear in both Thevet's and Belleforest's descriptions that language is not the only criterion; there are other ways in which Malta is more akin to Africa than to Europe. Thevet refers to the nature of the climate and the nature of the people, the most important markers for defining Europe: 'la nature du terroir ressent les humeurs d'Afrique, plustost que la douceur de l'Italie: et le peuple [...] est, sauf la religion, de mesmes mœurs et complexions que les Mores, gens vivans de peu, et fort addonnez au travail' (I, fol. 24^v; 'the nature of the land is affected by the humors of Africa rather than the sweetness of Italy: and the people [...] are, apart from religion, of the same customs and complexions as the Moors, folk living on little and mainly given to work'). The qualification about customs is significant: culturally, the people of Malta resemble the people of Africa even though they are Christian. The geographical limits of Europe and Christendom are not regarded as one and the same, with climactic theories of cultural difference taking precedence. Thevet's view is not unusual. Belleforest also underlines the negative impact of the climate on the people, who are summarised as inferior to the people of Europe despite sharing the Christian faith: 'le peuple y est assez farouche, et se ressentant des façons de faire d'Afrique, toutesfois bon Chrestien [...] il vit escharcement pour estre l'isle si peu fertile, que elle ne suffit a le nourrir' (III, p. 1880; 'the people there are rather wild and have the same manner of doing things as in Africa, although being good Christians [...] they live miserably because the island is so scarcely fertile that it is not sufficient to feed them'). The consideration that both Thevet and Belleforest give to categorising Malta as African speaks of a great preoccupation with delimiting the boundaries of Europe and defining the cultural meanings of the continent.

The attention paid to Malta also reflects the increased significance afforded to the island following the siege of 1565. The Ottomans' failure to capture the island from the Knights Hospitaller prevented Ottoman control of the western Mediterranean and was celebrated throughout the continent as a victory for Christianity over Islam.[17] Writing after the siege, Belleforest dedicates more space to Malta than Münster did, noting the island's fame: 'Ce qui plus donne a present de lustre a cette Isle, est le siege, et demeure qu'y font les freres, et seigneurs Chevaliers de l'hospital de saint Jean de Jerusalem' (III, p. 1879; 'What at present gives lustre to this island is the siege and the residence by the brothers and ennobled knights of the Hospital of St John of Jerusalem'). Thevet goes further, describing the knights and the siege at length. He closes the chapter of his *Cosmographie universelle* on 'la fameuse isle de Malte' ('the famous island of Malta') by distinguishing the Knights Hospitaller from the Maltese people: 'Voyla quant au people, et assiette d'icelle. Reste à parler des Chevaliers, qui à present la tiennent, et servent là de boulevert contre l'incursion des Turcs et Barbares, ennemis de la religion Chrestienne' (I, fol. 27ᵛ; 'That is all for the people and situation of the island. It remains to speak of the knights who at present hold it and serve there as a bulwark against the incursion of the Turks and Berbers, enemies of the Christian religion'). This is followed by a chapter on the history of the Knights of St John and then a chapter on the 1565 siege. Even within a view of the world focused on its division into four discrete geographical parts, such as is presented in Thevet's cosmography, the symbolic value of Christendom remains important. Malta stands as an important outpost because the rulers are Christians from Europe, not because the people are Christian. The historical dimension is paramount in that Malta may now be ruled by a Christian order and the people may in ancient times have received the Christian faith from Saint Paul (I, fol. 24ᵛ), but the period in between was inconsistent, with rule by the Carthaginians, then the Romans, and afterwards coming 'entre les mains des Afriquains' ('into the hands of Africans') before becoming part of the Kingdom of Sicily, as Thevet explains (I, fol. 25ʳ). As noted above, geographical boundaries were considered to have historical stability. Therefore, Malta's culturally diverse history was perhaps understood as a further reason for pushing the island outside the boundaries of Europe.

Thevet's description of Malta in the *Cosmographie universelle* hints at the conceptual difficulties that the four-part division of the world attempts to ignore. Just as the Mediterranean seems a coherent geographical border between continents until the bird's-eye view zooms in to acknowledge the existence of islands in the sea, a closer look at places carefully assigned to one continent unsettles the overarching and simplified cultural meanings that the continent was supposed to represent. While Thevet writes on one page of the Maltese people looking and behaving the same as Moors, on another he states, 'Ce people est aussi bon que le Sicilien, participant quelque peu de l'Afriquain' (I, fol. 26ᵛ; 'This people is as good as the Sicilian, adhering to a small extent with the African'). Though a Mediterranean island, Sicily does not cause the same intellectual anxieties as Malta; Thevet notes the ancient conventional wisdom that Sicily was separated from the Italian mainland by an earthquake (II, fol. 749ʳ). Likewise, Thevet notes that the sterility of Malta means the people 'tirent leurs vivres' ('bring their provisions') from Sicily (I, fols 25ᵛ–26ʳ). Malta's reliance on the larger island for its survival makes for an intimate connection between the two which transcends the continental frontier that separates them intellectually and within a book of cosmography. Thevet notes the connections between the two peoples when he compares them, granting that they are as good, as virtuous, as one another.

However, the schema that places Malta in Africa and Sicily in Europe requires an explanation in light of the similarities between the two peoples. Thevet's explanation is that the people are not fully African, even though Malta is in Africa. This seems unsatisfactory. The clear delimitation of the continents in cosmographical writing relates to environmental theory that posits that climate determines what a place is like, which in turn determines what the place's people are like. To make a comment about the geography of a place was by extension to make a comment about the people of the place. Such theory also meant that places near to each other were similar to each other, hence the perceived similarities between the Maltese and the Sicilians. However, the insistence on a four-part division of the world and each of the four parts as an important discrete category implies that each continent is a unity. The bird's-eye view of the world offered in cosmographies presents the unity of each of the four parts, but the closer views of the world's regions problematise that unity, as is evident in Thevet's admission that the Maltese people are somewhat African and, therefore, that there are degrees of being African. Thevet does not dwell on the issue.

This is an issue that underscores the significance of Africa in articulating an idea of Europe. Africa, like Europe, is an imagined concept as well as a physical reality.[18] Its imagined geography plays an important role in shaping the imagined geography of Europe. In writing their cosmographies and adhering to a four-part division of the world, Thevet and Belleforest were constructing interrelated ideas of the continents, such that Europe was defined as much by what it was not as by what it was, its unity deriving from being not Africa, not Asia and not America. Clarifying what Africa, Asia and America were served to clarify what Europe was. Belleforest writes of the peoples of Africa:

> Quant aux vertus et vices des Africans, ils sont si mal balancez, que qui mettroit l'un en conference de l'autre, le vice emporteroit le poids, non que ce people ne soit de bon naturel, mais la religion qu'il suit la perverty, et l'air aide quelque cas a le rendre fascheux, mal plaisant, et peu acostable. (III, p. 1820)

> As for the virtues and vices of Africans, they are so badly balanced that, if you compared one with the other, the vice would weigh more, not that this people are not naturally good, but the religion they follow corrupts them and the air in any case makes them offensive, rude and not very affable.

In this generalising comment on all Africans, Belleforest claims that their customs are determined by the environment and the cultural influence of religion. Read in the light of this, his description of the Maltese people as African and good Christians is contradictory. Such is the result of the essentialising discourse of a four-part division of the world. Indeed, elsewhere Belleforest is concerned with the divisions of land and people in Africa. He distinguishes between Africans who originated in the continent and those whose origins are outside as a result of 'migrations des peuples' ('migrations of peoples'), such as 'les Arabes, et Mahometans' (III, p. 1807; 'the Arabs and Mohammedans'). He also asserts that 'l'Afrique est divisee en Mores blancs et noirs' (III, p. 1800; 'Africa is divided into white Moors and black Moors'), using the term 'More' to refer to the whole of Africa and using colour to identify and racialise groups of people within the continent.[19] Similarly, Thevet highlights the diversity of Africa: 'ceste grande region Afriquaine est diversement influee, et a diversité de peuples, aussi a elle ses païsages, les uns fertils, les autres infecondes' (I, fol. 146ᵛ; 'this large African region has been shaped in different ways, and has a variety of peoples and also of landscapes, some fertile, others unfruitful'). In this sense, Africa presents a marked contrast with Europe, which is characterised more for its uniformity of fertility and people. In its diversity, Africa can stand for a range of differences from Europe, differences that come to the fore in Thevet's and Belleforest's descriptions of Malta. The Maltese people's adherence to the Church of Rome makes their other characteristics significant markers of difference, markers of what Africa is and what Europe is not: 'vivans de peu' and 'assez farouche'. In claiming they have the 'mesmes mœurs et complexions que les Mores', Thevet uses a racialised term to underscore difference and construct Europe through that difference. The notion of 'mœurs' is vague and loosely articulated, and communicates above all the feeling of difference.

Malta's location in the liminal space that is the Mediterranean allows for a border that is both geographical and cultural to be drawn around the island. Malta is conceived as outside Europe, both geographically and culturally. It poses for the imagined geography of Europe the problem of whether a place whose people are Catholic yet speak a Semitic language is in Europe. This is different from the problems posed by other Mediterranean islands. By 1575 Crete had been ruled by Catholic Venice for three and a half centuries and settled in by thousands of Venetians, yet Thevet categorises the island as a part of Asia.[20] He excoriates the people:

> je ne veis entre ceux qui ont quelque familiarité à l'estranger abordant en leur païs, peuple si brutal, meschant et desloyal, yvrongne, corrompu, et addonné à tout vice, que sont les païsans et le populaire de Candie [...] Ceux desquels je me suis plus scandalisé, c'est de leurs Prestres Grecs, lesquels quelque mine de saincteté exterieure qu'ils ayent, et qu'ils facent plus de la chatemite qu'un moine Abyssin, si est-ce qu'ils sont plus corrompuz et meschans que tous les autres, sans qu'ils prennent exemple à la bonne vie des Latins qui vivent entre eux: et pouvez vous asseurer, que j'aimerois mieux tomber à la mercy d'un Turc, ou d'un Arabe, voire d'un Sauvage des Indes, où j'ay esté, que du Candiot rustique. (I, fol. 216^v)

> As with those who have some familiarity with foreigners to their country, I have not seen a people so brutal, wicked and disloyal, drunken, corrupted and inclined to all vice as the peasants and common folk of Candia [...] Those who scandalise me the most are their Greek priests, who, whatever outward appearance of holiness they have and that they feign more than an Abyssinian monk, are surely more corrupted and wicked than all others, without them following the example of the good life of the Latins who live among them. You can be assured that I would prefer to fall at the mercy of a Turk or an Arab, even a Savage of the Indies, where I have been, than of a rustic of Candia.

The Cretans are placed in a cultural hierarchy below the Ottoman, Arabic and American peoples. Thevet draws a clear distinction between two ethnic groups in Crete, those he calls 'Candiots' and those he calls

Venetians: 'Au contraire, les Venitiens qui habitent en Candie, sont les plus humains et affables qu'on sçauroit trouver, et tels que par leur courtoisie à l'endroit de l'estranger recompensent l'incivilité et vilenie de leurs subjects' (I, fol. 216ᵛ; 'On the contrary, the Venetians who live in Candia are the most human and affable that one could find, and, such as with their courtesy towards the foreigner, recompense for the incivility and villainy of their subjects'). In making this ethnic distinction, Thevet distinguishes between peoples who derive historically from Crete, and therefore Asia in his view, and peoples who originate from abroad, from Europe. He is thus suggesting ethnicity as a constitutive element of Europe, which illuminates the exclusion of Malta: the 'mœurs' of the Maltese are the 'mœurs' of an ethnic other.

The importance of ethnic origin to imagined geography is most clearly elaborated in descriptions of the Ottoman Empire. Both Thevet and Belleforest stress that while the Ottomans are in Europe, they are outsiders from Asia. Belleforest follows Münster in writing of 'l'Europe qui comprend de nostre temps la Chrestienté, et aussi quelque chose de la seigneurie du Turc' (I, p. 81; 'Europe which in our time comprises Christendom and also something of the lordship of the Turk'). While the geography of Europe is in part culturally defined, cultural developments such as the expansion of the Ottoman Empire do not alter the geographical boundaries of the continent. But these cultural developments do strengthen the sense of Europe's values: 'Je parle des Turcs l'origine desquels j'ay à deduire estant sur le païs, où ils regnoyent avant que passer en Grece [...] Les Turcs eurent leur premiere et naturelle demeure en la Scythie Asiatique [...] et fut une gent et nation cruelle et infame, et adonnee à paillardise' (II, pp. 521–24; 'I speak of the Turks, the origin of whom I must deduce as being the land where they ruled before crossing into Greece [...] The Turks had their first and natural abode in Asian Scythia [...] and were a nation of people cruel and infamous and given to lechery'). Whereas Münster discussed Turkey at the end of his section on Europe, Belleforest reorganises his source material to underscore the Ottomans' status as outsiders by including Turkey in the section on Asia in his *Cosmographie universelle*. The key word here is 'origine'; the Ottomans are not of Europe, but rather descend from a people whose features – cruelty, infamy, lechery – are named in this way to articulate what Europe is not. Since antiquity, the Scythians had been used as markers of the ultimate barbarity.[21] Like Belleforest, Thevet also uses the Scythians to distinguish the civilised from the uncivilised, Europe from Asia, and present the Ottomans as foreign to the place and values of Europe: 'Les Turcs donc sont Scythes, ou Tartares Levantins, lesquels vivoient en leur païs naturel plus de larcin que d'autre chose, peuple farouche et cruel, addonné à toute espece de paillardise' (I, fol. 359ᵛ; 'The Turks therefore are Scythians, or Levantine Tatars, who in their natural land live more on theft than anything else, a people wild and cruel, given to all kind of lechery'). In commenting on where the Turks came from, Thevet and Belleforest were reflecting on contemporary debates about the origins and nature of the Ottomans, dismissing the idea that they descended from Trojans and were therefore related to the royal houses, including the French, that claimed Trojan ancestry.[22]

The ethnic difference in Crete that Thevet emphasises aligns with the religious difference of Latin and Orthodox Christianity, a significant fault line in the meaning of Europe. Unlike Thevet, Belleforest locates Crete in Europe, alongside the Greek mainland and islands, but he does stress the significant difference of religion. The Cretans are a 'peuple non guere affectionné aux Chrestiens Latins' (III, p. 313; 'people bearing little good will towards Latin Christians'). He highlights the negative qualities of all Greek peoples: 'La legereté, l'inconstance et l'infidelité ont esté reprochees comme vices familiers aux Grecs' (III, p. 24; 'Levity, inconstancy and infidelity have been admonished as the familiar vices of the Greeks'). Indeed, he blames the Greeks for the Ottoman advance into Europe: 'nous avons (ou à tout le moins nos peres) veu, que la trahison Greque, et la sedition mutuelle des citoyens Gregeois a servy de pont au Turc pour passer en Europe' (III, p. 25; 'we (or nevertheless at least our fathers) have seen that Greek treachery, and the collective sedition of the Greek people, has served as a bridge for the Turk to cross into Europe'). The Greeks are condemned in forceful terms that disassociate them from western Christians; geographically they are of Europe but culturally they fail to meet the continent's values. Similarly, Muscovy highlights the discrepancy between the geographical and cultural boundaries of Europe. Belleforest maps Muscovy within Europe yet condemns the people:

> C'est un peuple fort addonné à paillardise, et yvrongnerie. L'yvrongnerie leur est vertu, et la paillardise leur est licite, ce disent ils, moyennant que cela se face sans offencer le mariage. Quant aux articles de la foy, ils suyvent les Grecs, ils accordent avec eux touchant les ceremonies, et la veneration des Saincts. (II, p. 1823)

> They are a people strongly given to lechery and drunkenness. Drunkenness to them is virtue, and lechery to them is lawful, they say, so that it is done without harming marriage. As for the articles of faith, they follow the Greeks; they concur with them about the rites and the veneration of Saints.

His vocabulary serves to liken the Muscovites to both the Ottomans, whom he also accuses of being 'addonné à paillardise', and the Greeks, who share a religion with the Muscovites and whom he suggests are also guilty of 'yvrongnerie' (III, pp. 24–25). Likewise, Thevet categorises Muscovy as within Europe but refers to Poland as 'ce Royaume le dernier de l'Europe, et qui sert de mur aux autres: de sorte que si le Turc, les Tartares ou les Moscovites le rompoient une fois, l'Allemaigne et les autres Provinces auroient bien des affaires' (II, fol. 877ʳ; 'this Kingdom, the last of Europe and which serves as the wall of the others, so that if the Turk, the Tatars or the Muscovites breached it, Germany and the other Provinces would have real troubles'). This presents Muscovy as on a par with the Ottomans and the Tatars as a threat external to Europe.[23] While the bird's-eye view of Europe's borders offered in Thevet's *Cosmographie universelle* encompasses Muscovy, the image of Europe appears different when viewed from Poland, characterised here as the walls of Europe. Such a view was not peculiar to Thevet or even to the sixteenth century; as Norman Davies has noted, 'At any point between AD 1000 and 1939, quotations can be found to illustrate the conviction that Poland was, is, and always will be, the last outpost of western civilization.'[24] It is in Thevet's textual engagement with Poland that a clear split emerges between geographical Europe and cultural Europe, one which, in representing Poland as an end point, considers Europe as coterminous with Latin Christianity.

Emphasising differences in the morals of Latin Christians and Orthodox Christians, as both Thevet and Belleforest do, constructs Europe from a particular viewpoint, from that of Latin Christianity, its self-image mapped onto the geographical expanse of Europe. This imagined geography that equates Europe with western Christianity excludes certain communities within the boundaries. Roberto Dainotto has traced the emergence in the eighteenth century of the representation of the south of Europe – Portugal, Italy, Greece, Spain – as Europe's internal other, that is, as symbolising the negative values against which a conception of Europe is articulated according to the ideas associated with the northern part of the continent.[25] The cosmographies of Belleforest and Thevet show the same process of constructing a dominant image of Europe against a part of Europe, in this case of Europe as Latin Christendom versus Orthodox Christendom, as west versus east. It is an idealised image of Europe that excludes the Orthodox Christians and Muslims in its boundaries.[26] This image is clearest in the broad view of the world offered in cosmographies. It is when the view moves closer in to a particular place that Europe looks different. The views from Malta, Crete, Muscovy and elsewhere problematise the generalising definition of Europe.

Travels to Malta

In writing about Malta in his *Cosmographie universelle*, Thevet was returning to the island he had visited in 1552 and written about in his *Cosmographie de Levant* of 1554. Thevet had travelled from Venice in 1549 through the eastern Mediterranean, visiting Crete, Constantinople, Rhodes, Egypt and Jerusalem before returning to Marseille via Malta in 1552.[27] Prior to the Great Siege of 1565 and the island's subsequent fame, travel to Malta was not common.[28] This section examines the accounts of Thevet and another voyager, Nicolas de Nicolay, whose *Les Quatre Premiers Livres des navigations et peregrinations orientales* was published in 1567, fifteen years after he returned from Constantinople. These travel accounts reveal ways of conceptualising Europe that are different from universal cosmographies, demonstrating that the work of imagining geography is in large part contingent on genre.

Thevet's journey provides the narrative framework of the *Cosmographie de Levant*, but the text offers little in the way of a personal travel account. Rather, as Frank Lestringant has shown, it draws on the literary models of pilgrimage accounts and Gaius Julius Solinus's *Polyhistor*, a geographical compendium, and was written in collaboration with his later rival François de Belleforest.[29] For each place he describes, he focuses on the history and environmental features and the curiosities to be seen there. Instead of personal observation, Thevet's descriptions consist of a *bricolage* of humanist sources that offers the reader a compilation of scholarly knowledge.[30] For this project of synthesis, Thevet has been compared to the fourteenth-century John Mandeville.[31] Nonetheless, the framing device of an actual journey leads to ways of representing Malta and Europe that differ from his later *Cosmographie universelle*.

Where in Thevet's *Cosmographie universelle* the focus is on explaining Malta's position in Africa, in the *Cosmographie de Levant* there is not the same concern with delimiting the boundaries of the continents. The voyage structure provides a different framework from the *Cosmographie universelle*, one that sees the world not from above, but from the perspective of the traveller as he moves from place to place. The bird's-eye view emphasises the four-part division of the world; the traveller's-eye view sees what is before it, not the world in its entirety. From this more personal perspective, even with Thevet's reliance on scholarly sources, the continents are not a meaningful geographical unit. In the *Cosmographie de Levant* Thevet describes Malta as 'entre Sicile et Afrique, quasi au milieu de la Mer, celebre et de grand renom, pour cause du Naufrage que fit là S. Paul' (p. 205; 'between Sicily and Africa, almost in the centre of the sea, famous and of great renown because of St Paul's Shipwreck there'). Africa is cited as a geographical landmass to help the reader locate Malta, not as a cultural frame of reference. What is significant geographically to the narrator-traveller is the biblical itinerary of the Apostle Paul. Malta continues to be important in the present day as 'le lieu ou demeurent maintenant les Chevaliers Rhodiens, depuis le tems que les Turqs leur oterent Rhodes' (p. 205; 'the place where the Rhodian Knights reside since the time that the Turks expelled them from Rhodes').

Thevet's comments in the *Cosmographie de Levant* on culture and environment are made without reference to a systematising framework as they are in the *Cosmographie universelle*. There are inconsistencies in the text, such that an assertion of Malta's fecundity that draws on the *Fasti*, 'Ce païs est moult fertile, comme dit Ovide' (p. 206; 'This land is exceedingly fertile, as Ovid says'), is contradicted just several pages later when it is claimed that the people 'vivent pourement, comme aussi la sterilité du lieu le porte' (p. 208; 'live wretchedly, as much as the sterility of the place can sustain'). This speaks to tensions in the compositional practice of the *Cosmographie de Levant* between the array of sources used, and between those written sources and Thevet's personal experiences.[32] The narrative structure of travel frees the text from the coherence imposed in cosmographies by situating each locale in relation to a wider one (town to region, country to continent). A remark stands only for itself, a point of interest to the author and to the reader, and contradictory remarks do not have a wider frame of reference with which they ought to be rationalised. Malta and its people are not viewed through the lenses of Africa and Europe but are instead comprehended more directly. In terms of the people, the identifying markers perceived to be the most important are ethnicity and religion: 'cette isle de Malte est habitee des Maures blancs, qui sont Cretiens, faisans leurs service selon l'Eglise Rommeine' (p. 208; 'this isle of Malta is inhabited by white Moors who are Christians following the religious practice of the Roman Church'). These two aspects that most strike the author-traveller are joined smoothly by the relative pronoun 'qui', whereas in the *Cosmographie universelle* they stood in tension with one another, connected by the preposition 'sauf'.

Where the *Cosmographie universelle* aligned ethnicity and religion on continental lines, the *Cosmographie de Levant* applies categories without relating them to an overarching framework. Indeed, Georges Van Den Abbeele has argued that the *Cosmographie de Levant* resists an essentialising discourse of the east through its range of source materials that explore historical interactions and cross-fertilisation between cultures.[33] The chapter on Malta bears this out:

> S. Luc apelle ceus, lesquels du tems de l'Apotre y demeuroient, Barbares, pource seulement qu'ils estoient Africains, et non pour leur meurs et vie: car ils exercerent grande liberalité envers S. Paul, le nourrissant, et logeant par l'espace de trois mois. Au dit lieu pareillement estoient plusieurs Colonies Rommeines, qui là avoient esté envoyees pour habiter [...] Et n'est de merveille, que nacions estranges, et gens de diverses regions habitent ensemble, combien qu'il n'est pas sans danger. (p. 205)

> St Luke calls those who lived there at the time of the Apostle Barbarians, only because they were Africans and not because of their customs and way of life, since they practised great generosity towards St Paul, feeding him and lodging him for the space of three months. Likewise, in the said place there were many Roman settlers who had been sent there to live [...] And it is not strange that foreign nations and people from different regions live together, although it is not without danger.

The information on Malta's inhabitants at the time of Paul's shipwreck is taken from the *Epitome trium terrae partium* of 1534 by the humanist Joachim Vadian, but the comment on diversity that follows and steers the reader towards a positive interpretation of this is Thevet's.[34] Ethnicity is a feature of cultural understanding in that the Romans and the 'Barbares' are different and in that the Maltese are 'Barbares' because they are African, but value judgement is not the driving force that it is in the *Cosmographie universelle*.

The word 'Europe' is little used in the *Cosmographie de Levant*, appearing only ten times. The imagined geography of the continent with its cultural associations of unity and superiority that was central to the *Cosmographie universelle* and the *Singularitez* does not feature in Thevet's first publication. It is not a useful reference point to anchor the narrative. Seven of the ten uses of the term feature in relation to Constantinople, the city that sits across the Bosporus. There, on a geographical boundary of the continent, 'Europe' is a useful term. On the approach to Constantinople, Thevet notes that the Hellespont (the Dardanelles) 'avec le fleuve Thanais, divise et separe l'Europe de l'Asia' (p. 57; 'with the river Tanais divides and separates Europe from Asia'). He also mentions that in the Hellespont there are 'quatre viles oposites, deus en Europe, Calipoli et Seste: Les autres en Asie, Lampsaque et Abyde' (p. 57; 'four towns opposite from one another, two in Europe (Gallipoli and Sestos), the others in Asia (Lampsacus and Abydos)'). In this context, 'Europe' is a term of geographical, not cultural, significance. The Hellespont, to the traveller moving through it, is a geographical boundary between two continents.[35] To the same traveller, the

Mediterranean, as he moves through it, does not represent a boundary. Outside the context of Constantinople, the word 'Europe' is used once to note that Greece 'est une region d'Europe' (p. 85; 'is a region of Europe') and twice in the final chapter on Marseille at journey's end to argue that the city was founded by the Phocaeans, 'qui estoient peuple d'Asie et nom de l'Europe' (p 215; 'who were people of Asia and not of Europe'). This is another example of Thevet's interest in historical cross-cultural exchange. Used here in relation to Europe, it suggests a very different picture of the continent from the unity and integrity represented in the *Cosmographie universelle*.

France is in the narrator's thoughts little more than Europe is, but when there is textual acknowledgement of the country it is invested with an emotional significance that is absent in the few references to the continent. Thevet's feelings about France are clearest as the narrative approaches Marseille and the end of his voyage:

> [N]ous commencions aprocher de Marseille, ou nous arrivames tous bien joyeus, et alaigres: et n'estime point, que Agamemnon fust tant joyeus, quand il vit la ruïne de Troye la grande: ou Electra, quand elle vit Oreste: ou Ulysse, quand il vit le rivage d'Ulichie, que je fus, apres avoir connu, que j'estois en mon païs, lequel j'avois tant de fois souhaité. (pp. 213–14)[36]

> We began to approach Marseille, where we all arrived full of joy and cheer; and I don't at all consider that Agamemnon was as joyful when he saw the ruin of the great Troy, or Electra when she saw Orestes, or Ulysses when he saw Dulichium, as I was after learning that I was in my country, which I had desired for so long.

Thevet was from Angoulême in the west of the country, yet his joy at reaching Marseille positions his text as an account of a journey back to France. Thevet writes himself as a Frenchman for whom home is not town or region but the wider imagined geography of the nation.[37] This final scene closes the circle that began in the preface, where Thevet describes himself as 'natif' ('native') to France and justifies his reasons for wanting to travel outside of his country (p. 15). In his next work, *La Singularitez de la France antarctique*, Thevet situates Europe as his return destination (as explored in Chapter 2 of this book), but in this first publication the location of Thevet's cultural affections is France.

Similarly, another Renaissance account of a journey to the Levant that took in Malta on the itinerary, Nicolas de Nicolay's *Navigations*, stages France as the voyage's emotional point of departure and return, as Marcus Keller has argued.[38] Like Thevet, Nicolay was appointed an official cosmographer at the royal court.[39] In 1551 Nicolay joined Gabriel d'Aramon, French ambassador to the Ottoman court, on his mission to Constantinople. Nicolay's function was probably as a spy for

King Henri II as he had performed this role before.⁴⁰ The party stopped in Algiers, Malta and Tripoli before navigating through the Aegean Sea. Nicolay returned to France in 1552 but did not publish his account for fifteen years. One of his stated aims of the *Navigations* was to promote mutual understanding across different cultures.⁴¹ There are also traces of his work as a spy, with comments on information gathered about sites of military interest, such as fortifications and ports.⁴² The *Navigations* consists of four books. The first offers a chronological account of the voyage from France to Tripoli and then back to Malta following the successful Ottoman Siege of Tripoli. The first half of the second book concludes the journey to Constantinople. The narrative mode then moves away from a chronological structure. The remainder of the second book and all of the third describe the politics, culture and environment of the Ottoman Empire.⁴³ The fourth book offers another change in mode, describing Persia, Arabia, Armenia and Greece, regions under Ottoman control that Nicolay did not visit. This last book draws mostly on existing sources on these lands.⁴⁴ The *Navigations* is thus a hybrid work, and its range of styles shapes the imagined geographies it articulates.⁴⁵

The reader of the *Navigations* encounters Malta as part of Nicolay's chronological account and so encounters Malta as a site of action. Chapter 15 of book 1 ('Partement de l'isle Pantalarée pour aller à Malte', 'Departure from Pantelleria to go to Malta') begins:

> Le pénultième du même mois de juillet, nous partîmes de Pantalarée avec vent si propice que le premier jour d'août, après avoir passé l'île de Goze, vînmes surgir environ le vêpre à la rade de Malte, où, incontinent fûmes visités par messieurs les chevaliers Parisot et Villegaignon, et de plusieurs autres de diverses nations.⁴⁶

> The penultimate day of the same month of July, we left Pantelleria with a wind so favourable that the first day of August, after passing the island of Gozo, around evening we came ashore at the harbour of Malta, where we were immediately met by the knights, Lords Parisot and Villegaignon, and many others of different nations.

Shortly afterwards, the voyagers learn that only a few days earlier the 'Barbares' Ottomans had attacked Malta and successfully invaded Gozo, capturing around 6,300 prisoners (p. 75). Nicolay's first experience of Malta is this meeting with the knights of the island, not the native inhabitants, and this frames his perception of the place as one of activity, where the political, diplomatic and military dynamics of the world are being contested and where the knights of this strategic island are a multicultural blend 'de diverses nations'. These different cultures share a common Christianity, and so Malta is represented as an important site of conflict between Islam and Christianity.⁴⁷

It is the following shorter chapter ('Description de l'isle de Malte' ('Description of the Island of Malta')) that considers Malta as a static object of geographical and cultural knowledge. Nicolay's conception of Malta reflects his initial sense of the island as a site of cross-cultural interaction. He does not define it as part of either Europe or Africa since such geographical units are not relevant to his narrative of moving from place to place. He identifies Malta as 'une île en la mer Méditerranée entre Sicile et Tripoli' (p. 76; 'an island in the Mediterranean Sea between Sicily and Tripoli'), and what follows in his brief description of the island focuses on it as an in-between place where cultures mix. Nicolay does not, unlike Thevet, characterise the island's native inhabitants as followers of the Roman Church. Instead, he simply points out what he sees: 'plusieurs belles églises grecques et latines' (p. 76; 'many beautiful Greek and Latin churches'). His remark on the people of Malta emphasises the different groups who dwell there, including the comment that the island 'est peuplé de grand nombre de commandeurs, chevaliers et marchands de toutes nations. Mais surtout, y a abondance de courtisanes, tant grecques, italiennes, espagnoles, maures que maltaises' (pp. 76–77; 'is peopled with a great number of commanders, knights and merchants of all nations. But above all there are plenty of courtesans, as many Greek, Italian, Spanish and Moorish as there are Maltese'). It is these labels that refer in part to country and in part to ethnicity – *nation* in its meaning of a grouping of people – that Nicolay finds most useful when describing the world as he encounters it on his journey across the Mediterranean. People move, taking their cultural identities with them; continents do not move.

It is in the fourth book of the *Navigations* that Nicolay articulates an imagined geography of Europe, the fourth book being the one where he describes places he had not visited. To Nicolay's cosmographical eye, which sees the world through books and in the imagination, 'Europe' is a useful term. To Nicolay's travelling eye, which directly sees a part of the world like a Maltese port, 'Europe' is not a useful term. The exception is the same as with Thevet's travelling eye in the *Cosmographie de Levant*, that is, when he is travelling through the Dardanelles to Constantinople. There, where he sails between two landmasses and can see a fortress on either side, he explains that one is in Europe, the other in Asia: 'dans le détroit de l'Hellespont [...] y a deux forts châteaux [...] l'un du côté d'Europe [...] et l'autre en la petite Asie' (p. 116; 'In the Dardanelles strait [...] there are two fortified castles [...] one on the coast of Europe [...] and the other in Asia Minor'). In the Dardanelles, Nicolay has an experiential sense of Europe; he can point it at, seeing both it and Asia and the water separating them. As in Thevet's *Cosmographie de*

Levant, the use of the term 'Europe' in this context is a geographical one. Nicolay uses the word with more elaborate cultural significance only later in the *Navigations* in relation to Greece. He describes Greece as 'entre les autres provinces de l'Europe la plus noble et la plus fameuse' (p. 256; 'among the other provinces of Europe the most noble and the most famous'), but, crucially, the greatness of Greece is in the past:

> Donc, tant pour leurs erreurs que pour plusieurs vices desquels ils ont été et sont encore pour le jourd'hui entachés, ne se faut émerveiller si cette jadis tant célébrée nation grecque qui a été la plus florissante de toutes les nations de l'Europe [. . .] est pour le jourd'hui par le variable cours de nature et instabilité de fortune, la plus déserte, barbare et désolée province de la terre habitable, pour être tombée en si ignominieuse calamité et servitude misérable envers les plus que barbares. (pp. 272–73)
>
> Therefore, as much for their errors as for the many vices by which they have been, and still today are, polluted, you should not be astonished that this Greek nation, so celebrated in times past, which has been the most flourishing of all the nations of Europe [. . .] is today, by reason of the changeable course of nature and the instability of fortune, the most forsaken, barbarous and desolate province of the inhabitable earth, for having fallen into such infamous calamity and miserable servitude among those worse than barbarians.

Nicolay places the blame for Greece's ruin squarely on the Greeks themselves: they 'tombèrent en si grand orgueil et présomption, que ne pouvant plus nourrir paix les uns envers les autres, eurent ensemble plusieurs longues et cruelles guerres, par lesquelles s'en ensuivit la ruine, saccagement et désolation de leur pays' (p. 276; 'fell into such great pride and presumption that, no longer able to foster peace among each other, they had many long and cruel wars against each other, from which followed the ruin, sacking and desolation of their country'). Tellingly, this view is outlined in Nicolay's chapter on the 'Moderne religion des Grecs' ('Religion of the Greeks in our Times'). Nicolay is articulating the same conception of Greece as in Belleforest's *Cosmographie universelle*. Greece is in Europe, was once the best of Europe, but is now no longer. This view associates western Christianity with cultural superiority and underscores eastern Christianity's divergence by claiming Greece to be the most barbarous place on earth. It is a view of the world that emerges in Nicolay's text when he shifts narrative mode from the real voyage he undertook to the imagined voyage through Ottoman lands. Europe is elaborated as an imagined geography not through the process of travel but through the process of imagining travel.

Conclusion

The task of Renaissance cosmography was to make the world legible, to describe the whole world in the pages of a book. Boundaries were key to this project. The cosmographies of Thevet and Belleforest described and explained the boundaries of cities, provinces, countries and continents. These geographical boundaries were elaborated with cultural meaning so that Europe was imagined as different from Africa, Asia and America. Europe stood for the superiority of people and environment. Europe in these texts is a meaningful concept that helps the cosmographer to explain cultural difference. In the travel accounts of Thevet and Nicolay, Europe is a much less meaningful concept. Travellers have a different sense of geography from a cosmographer; Thevet the traveller writes geography differently from Thevet the cosmographer. The Mediterranean Sea is a fixed frontier to a cosmographer, a malleable contact zone to a traveller. To a cosmographer, Malta is a place from which to articulate Europe. To a traveller, Malta is a place to be understood on its own terms. Europe is a meaningful concept to a traveller when it can be seen from the Bosporus as a distinct landmass from Asia. Its cultural meanings are articulated in Nicolay's *Navigations* only when the narrative mode switches from an experiential account to a description drawing on other books. Europe is constructed differently according to genre and narrative style.

In showing that Europe was less significant to the real traveller than to the armchair traveller, Thevet's *Cosmographie de Levant* and Nicolay's *Navigations* emphasise the significance of ethnic, national and religious identities as ways of understanding the world. As they travel, they take these identities with them and they understand other cultures through those lenses. Similarly, the imagined journeys on which cosmographies take readers incorporate views on ethnicity, nationality and religion which reshape the imagined geography of Europe constructed in the totalising bird's-eye view of the world. In disassociating Greece and Muscovy from the culture of Europe, Thevet and Belleforest write Europe as Latin Christendom. In delimiting Catholic Malta as in Africa, Thevet and Belleforest write Europe on ethnic lines. Europe is mapped as an extension of the culture of the writer, which for both Thevet and Belleforest was Catholic and French. France is, in Thevet's words, 'situee au milieu de l'Europe, comme le cœur de la Chrestienté' (II, fol. 508ʳ; 'situated in the centre of Europe as the heart of Christendom'). Yet France was, as Thevet attests, mired in civil war: 'nostre France, affligee et tourmentee de guerres civiles et seditions' (II, fol. 580ʳ; 'our France, afflicted and tormented by civil wars and seditions'). The possessive adjective 'nostre' takes it for granted that France is a geographical and cultural unit that transcends differences. The imagined geography of France was constructed in tandem with the imagined geography of Europe, the values of one representing the same values of the other. Both France and Europe signalled a unity that was fragile and could exist only in the imagination.

Notes

1. This thesis can be traced back to Henri Pirenne's 1937 *Mohammed and Charlemagne* and has endured in studies of the conflict between Islam and Christianity. For an overview of the historiography, see Eric R. Dursteler, 'On Bazaars and Battlefields: Recent Scholarship on Mediterranean Cultural Contacts', *Journal of Early Modern History*, 15 (2011), 413–34 (pp. 413–15).
2. Fernand Braudel, *La Méditerranée et le monde méditerranéen à l'époque de Philippe II* (Paris: Colin, 1949). On this recent scholarship and the influence of Braudel, see Dursteler, pp. 415–19, and the essays in *Braudel Revisited: The Mediterranean World 1600–1800*, ed. by Gabriel Piterberg, Teofilo Ruiz and Geoffrey Symcox (Toronto: University of Toronto Press, 2010).
3. See, for instance, Peregrine Horden and Nicholas Purcell, *The Corrupting Sea: A Study of Mediterranean History* (Oxford: Oxford University Press, 2000); David Abulafia, *The Great Sea: A Human History of the Mediterranean* (London: Allen Lane, 2011); Kate Fleet, *European and Islamic Trade in the Early Ottoman State: The Merchants of Genoa and Turkey* (Cambridge: Cambridge University Press, 1999); Molly Greene, *A Shared World: Christians and Muslims in the Early Modern Mediterranean* (Princeton: Princeton University Press, 2000); E. Natalie Rothman, *Brokering Empire: Trans-Imperial Subjects between Venice and Istanbul* (Ithaca, NY: Cornell University Press, 2011); Steven Hutchinson, *Frontier Narratives: Liminal Lives in the Early Modern Mediterranean* (Manchester: Manchester University Press, 2020).
4. Megan C. Armstrong and Gillian Weiss, 'France and the Early Modern Mediterranean', *French History*, 29 (2015), 1–5 (p. 1). For work on France's Mediterranean interactions in the early modern period, see Peter N. Miller, *Peiresc's Mediterranean World* (Cambridge, MA: Harvard University Press, 2015); Junko Takeda, *Between Crown and Commerce: Marseille and the Early Modern Mediterranean* (Baltimore: Johns Hopkins University Press, 2011); Gillian Weiss, *Captives and Corsairs: France and Slavery in the Early Modern Mediterranean* (Stanford: Stanford University Press, 2011). Work on the nineteenth and twentieth centuries is represented by the essays in *French Mediterraneans: Transnational and Imperial Histories*, ed. by Patricia M. E. Lorcin and Todd Shepard (Lincoln: University of Nebraska Press, 2016).

5. For a history of early modern Malta, see Carmel Cassar, *Society, Culture and Identity in Early Modern Malta* (Msida: Mireva, 2000). On the impact of the Order of St John on Malta and the Maltese people, and Malta's growing fame, see George Cassar, 'Malta and the Order of St John: Life on an Island Home', in *Islands and Military Orders, c.1291–c.1798*, ed. by Emanuel Buttigieg and Simon Phillips (Farnham, Surrey: Ashgate, 2013), pp. 75–83. For an examination of Hospitaller Malta's connections with the wider world, see Emanuel Buttigieg, 'The Maltese Islands and the Religious Culture of the Hospitallers: Isolation and Connectivity c.1540s–c.1690s', in *Islands and Military Orders, c.1291–c.1798*, ed. by Emanuel Buttigieg and Simon Phillips (Farnham, Surrey: Ashgate, 2013), pp. 39–49.
6. While all quotations from Nicolay's text are taken from the critical edition prepared by Marie-Christine Gomez-Géraud and Stéphane Yérasimos under the title *Dans l'empire de Soliman le Magnifique* (Paris: Presses du CNRS, 1989), I will refer to Nicolay's work as *Les Quatre Premiers Livres des navigations et peregrinations orientales* or the *Navigations*.
7. Frank Lestringant has studied Thevet's cosmographical practice at length. See *L'Atelier du cosmographe: Ou l'image du monde à la Renaissance* (Paris: Albin Michel, 1991).
8. Matthew McLean, *The 'Cosmographia' of Sebastian Münster: Describing the World in the Reformation* (Aldershot: Ashgate, 2007), p. 175.
9. For an account of the research and composition of Münster's *Cosmographia*, see McLean, pp. 143–73. For a comparison of Thevet's and Belleforest's styles of composition see Tom Conley, *The Self-Made Map: Cartographic Writing in Early Modern France* (Minneapolis: University of Minnesota Press, 1996), pp. 178–204.
10. Lestringant puts it well in *L'Atelier du cosmographe* (p. 11) when he refers to Thevet's 'chaos encyclopédique' ('encyclopaedic chaos'). On Thevet's style, see Frédéric Tinguely, 'Le Vertige cosmographique à la Renaissance', *Archives internationales d'histoire des sciences*, 59 (2009), 441–50. Tom Conley's study of *La Cosmographie universelle* focuses on the disarray of Thevet's composition in 'collecting and arranging the sum of the world's mosaic pieces': *The Self-Made Map*, pp. 187–96 (p. 188). I would argue that in his generalising descriptions of each continent, Thevet tries to make the sum add up to a coherent image of a four-part world.
11. André Thevet, *La Cosmographie universelle d'André Thevet, cosmographe du roy, illustrée de diverses figures des choses plus remarquables veuës par l'auteur, & incogneuës de noz anciens et modernes*, 2 vols (Paris: Guillaume Chaudiere, 1575), I, fol. 7^v. All references will be to this edition, and further references to it are given in parentheses after quotations in the text.
12. On the increasing importance afforded to the continents in intellectual thought, see Numa Broc, *La Géographie de la Renaissance (1420–1620)* (Paris: Bibliothèque Nationale, 1980), p. 209.
13. Lancelot Voisin de La Popelinière, *Les Trois Mondes de La Popelinière*, ed. by Anne-Marie Beaulieu (Geneva: Droz, 1997). On geographical divisions of the world as cultural constructs, see Martin Lewis and Kären Wigen, *The Myth of Continents: A Critique of Metageography* (Berkeley: University of California Press, 1997).

14. François de Belleforest, *La Cosmographie universelle de tout le monde, augmentee, ornée et enrichie par F. de Belle-Forest*, 3 vols (Paris: Michel Sonnius, 1575), I, p. 28. Further references to this edition are given in parentheses after quotations in the text.
15. On Strabo's description of Europe and how Renaissance cosmographers use it, see Jean Céard, 'L'Image de l'Europe dans la littérature cosmographique de la Renaissance', in *La Conscience européenne au XVe et au XVIe siècle: Actes du colloque international organisé à l'École Normale Supérieure de Jeunes Filles (30 septembre – 3 octobre 1980)* (Paris: École Normale Supérieure de Jeunes Filles, 1982), pp. 49–63.
16. On early modern environmental theories, see Clarence J. Glacken, *Traces on the Rhodian Shore: Nature and Culture in Western Thought from Ancient Times to the End of the Eighteenth Century* (Berkeley: University of California Press, 1967), pp. 429–60, and Frank Lestringant, 'Europe et théorie des climats dans la second moitié du XVIe siècle', in *La Conscience européenne au XVe et au XVIe siècle: Actes du colloque international organisé à l'École Normale Supérieure de Jeunes Filles (30 septembre – 3 octobre 1980)* (Paris: École Normale Supérieure de Jeunes Filles, 1982), pp. 206–26.
17. For a comprehensive account of the siege, see Ernle Bradford, *The Great Siege* (London: Hodder and Stoughton, 1961).
18. On the idea of Africa as invented by western/European discourses, see V. Y. Mudimbe, *The Invention of Africa: Gnosis, Philosophy, and the Order of Knowledge* (Bloomington: Indiana University Press, 1988) and V. Y. Mudimbe, *The Idea of Africa* (Bloomington: Indiana University Press, 1994).
19. On the term 'Moor' in French writing of the period, see Brian Sandberg, '"Moors Must Not Be Taken for Black": Race, Conflict, and Cultural Translation in the Early Modern French Mediterranean', *Mediterranean Studies*, 29 (2021), 182–212. There is also a useful discussion of the term in English in Nandini Das and others, *Keywords of Identity, Race, and Human Mobility in Early Modern England* (Amsterdam: Amsterdam University Press, 2021), pp. 40–51.
20. On Venetian Crete and the relations between Greek Cretans and Latin Cretans, see Sally McKee, *Uncommon Dominion: Venetian Crete and the Myth of Ethnic Purity* (Philadelphia: University of Pennsylvania Press, 2000).
21. Phillip John Usher, *Errance et cohérence: Essai sur la littérature transfrontalière à la Renaissance* (Paris: Garnier, 2010), pp. 71–72.
22. On these debates and their political significance, see James Hankins, 'Renaissance Crusaders: Humanist Crusade Literature in the Age of Mehmed II', *Dumbarton Oaks Papers*, 49 (1995), 111–207 (pp. 135–44).
23. Jean Céard has noted that Orthodox Christians are included in Europe geographically but excluded geopolitically: 'L'Europe en quête de son identité, selon les cosmographes de la fin de la Renaissance', in *Renaissances européennes et Renaissance française*, ed. by Gilbert Gadoffre (Montpellier: Éditions Espaces 34, 1995), pp. 53–67 (p. 63).
24. Norman Davies, *God's Playground: A History of Poland*, 2 vols (Oxford: Oxford University Press, 2005), I, p. 125. Another of Davies's works refers

to Poland as the 'heart of Europe', suggesting its importance to conceptions of Europe's ideological and cultural meanings: *Heart of Europe: A Short History of Poland* (Oxford: Oxford University Press, 1984).
25. Roberto M. Dainotto, *Europe (in Theory)* (Durham, NC: Duke University Press, 2007).
26. Jean Céard, 'L'Image de l'Europe dans la littérature cosmographique' in *La Conscience européenne au XVe et au XVIe siècle: Actes du colloque international organisé à l'École Normale Supérieure de Jeunes Filles (30 septembre – 3 octobre 1980)* (Paris: École Normale Supérieure de Jeunes Filles, 1982), pp. 60–61.
27. On Thevet's life, see Frank Lestringant, *André Thevet: Cosmographe des derniers Valois* (Geneva: Droz, 1991).
28. On accounts of later travellers to Malta in the seventeenth and eighteenth centuries, see Patricia Micallef, 'The Vision of the Island of Malta and its Role in the Transformation of the Order's Mission as Seen by the Seventeenth- and Eighteenth-Century Traveller', in *Islands and Military Orders, c.1291–c.1798*, ed. by Emanuel Buttigieg and Simon Phillips (Farnham, Surrey: Ashgate, 2013), pp. 115–25. Malta became a destination on the Grand Tour; see Thomas Freller, *Malta and the Grand Tour* (Malta: Midsea Books, 2009).
29. On Thevet's working relationship with Belleforest, see Frank Lestringant's introduction to his critical edition of Thevet's *Cosmographie de Levant* (Geneva: Droz, 1985), pp. xxi–xliii; on Thevet's sources, see pp. xlv–lx. Further references to this edition are given in parentheses after quotations in the text.
30. On the style of the *Cosmographie de Levant*, see Lestringant, *L'Atelier du cosmographe: Ou l'image du monde à la Renaissance* (Paris: Albin Michel, 1991), pp. 59–77. Frédéric Tinguely examines the *Cosmographie de Levant*'s relationship with pilgrimage accounts in *L'Écriture du Levant à la Renaissance: Enquête sur les voyageurs français dans l'Empire de Soliman le Magnifique* (Geneva: Droz, 2000), pp. 54–69.
31. Joan-Pau Rubiés, 'New Worlds and Renaissance Ethnology', *History and Anthropology*, 6 (1993), 157–97 (p. 181).
32. In this sense I am departing from the view of Georges Van Den Abbeele, who argues that the use of existing texts means that the *Cosmographie de Levant* could have been written without leaving a library: 'Duplicity and Singularity in André Thevet's *Cosmographie de Levant*', *L'Esprit créateur*, 32 (1992), 25–35 (p. 33). I suggest that while this is true for the most part, Thevet's experience of travel did play some role in shaping the text.
33. Van Den Abbeele, p. 34.
34. On the borrowings from Vadian, see Lestringant's introduction to his critical edition of Thevet's *Cosmographie de Levant*, pp. lxv–lxvi.
35. The Bosporus and Dardanelles were commonly understood as a natural boundary between Europe and Asia. On their representation in geographical texts, see Georges Tolias, 'Seuils de l'espace – seuils de pouvoir: Les détroits dans la pensée cosmographique', in *La Renaissance au grand large: Mélanges en l'honneur de Frank Lestringant*, ed. by Véronique Ferrer, Olivier Millet and Alexandre Tarrête (Geneva: Droz, 2019), pp. 361–72.

36. Frédéric Tinguely has shown how Renaissance travellers used the figure of Ulysses to legitimise their travel and writing: *Le Voyageur aux mille tours: Les ruses de l'écriture du monde à la Renaissance* (Paris: Champion, 2014), pp. 11–20; on the use of Ulysses in the *Cosmographie de Levant*, see pp. 12–13.
37. For an alternative reading of Thevet's return to France, see Wes Williams, *Pilgrimage and Narrative in the French Renaissance: The Undiscovered Country* (Oxford: Oxford University Press, 1998), pp. 266–70. Williams explores the scene as the articulation of Thevet's new professional identity as an author.
38. Marcus Keller, 'Nicolas de Nicolay's *Navigations* and the Domestic Politics of Travel Writing', *L'Esprit créateur*, 48 (2008), 18–31 (pp. 23–24).
39. On the rivalry between Nicolay and Thevet, see Lestringant, *André Thevet*, pp. 259–74.
40. Antónia Szabari reads the *Navigations* as Nicolay's attempt at self-representation and self-identity as a spy in 'The Ambassador, The Spy, and the *Deli*: Self-Representation and Anti-Diplomacy in Nicolas de Nicolay's *Navigations*', *MLN*, 131 (2016), 1002–22.
41. On Nicolay's approach to cross-cultural understanding, see Keller, 'Nicolas de Nicolay's *Navigations*', pp. 19–23. For a study of the specific example of Nicolay's 'dispassionate approach toward Islam', see David Brafman, 'Facing East: The Western View of Islam in Nicolas de Nicolay's *Travels in Turkey*', *Getty Research Journal*, 1 (2009), 153–60.
42. Lestringant, *André Thevet*, p. 265; Szabari, p. 1006.
43. On the representation of the Ottomans in Nicolay's *Navigations*, see Tinguely, *L'Écriture du Levant à la Renaissance*, pp. 198–209.
44. For a study of Nicolay's narrative style and his mixing of empirical observation and textual sources, see Michael Harrigan, 'The *Navigations* of Nicolas de Nicolay and the Economics of Ethnology in the Early Modern Mediterranean Basin', in *Anthropological Reformations – Anthropology in the Era of Reformation*, ed. by Anne Eusterschulte and Hannah Wälzholz (Göttingen: Vandenhoeck & Ruprecht, 2015), pp. 541–56.
45. Szabari (p. 1003) calls the *Navigations* a 'curious hybrid' of travel book, costume book and account of a diplomatic mission.
46. Nicolay, *Dans l'empire de Soliman le Magnifique*, p. 74. In this annotated critical edition, the orthography has been modernised and regularised. Further references to this edition are given in parentheses after quotations in the text.
47. Szabari (p. 1016) suggests that Nicolay uses Malta to 'narrate a kind of crusading story about a Mediterranean war zone divided into Christian and Muslim forces'.

Chapter 5

Views from Geneva

At the Estates General at Orléans in 1560, the first assembly of the representatives of nobility, clergy and commoners in the sixteenth century, religious division was high on the agenda. Calvinism had been growing in France, and tensions between Protestants and Catholics would eventually lead to the outbreak of the Wars of Religion in 1562. In his address at the opening of the Estates General, Michel de l'Hospital, the chancellor of France, highlighted the emotive power of religion in shaping collective identity:

> Nous l'experimentons aujourd'huy, et voyons que deux François et Anglois qui sont d'une mesme religion, ont plus d'affection et d'amitié entre eux, que deux citoyens d'une mesme ville, subjects à un mesme seigneur, qui seroyent de diverses religions: tellement que la conjonction de religion passe celle qui est à cause du pays. Par contraire, la division de religion est plus grande et loingtaine que nulle aultre. C'est ce qui separe le pere du fils, le frere du frere, le mari de la femme.[1]

> We are experiencing it today and see that a Frenchman and an Englishman who are of the same religion have more goodwill and friendship for each other than two citizens of the same town, subjects of the same lord, who are of different religions, so much does the connection of religion surpass that which is caused by country. However, division of religion is greater and further than any other. It's what separates father from son, brother from brother, husband from wife.

As his usage of the emotionally charged vocabulary of friendship and family life makes clear, he feared for a nation whose people were divided along confessional lines. From his appointment as chancellor in 1560 until his dismissal in 1568, French royal policy was aimed at religious accord, preferring to heal confessional disputes by persuasion rather than oppression.[2] To this end, he began to promote tolerance of the Huguenot minority and appeal to a model of national citizenship separate from religion, but this move was designed as a temporary strategy, religious unity remaining l'Hospital's ultimate goal.[3]

The confessional strife of the Reformation tore apart not only France, but societies across the continent. How could an imagined geography of Europe as a Christian community withstand the violent realities of religious division? It is generally accepted that it could not and that the ideal of Christendom as an overarching marker of identity was replaced by the idea of Europe as a unifying culture.[4] This chapter examines the conceptions of Europe and Christendom from the vantage points of two Calvinist writers who lived and suffered through the tumultuous Wars of Religion in France before fleeing to the safety of Switzerland, Jean de Léry (1536–1613) and Théodore-Agrippa d'Aubigné (1552–1630). It explores how the violence of the Reformation shaped their understandings of the geographies of Europe, Christendom and France. The texts analysed here – Léry's *Histoire d'un voyage faict en la terre du Brésil* (*History of a Voyage Made to the Land of Brazil*, 1578) and d'Aubigné's *Histoire universelle* (*Universal History*, 1616–19) – represent different genres of writing. The latter is an account of the bloody progression of the Reformation, published in three volumes between 1616 and 1619. It is *universelle* in space, not time, examining events that took place throughout the world.[5] Unlike in his epic poem about the French Wars of Religion, *Les Tragiques*, d'Aubigné in the *Histoire universelle* attempts to offer an impartial account.[6] In that sense, the work is influenced by contemporary developments in history writing, such as that of Jacques Auguste de Thou, who aimed for an unbiased account in his *Historia sui temporis*.[7] By contrast, Jean de Léry's *Histoire d'un voyage* of 1578 makes no attempt at impartiality. Léry offers a personal account of his journey to the New World and a passionate defence of his coreligionists.[8] He travelled as part of a group of Calvinists to the fort established as the colony of *France antarctique* in Guanabara Bay. Religious disputes in the fort led to the Calvinists seeking refuge among the Tupinambà on the mainland. His *Histoire* is a response to André Thevet's 1575 *Cosmographie universelle*, which condemns the Calvinist party for the failure of the French colony in Brazil (1555–67).[9] In setting down his testimony in print and countering Thevet's arguments, Léry gives voice to a community of Huguenots, living and dead, who travelled to Brazil, but it is an account that remains very personal, as much about the 'je' as it is about the Calvinist 'nous'. His travel journal thus offers a different perspective on France and Europe from that of d'Aubigné's *Histoire universelle*. He writes from the perspective of having travelled from France to Brazil and back, whereas d'Aubigné writes of places he has journeyed to only in his mind. What the two men share is the experience of exile, a fate that befell so many in the period that historians have written of the 'Reformation of the refugees'.[10]

Europe and Christendom

As d'Aubigné's *Histoire universelle* is concerned with 'toutes les parties du monde' ('all parts of the world'), the space of the world must be organised within the space of the text.[11] Although d'Aubigné takes the whole globe as his object, France is at the centre of the work. Each book of the *Histoire* concerns a given time period, first relating the affairs of France before giving some, yet notably less, consideration to 'nos voisins' ('our neighbours') (Germany, Italy, Spain and England) and then the rest of the world, arranged according to the compass points, 'Orient', 'Midi', 'Occident' and 'Septentrion'. The survey of the other parts of the world does not direct attention away from French affairs, but rather reinforces the narrative of religious conflict in France by highlighting how confessional disputes are playing out across national and even continental boundaries.[12] Although Europe is not an organising principle in the *Histoire universelle*, unlike in the genre of cosmography, the word nonetheless appears not infrequently. It is used as a spatial term which can be divided into several parts: d'Aubigné refers to 'toute l'Europe' (II, p. 157; 'all of Europe'), the 'divers endroits de l'Europe' (II, p. 163; 'the different places of Europe') and 'l'Europe Occidentale' (IX, p. 268; 'western Europe'). In another contrast to cosmographies, the boundaries of the continent are never explicitly delimited. There is a reference to the Iberian peninsula as 'la teste de l'Europe' (V, p. 298; 'the head of Europe'), which alludes to the anthropomorphic maps that tended to depict Europe as a queen with Spain as the head, but no specific reference to the continent's eastern end point.[13]

Beyond France and the neighbouring countries, the boundaries articulated in the *Histoire universelle* become geographically fuzzy, more cultural than spatial. The political border between the Polish-Lithuanian Commonwealth and Muscovy is imagined as an eastern frontier of Europe:

> Les Polonnois se servent ordinairement vers la frontiere de Moscovie d'une sorte de gens de guerre qui s'appellent Cosakes, la pluspart Polonnois de nation, et sont les gens de cheval les plus redoutez de tout le Septentrion, accoustumez à chastier les Tartares et brider les courses que sans eux ils feroyent plus frequentes en l'Europe. (V, p. 35)

> The Polish commonly use near the frontier of Muscovy a sort of warrior called Cossacks, the majority Polish by birth, who are the most feared horsemen throughout the whole North, accustomed to punishing the Tatars and keeping in order the roads that, without them, would be the most used in Europe.

Rather than an explicit definition of where the continent's eastern boundary lies, this description articulates the sentiment that Poland represents the end point of the continent, with the neighbouring Muscovite and Tatar lands outside Europe. The Cossacks are represented as warriors who police and protect Europe's borderlands from external threats.[14] The imagined frontier is a religious one as both the Muslim Tatars and the Orthodox Muscovites signal religious difference. According to d'Aubigné, Catherine de Medici is supposed to have said, 'Si donc nous ne nous fions en notre Roi, serons nous pas pires que Perses, Turcs, Moscovites et Barbares, nous qui nous disons Chrestiens?' (v, p. 344; 'if therefore we don't put trust in our King, are we, who call ourselves Christians, not worse than Persians, Turks, Muscovites and Barbarians?'). The term 'Moscovite' is given an equivalence to 'Perse', 'Turc' and 'Barbare', all denigratory expressions used to distinguish 'nous' from them. With the suggestion that the Orthodox Muscovites were not Christian, the imagined geography of Europe constructed here is shaped by the culture of Latin Christianity, a culture that includes not only religious but also political associations that are believed to distinguish it from the world beyond.

In this way, the word 'Christendom' as it is used in the *Histoire universelle* overlaps with the signification of the word 'Europe'. 'Christendom' has a spatial dimension, as the use of the phrase 'les frontieres de la Chrestienté' (I, p. 86; 'the frontiers of Christendom') makes clear. The two words are often used interchangeably, as in this comment on a pamphlet about the Spanish Armada of 1588: 'Sa description imprimee à Lisbonne, fut traduite en François, en Latin, en Aleman et en Italien, et ainsi curieusement publiee par toutes les bornes de la Chrestienté; ce grand soin d'en espouventer l'Europe m'a donné celui de la descrire' (VII, p. 210; 'Its description printed in Lisbon was translated into French, Latin, German and Italian, and so was diligently made known to all the limits of Christendom; this great care to amaze Europe gave me that to describe it').[15] Stylistic concerns seem to have motivated d'Aubigné to opt for the term 'Europe' to avoid repetition of 'Chrestienté'. Although the referents of the two words here differ somewhat – 'Christendom' signifies a geographical space only while 'Europe' refers to place and people – it is unlikely that d'Aubigné includes the Ottoman Europe within this mention of 'Europe'. Rather, he takes the two to be geographically coterminous, limiting the scope of Europe to its Christian-ruled areas. Thus, Europe in the *Histoire universelle* is made, in part, by its cultural identification with Christianity and by the perception of the world outside as non-Christian.

Nevertheless, there are instances in the *Histoire universelle* where d'Aubigné does make distinctions between Europe and Christendom.

He can eschew a cultural association of the two and play upon a geographical difference between their boundaries to write of 'l'Europe Chrestienne' (IV, p. 112; 'Christian Europe'). In doing so, he alludes to the expansion of the Ottoman Empire into Europe, a recurrent motif in the *Histoire*. For example, the reader is told that Suleiman I 'vint prendre en l'Europe Bellegrade' (I, p. 84; 'came into Europe to seize Belgrade'), and that Pope Gregory XIII 'esper[ait] profiter sur la foiblesse des Turcs en Europe' (V, p. 296; 'hoped to profit from the weakness of the Turks in Europe'). The disparity in the geographical boundaries of Christendom and Europe, downplayed elsewhere in favour of a cultural concurrence, is emphasised when d'Aubigné writes of the expansionist aims of the Ottomans or the desire for a crusade to combat them. He thereby indicates that while Europe and Christendom are different notions geographically, they are, or ought to be, the same culturally. The underlying idea is that the Ottomans should be pushed back to Asia in order to remake Europe and Christendom as one and the same.

The threat from the east thickens the boundaries of the imagined geography of Christendom. The threat runs throughout the *Histoire universelle*: 'Soliman eut lors un beau temps pour enfoncer la Chrestienté' (I, p. 88; 'Suleiman had then a great opportunity to thrust far into Christendom'). Under constant peril, the borders of Christendom are fluid: 'une armee de cent cinquante mille Turcs combatans en Croatie, sous la charge du Bacha Assan, qui après un long siege prend Wittitski, metropolitaine, laquelle servoit de boulevart à la Chrestienté' (VIII, p. 325; 'an army of one hundred and fifty thousand Turks fighting in Croatia, under the command of Hasan Pasha, which after a long siege took Bihać, a free city, which had served as a bulwark of Christendom'). This fear of the buffer zone moving ever closer west shapes the sentiment of a unified Christendom: 'Le Turc [Murad III] [. . .] fit peur aux Venitiens et au reste de la Chrestienté par une très-grande armee' (V, p. 303; 'The Turk created fear in the Venetians and in the rest of Christendom with his very great army'). An Ottoman attack is interpreted as a danger not only to those on the front line but also to countries further west and north who feel a solidarity with the Venetians, a solidarity conceptualised as Christendom. This term includes Protestant and Catholic powers; the 1570 Peace of Stettin between Lutheran Denmark and Sweden, brokered by the Catholic Maximilian II, Holy Roman Emperor, was, in d'Aubigné's words, 'signee presque par tous les Rois et Souverains de la Chrestienté' (III, p. 271; 'signed by almost all the Kings and Sovereigns of Christendom'). It is significant that when the *Histoire universelle* evokes unity, it does so with the word 'Chrestienté' and not 'Europe'. The Grand Seigneur is 'l'ennemi de la Chrestienté' (V, p. 57; 'the enemy of Christendom'), not the enemy of Europe. D'Aubigné writes of the 'forces de la Chrestienté' (II, p. 317; 'forces of Christendom') and 'les progrez de la Chrestienté' ('the proceedings of Christendom') against the Ottomans (IX, p. 196). The failure of the 1565 siege of Malta by Suleiman's Ottomans is greeted with 'la joye du peril passé: laquelle s'estendit par toute la Chrestienté' (II, p. 336; 'joy at the passing of the peril, which extended to all of Christendom'). When describing battles with the Ottomans, d'Aubigné writes of 'l'armee Turquesque' ('the Turkish army') against 'l'armee Chrestienne' (III, p. 237; 'the Christian army') or 'l'armee des Chrestiens' (I, p. 350; 'the army of Christians'). 'Européen' is a term missing from the *Histoire universelle*, despite the adjective existing in both Latin and vernacular languages by the seventeenth century. By contrast, the phrase 'des Africains' ('Africans') is used (I, p. 95).

Whereas both 'Europe' and 'Chrestienté' are common terms in d'Aubigné's *Histoire universelle*, the word 'Chrestienté' makes no appearances in Léry's *Histoire d'un voyage*. 'Europe' is found eleven times. The word is used to make explanatory comparisons with the New World for the benefit of Léry's readership. The statement that 'il faudroit là user de façons de vivre, et de viandes du tout differentes de celle de nostre Europe' ('it would be necessary to adopt means of living and sustenance wholly different from those of our Europe') points to a sense of radical difference between the Old World and the New.[16] Since Léry wrote in French and is concerned in his writing with the course of the Reformation in France, his use of the term 'Europe' is notable, indicating the perception of shared cultural characteristics across national and religious divides within the continent. Much of Léry's writing is ethnographic in style, concerned to document in detail the cultural practices of the Tupinambà people, and the first comment he makes on them includes 'Europe' as a marker of comparison: 'les sauvages de l'Amerique [...] n'estans point plus grans, plus gros, ou plus petits de stature que nous sommes en l'Europe, n'ont le corps ny monstrueux ny prodigieux à nostre esgard' (p. 211; 'the savages of America [...] not being taller, fatter or smaller in stature than us in Europe, don't have bodies that are monstruous or prodigious by our reckoning').[17] The natural world too is explained by reference to Europe, although, unlike the people, the flora and fauna are regarded as distinctive.[18] Léry writes of 'des chairs, poissons, fruicts et autres viandes du tout dissemblables de celles de nostre Europe' (p. 246; 'flesh, fish, fruits and other foods totally unlike those of our Europe'). Some animals are described as 'estrangement defectueux, eu esgard à ceux de nostre Europe' (p. 275; 'strangely defective in consideration with those of our Europe'). The birds are said to be 'different en especes à ceux de nostre Europe'

(p. 286; 'different in sort from those of our Europe'). And the word 'Europe' is right there at the close of Léry's sketch of the flora and fauna of the New World: 'il n'y a bestes à quatre pieds, oyseaux, poissons, ny animaux en l'Amerique, qui en tout et par tout soyent semblables à ceux que nous avons en Europe' (pp. 333–34; 'there are no four-footed beasts, birds, fish or other animals who are wholly and completely like those we have in Europe'). Léry's preference for 'Europe' over 'Chrestienté' can be explained in part by the pairing of two geographical terms, 'Amerique' and 'Europe', both of which have a continent as the primary denotation.

Although the word 'Europe' is used in the *Histoire d'un voyage*, it does not appear to be of particular importance in Léry's thinking. The eleven appearances of the term are not frequent when compared with the more than thirty occurrences in André Thevet's shorter account of a voyage to Brazil, *Les Singularitez de la France antarctique* (discussed in Chapter 2 of the present book), nor when compared with the more than 100 references in the *Histoire* to France and the French. Léry refers more commonly to France than to Europe in his comparative remarks, and more specific localisation is also expressed, as in his noting that the scorpions of Brazil 'soyent beaucoup plus petits que ceux qu'on voit en Provence' (p. 294; 'are smaller than those that can be seen in Provence'). As he describes his company's approach to Brazil, he comments on the climate, using Europe as a conceptual category to help make sense of it, but in a manner that downplays its significance:

> Nous commençasmes aussi lors de voir premierement, voire en ce mois de Febvrier (auquel à cause du froid et de la gelée toutes choses sont si reserrées et cachées par deçà, et presque par toute l'Europe au ventre de la terre), les forests, bois et herbes de ceste contrée là aussi verdoyantes que sont celles de nostre France és mois de May et de Juin. (p. 147)
>
> We also started to see then before all other things, even in that month of February (when because of the cold and the frost all things are so closed and hidden, over here and almost all of Europe, in the belly of the earth) that the forests, woods and plants of that country are as flourishing as those of our France in the months of May and June.

'Europe' is here one of a number of lexical items deployed for the purposes of explanation, with the adverbial expression 'par deçà' ('over here') and the noun 'France' also serving to perform this illustrative function. 'Europe' and 'par deçà' are not equivalent terms; rather the latter is a part of the former. Thus, Europe is not the deictic centre of the statement. The 'par deçà' articulates a geographical community that includes Léry and his intended readership, probably France and Geneva. Europe is not used as a marker of cultural identity. Indeed, an overarching sense of unity that comes to the fore in d'Aubigné's *Histoire universelle* in the face of opposition to the Ottoman Empire is absent from Léry's *Histoire d'un voyage*.[19] Accordingly, Léry tends to adopt a more narrowly spatial denotation in his usage of the word 'Europe'. He does not refer to people as 'européen'; the word is absent from the text, whereas there is mention of 'Afriquains' (p. 130; 'Africans') and 'Ameriquains' (p. 217; 'Americans'). Travellers to the New World are identified by nation and religion: 'les François et Portugais ont frequenté ce pays-là' (p. 341; 'the French and Portuguese have frequented that land') and 'les Chrestiens ont frequenté ce pays-là' (p. 363; 'the Christians have frequented that land').

The Politicised Language of Christendom

Naming a group of people is a political act. Responding to the brewing threat of civil war, Michel de l'Hospital appealed to the name Christian as a marker of overarching identity: 'Ostons ces mots diaboliques, noms de parts, factions et séditions, luthériens, huguenots, papistes: ne changeons le nom de chrestien' (p. 403; 'Let's lay aside these diabolical words, the names of parties, factions and seditions: Lutherans, Huguenots, Papists. Let's not change the name Christian'). His rejection of such labels entails a refusal to accept confessional division.[20] It underscores how the vocabulary used to name groups serves to unify people or to divide them and, therefore, how the use of such vocabulary is inherently politicised. Equally, not using a particular word like 'chrestien' is significant. The absence of 'Chrestienté' from Léry's *Histoire d'un voyage* may be understood as a rejection of the political and cultural significance of the term since it appeals to an overarching Christian unity which the Calvinist Léry considered illusory. This section examines the political uses of language in Léry's text and d'Aubigné's *Histoire universelle*, focusing on the implications of religious division for the idea of a unified Christendom.

Léry's *Histoire d'un voyage* is a polemical text that is designed, in part, to argue a Calvinist point of view. In that sense, it forms part of the war of words that was waged during the French religious crisis of the sixteenth century.[21] Léry highlights the contentious nature of the language of Christianity in this comment about some birds that the company kill on an uninhabited island on their way to Brazil:

> Tellement qu'encores que ce fust le jour qu'on appelloit les Cendres, nos matelots neantmoins, voire les plus catholiques Romains, ayant prins bon appetit au travail qu'ils avoyent eu la nuict precedente, ne firent point de dif-

ficulté d'en manger. Et certes aussi celuy qui contre la doctrine de l'Evangile a defendu certains temps et jours l'usage de la chair aux Chrestiens, n'ayant point encores empieté ce pays-là, où par consequent il n'est nouvelle de pratiquer les loix de telle superstitieuse abstinence, il semble que le lieu les dispensoit assez. (p. 158)

So even though it was the day that is called Ash Wednesday, our sailors nevertheless, even the most Roman Catholic, having got a good appetite from the work they had done the night before, had no problem with eating them. And, truly, as the one who, contrary to the doctrine of the Gospel, has forbidden the eating of meat by Christians at particular times and on particular days, has not yet seized hold of that land, where, as a consequence, there have been no reports about following the laws of such superstitious abstinence, it seems that the place was dispensation enough.

Léry's ironic tone here condemns the Catholic practice of abstaining from meat during Ash Wednesday. He mocks the pope ('celuy') as a figure who dictates false doctrine to 'Chrestiens' yet who is powerless to spread his rules to the New World. The inclusion of the word 'Chrestiens' within this context serves to illustrate its troublesome quality. Léry and his co-religionists would not subscribe to the pope's views on alimentary prohibition but would equally lay claim to the title of 'Chrestien'. The term, as Michel de l'Hospital would have it, is an all-encompassing one that could unite Calvinists and Catholics, but its inclusivity is a chimera, obscuring the intractable differences between the two confessions.

Léry is consequently distrustful of such inclusive language. Christianity can be taken as a badge of identity by those who, in his eyes, do not merit it: 'ceux qui portent le titre de Chrestiens [...] lesquels ne s'estans pas contentez d'avoir fait cruellement mourir leurs ennemis, n'ont peu rassasier leur courage, sinon en mangeans de leur foye et de leur cœur' (p. 375; 'those who carry the title of Christian [...] who, not being content to have their enemies cruelly killed, have not been able to sate their appetite, save by eating their livers and their hearts'). Léry portrays Villegaignon as a person who speaks the inclusive language of Christianity, referring to 'la Religion Chrestienne' (pp. 72, 172; 'the Christian Religion') in both his reported letter to Calvin and in a reported prayer but nonetheless '[il] se fust revolté de la Religion reformée' (p. 413; 'he had rebelled against the Reformed Religion'), killing three of them (p. 511). Violence shapes the attitudes of religious communities towards one another, strengthening confessional identity through hostility and collective memory.[22] Accordingly for Léry, 'Chrestien' has become an ambiguous and ambivalent term. The labels 'catholiques Romains' (p. 158; 'Roman Catholic') and 'de la Religion reformée' (p. 107; 'of the reformed religion') are more specific and thus more appropriate as markers of identity. Christendom has no place at all.

Léry's usage of religious terminology is partisan; he does not seek to promote Christian unity but to bear witness to his faith and to articulate a confessional identity. In doing so, he dismisses the sorts of appeals made by Michel de l'Hospital. He does not share l'Hospital's faith in an overarching 'chrestien' identity. He has suffered too much danger at the hands of other so-called Christians whose religious views he does not accept:

> Villegagnon, sans que nous en sceussions rien, ayant baillé au maistre du navire où nous repassasmes (qui l'ignoroit aussi) un proces lequel il avoit fait et formé contre nous, avec mandement expres au premier Juge auquel il seroit presenté en France, non seulement de nous retenir, mais aussi faire mourir et brusler comme heretiques qu'il disoit que nous estions. (pp. 545–46)

> Villegaignon, without us knowing anything about it, had, when we returned, given the master of the ship (who also didn't know about it) a lawsuit in which he had indicted us, with the express charge to the first Judge to whom it would be presented in France, not only to detain us, but also to have us put to death and burned like the heretics that he said we were.

Léry goes on to reassure the reader of his safety and then describe the fate of those of 'nostre compagnie' ('our company') who remained in Brazil, three of whom were drowned by Villegaignon (p. 548). 'Heretiques' they may have been to Villegaignon, but Léry redescribes them as 'fideles serviteurs de Jesus-Christ' (p. 548; 'faithful servants of Jesus Christ'). In doing so, he asserts his interpretation of Christianity over and above that of Villegaignon, and promotes the righteousness of the 'gens [...] de nostre Religion' (p. 193; 'people [...] of our religion') vis-à-vis the 'Catholiques', a word, coming from Léry's pen, full of derision. He writes elsewhere of 'vrais Chrestiens' (p. 181; 'true Christians') and 'la vraye Religion' (p. 411; 'the true Religion') and condemns 'ces Atheistes' (p. 337; 'those Atheists'), each time promoting the views of his confessional group, claiming the primacy of his definitions of these words. In Léry's parlance 'vrai Chrestien' is an exclusionary marker, expressing a narrow Protestant community that wants to purify and restore Christianity to what they regard as its original meaning. His usages of such vocabulary demarcate the boundaries of religious communities and frame a view of the world as fragmentary and conflictual. He makes a claim to speak for only one of the fragments into which Christendom has broken, not the whole.

By contrast, d'Aubigné in the *Histoire universelle* tries to avoid such partisan terminology in his pursuit of an impartial authorial voice: 'Que si les termes de Papiste et de Huguenot se lisent en quelque lieu, ce sera en faisant parler quelque partisan passionné et non du stil de l'Autheur' (I, p. 130; 'That where the terms Papist and Huguenot can be read in some place, they are a rendering of the speech of a particular impassioned adherent and not the use of the Author'). D'Aubigné here draws attention to the inherently political nature of words like 'Papiste' and 'Huguenot', the very words that Michel de l'Hospital criticised. These words and others such as 'heretiques' ('heretics') and 'luthériens' ('Lutherans') denigrate people and ideas, represent certain communities as other and thereby reinforce ideological divisions. Conversely, appeals to the rhetoric of Christendom may obscure division, rather than overcome it, as this comment on the 1559 treaty of Cateau-Cambrésis indicates:

> une paix en effect pour les Royaumes de France et d'Espagne, en apparence de toute la Chrestienté, glorieuse aux Espagnols, desavantageuse aux François, redoutable aux Reformés: car, comme toutes les difficultés qui se presenterent au traicté estoyent estouffees par le desir de repurger l'Eglise, ainsi après la paix establie, les Princes, qui par elle avoyent la paix du dehors travaillerent par æmulation à qui traicteroit plus rudement ceux qu'on appelloit heretiques. (I, pp. 126–27)[23]
>
> a peace indeed for the Kingdoms of France and Spain, in appearance for all of Christendom, glorious for the Spanish, disadvantageous for the French, fearful for the Reformers, since, as all the difficulties that the treaty presented were smothered by the desire to cleanse the Church anew, so after the peace was established, the Princes, who with the treaty had achieved peace abroad, set to work to outdo one another in treating more harshly those that they called heretics.

The word 'Chrestienté' is split into some of its constituent parts – 'Espagnols', 'François' and 'Reformés' – thereby parsing the 'apparence' of unity into disunity and factionalism. There is a gap between the ideal of Christianity and the reality: the name 'Christendom' can be invoked to justify political action, even though the outcome may favour one country and one religious group over others. Theologically, 'Chrestienté' is associated with peace, but politically, it involves redirecting violence towards heresy: 'le pretexte de presser la paix entre les Rois, estoit le dessein d'exstirper les heretiques' (I, p. 244; 'the pretext of urging peace between the Kings was the project to root out the heretics'). The concept of Christendom offers an illusionary ideal of peace, an all-embracing notion that does not represent peace for all. Such is the slipperiness of the notion, its potential for constant rewriting according to shifting circumstances, that the Christendom conceived by the architects of the treaty of Cateau-Cambrésis excludes many who would be included when the idea was put to use as anti-Ottoman rhetoric.

Ostensibly a marker of unity, Christendom as it is presented in d'Aubigné's *Histoire universelle* is more of an exclusionary concept. The term is used as a rhetorical device to promote religious orthodoxy and to intensify conflict by promoting animosity towards those defined as enemies. In 1567 the Reformers are told that 'c'estoit folie à eux d'alleguer [...] qu'un Roi de France (sans se bander contre la Chrestienté) puisse establir en son Royaume deux religions' (II, p. 247; 'it was folly on their part to urge that [...] a King of France could, without opposing himself against Christendom, establish in his Kingdom two religions'). The argument made here by the French crown against extending the rights of the Reformed Church is the attitude of Christendom, here clearly referring to Catholic Christendom. The pope especially, d'Aubigné demonstrates, makes political use of the idea of Christendom. Supposedly the symbol of a unified Church, the 'Prince de la Chrestienté' (I, p. 33; 'Prince of Christendom') in fact fosters division: 'il proceda aux excommunications des Princes reformez' (VI, p. 264; 'he proceeded with the excommunications of the Reformed Princes'). The papal power of excommunication allows the pontiff to construct his own definition of Christendom, naming those who are within the Church and those who are considered heretics. D'Aubigné writes of Pope Paul III with regard to the build-up to the Council of Trent: 'En l'an 1537 pour remedier (dit-il) aux heresies, dissensions en la Religion, guerres et troubles en la Chrestienté [...] assigna un Concile general à Mantouë au 23ᵉ jour de Mai' (I, pp. 77–78; 'In the year 1537 to remedy (he said) heresy, religious strife, wars and disturbances in Christendom [...] he called for a general Council in Mantua on the 23rd of May'). One of his stated aims is to pacify Christendom; yet another is to clamp down on heresy, an ambition which in itself reshapes the contours of Christendom according to his own definition.

In spite of d'Aubigné's goal of objectivity in the *Histoire universelle*, his personal comprehension of Christendom emerges in the text. It is a vision focused on peace. He labels the Augsburg Settlement, which established the legality of Lutheranism in the Holy Roman Empire, 'le nœud de la paix d'Allemagne, qui a duré jusques aujourd'hui' (I, p. 53; 'the hinge on which rests the peace of Germany, which has endured up to today'). The note of praise in this statement is evident. The treaty was negotiated by the future Ferdinand I (Holy Roman Emperor from 1558 to 1564), about whose death d'Aubigné writes: 'l'Empereur Ferdinand mourut d'hydropisie, Prince regretté des vrais Chrestiens, ami de paix, ennemi des cruautez, prudent, justicier et vigilant' (II, p. 346; 'the Emperor Ferdinand died of dropsy, a Prince lamented by true Christians, a friend of peace, an enemy of cruelties, prudent, an upholder of the law, and vigilant'). The phrase 'vrais Chrestiens' is d'Aubigné's own political use of language in which he offers a definition of what it means to be a true Christian. Of course, it is not a view that would have been universally shared. D'Aubigné refers to the 'grand dessein' ('grand strategy') of the Jesuits 'de mettre la Chrestienté sous un Roi Katholique et sous un seul Pasteur' (VI, p. 141; 'to put Christendom under a Catholic King and under a single pastor') – a post-Tridentine and exclusionary view of the Church which privileges political and theological uniformity and an attachment to Rome. His description of the Catholic Ferdinand as a 'vrai Chrestien' displays a willingness to conceive of a Christian community that is based on peace and can respect, not erase, confessional difference.

Calvinist Double Discourse: Religion and Nation as Competing Allegiances

The world that d'Aubigné depicts in the *Histoire universelle* is far from his ideal of peace. The first chapter of the first book opens in the middle of the sixteenth century with the birth of the future Henri IV and describes Europe as follows: 'Durant le berceau de ce Prince, l'Europe, comme ayant lors pour ascendant un astre ignée et belliqueux, fut esmeuë et rechauffée de toutes parts par diverses guerres' (I, p. 24; 'During the infancy of this Prince, Europe, as it then had in the ascendant a fiery and warlike star, was affected and heated up all over by different wars'). The vision of Europe that d'Aubigné offers here at the word's first appearance is of a place marked above all by conflict. The inclusion of this description as the background to the birth of Henri flags the supposed destiny of the prince to transform this divided Europe. Conflict acts as the structuring device of the whole work, which presents an inexorable cycle of war and peace, each book of the *Histoire universelle* ending with the description of a truce that inevitably erupts into violence in the next.[24] D'Aubigné's style has been labelled polyphonic for the way it aims to avoid particular viewpoints and present a range of views.[25] As well as offering a more impartial and measured tone, d'Aubigné's polyphonic composition indicates a world of irreconcilable perspectives, where one chapter offers an 'Abregé du dire des Catholiques' (I, p. 164; 'Abridgement of the Speech of the Catholics'), and the next an 'Abregé du dire des Reformés' (I, p. 167; 'Abridgement of the Speech of the Reformers'). The disagreements that the *Histoire universelle* dramatise prove to be so violent since the lines of religious division do not match those of national boundaries.[26] Indeed, a sense of an international community of reformers is constructed by the shifts in the narrative's perspective from the religious conflicts in France to the parallel conflicts in the rest of the world.[27] For d'Aubigné and other Calvinists, Henri IV, as a Protestant and the heir to the French throne from 1584, represented a potential means of healing the fundamental tension between faith and country, and combining the two in a larger cultural unity that would allow for a reconciliation of loyalties after decades of civil war. This hope is signalled by the inclusion of Henri in the *Histoire universelle*'s opening chapter. Within a textual geography centred on France, Henri is figured as the central character, the man who can end civil war.

Ultimately, Henri did bring an end to the French Wars of Religion, but in order to secure his position on the throne he had to convert to Catholicism. The *Histoire universelle* charts the disillusionment of d'Aubigné and his fellow Calvinists. The figure of Henri IV is found at the end of the *Histoire universelle*, as at the start, alongside the word 'Europe'. D'Aubigné summarises Henri's foreign policy aims on the eve of his assassination in 1610 as to become 'un Empereur des Chrestiens, qui de sa menace arresteroit les Turcs, pour reformer l'Italie, dompter l'Espagne, reconquerir l'Europe et faire trembler l'Univers' (IX, p. 406; 'an Emperor of the Christians, who will stop the threat of the Turks, reform Italy, tame Spain, subdue Europe again and make the universal world tremble'). There is a confessional and a national dimension to what it means to be 'un Empereur des Chrestiens' since it involves reforming papal Italy and pacifying the old Catholic enemy Spain. More than that, it consists of a universal vision that will overcome divisions to unite an expansive Christendom, take back south-eastern Europe from the Ottomans and spread the Christian religion. Its presence towards the end of the text weighs heavily: it offers an imagined geography of what might have been, of Christendom and Europe as one and the same culturally, politically and geographically. As such, it marks an end to hopes of a unifying politics that could bring together country and religion in providing a systematic image of the world and of a Calvinist's place within France.

In the much more personal and partisan *Histoire d'un voyage*, Léry is able to offer a fuller exploration of split loyalties than d'Aubigné. Like d'Aubigné and other Protestant refugees, Léry remained attached to his country of birth.[28] A Calvinist pastor, he claims of himself, 'François naturel que je suis, jaloux de l'honneur de mon prince' (p. 77; 'native Frenchman that I am, envious of the honour of my prince'). Monarchy though is problematic from the point of view of confessional difference, as the figure of Henri IV testifies. Léry's writing explores the impact on the individual of the discord between religion and nation. What does it mean to be French for a Calvinist subject to a Catholic king? What does it mean to be Christian in an age of confessionalism? Attached to allegiances to both faith and country, Léry's identity is fragmentary.

Léry uses the paratextual framework of the *Histoire d'un voyage* to set the work within the context of the Wars of Religion, inviting the reader to regard it as concerned with the religious fragmentation of France as much as it is a recollection of a voyage. The preface frames the *Histoire* as a correction to the 'impostures de Thevet' (p. 63; 'falsehoods of Thevet'), thereby promoting the truth claims of Léry and his coreligionists. The text is dedicated to the Huguenot general François de Coligny, who was the son of Admiral Gaspard de Coligny, a supporter of Villegaignon's expedition to Brazil characterised by Léry as a 'Capitaine François et Chrestien' (p. 48; 'French and Christian Captain'). These two defining features proved incompatible in his lifetime and he was killed in the St Bartholomew's Day Massacre. In the dedicatory epistle, Léry is damning about the failure of the colony *France antarctique*, which he argues could have been a great national triumph:

> aussi est-il tres-certain, que si l'affaire eust esté aussi bien poursuivy, qu'il avoit esté heureusement commencé, que l'un et l'autre regne, spirituel et temporel, y avoyent si bien prins pied de nostre temps, que plus de dix mille personnes de la nation Françoise y seroyent maintenant en aussi pleine et seure possession pour nostre Roy, que les Espagnols et Portugais y sont au nom de leurs. (p. 48)

> it is also very certain that if the enterprise had been pursued as well as it had been blessedly started, one and the other realm, spiritual and temporal, would have gained such a strong foothold in our time that more than ten thousand people of the French nation would be there now, in as full and secure possession of it for our King as the Spanish and Portuguese are there in the name of theirs.

The failure of the spiritual and temporal domains to align represents the fundamental problem of Reformation-era discourses on community.[29] The struggle for a Calvinist Frenchman to resolve the contradiction provokes the dream of a refuge in the New World where his two allegiances can coexist in harmony.[30] The adverbial 'y' ('there'), repeated in the above quotation, is significant. Michel de Certeau's structural analysis of the *Histoire d'un voyage* points to the narrative opposition between 'y' / 'là-bas' (over there') / 'ailleurs' ('elsewhere') / 'par-delà' ('beyond') and 'ici' ('here') / 'par-deçà ('over here').[31] The task Léry sets himself is, in part, to offer a description of the 'par-delà', yet the work is haunted by the uncertainty of the 'par-deçà'. Certeau indicates the instability, perhaps unwittingly, by naming the 'par-deçà' first as France and later as Geneva.[32] Léry's deictic markers – 'par-deçà', 'nous' and so on – shift;

there is no sense of writing from a location that he feels is stable and coherent. He writes of returning from Brazil 'en France [...] ma patrie' (p. 507; 'to France [...] my fatherland'), but France is not a place of safety for a man of his religious convictions. His *Histoire* portrays the fragmentation of the individual caught within a fragmented world.

The violent antagonism between communities in the Old World is one of the focal points of the *Histoire d'un voyage*. Léry closes chapter 15 on the practice of anthropophagy in Brazil with a series of reflections on the bloodshed cleaving Europe apart. He writes that 'nos gros usuriers (sucçans le sang et la moëlle, et par consequent mangeans tous en vie [...] [...] sont encores plus cruels que les sauvages' (p. 375; 'our great usurers (sucking blood and marrow and consequently eating everyone alive) [...] are even crueller than the savages'); that 'durant la sanglante tragedie' ('during the bloody tragedy') of the St Bartholomew's Day Massacre the livers, hearts and other parts of corpses were eaten by the murderers (p. 376); and 'au milieu de nous [...] ceux-ci se sont plongez au sang de leurs parens, voisins et compatriotes' (p. 377; 'in the midst of us [...] these have plunged into the blood of their kinsmen, neighbours and countrymen'). The vocabulary Léry adopts here is inclusive, taken from the semantic field of community, but the reality is anything but inclusive as 'voisins et compatriotes', ostensible members of the same communities, violently turn against each other, carving out new communities in blood, reshaping the meanings of such inclusive terms.[33] In successive editions of the *Histoire d'un voyage*, Léry adds to the catalogue of cruelties, introducing Dracula and descriptions of Ottoman barbarities in the 1585 edition and an account of the Spanish in the New World in the edition of 1599 so that cannibalism is depicted as a practice throughout the world.[34] Whereas in his account of a voyage to Brazil André Thevet locates savagery and barbarity outside Europe, as seen in Chapter 2 of the present book, Léry does not consider cruelty to be an extra-European phenomenon. It has been argued that the equivalence Léry suggests between the Old World and the New indicates that the people of Europe do not have a privileged link to God or a surer path to salvation after death, the whole world falling short of God's ideal.[35] In this way, the *Histoire d'un voyage* unsettles an imagined geography of Europe grounded in the notion of superiority and association with Christianity.

Faced with a Europe in which he cannot reconcile his incompatible allegiances to both nation and religion, it is not so surprising that Léry is nostalgic about his time in the New World and expresses a yearning to return, claiming, 'je regrette souvent que je ne suis parmi les sauvages' (p. 508; 'I often regret that I am not among the savages').[36] The *Histoire d'un voyage* was written twenty years after Léry's return, and so his reflections on a Brazil experienced by his younger self are coloured by the hopes and setbacks of the intervening period. He is less nostalgic for the New World than he is elegiac for France, wracked as it is by religious civil war.[37] Looking back at Brazil through the lens of increasing pessimism, he considers it to represent the safe haven that might have been. In Léry's view, Villegaignon squandered that opportunity: 'j'ay opinion, si Villegagnon ne se fust revolté de la Religion reformée, et que nous fussions demeurez plus long temps en ce pays-là, qu'on en eust attiré et gagné quelques-uns à Jesus Christ' (pp. 413–14; 'I am of the opinion that if Villegaignon had not rebelled against the Reformed Religion and we had stayed longer in that land, we would have attracted some and gained them for Jesus Christ'). As well as a new religious society, America could also have been a theatre for French glory:

> je croy fermement si [. . .] Villegagnon eust tenu bon, qu'il y auroit à present plus de dix mille François, lesquels outre la bonne garde qu'ils eussent fait de nostre isle et de nostre fort (contre les Portugais qui ne l'eussent jamais sceu prendre comme ils ont fait depuis nostre retour) possederoyent maintenant sous l'obeissance du Roy un grand pays en la terre du Bresil, lequel à bon droit, en ce cas, on eust peu continuer d'appeler France Antarctique. (p. 506)
>
> I firmly believe that if [. . .] Villegaignon had remained constant, there would be at present more than ten thousand Frenchmen who, other than the good protection they would keep of our island and our fort (against the Portuguese who would never have had the cunning to take it as they did after our return) under obedience to the King, would now possess a great country in the land of Brazil, which in that case could with good reason have continued to be called Antarctic France.

For Léry, the Brazilian expedition was a chance to resolve the contradictions between religious and national allegiance. His feeling of regret shapes his depiction of Brazil. Though the souls of the peoples of the Old World and the New may be regarded as equal in the eyes of God, Léry stresses the differences between the societies separated by the Atlantic.[38] He stresses this as he wants America to be different from Europe; he wants to build a new community, not recreate Europe in America.[39] However, America has turned out to be too much like Europe: forced into exile in Geneva, Léry feels that he and his coreligionists are dominated by Catholics in Europe, in much the same manner as they were dominated by Catholics in Brazil.[40] The tragedy of the New World, and indeed of the Old World, is that the two worlds do parallel one another.

Conclusion

Léry's *Histoire d'un voyage faict en la terre du Brésil* and d'Aubigné's *Histoire universelle* offer views on Europe from the perspective of exile in Geneva. From there, it is the Reformation that dominates the landscape; the geography of Europe looks fragmented. Léry saw more of the world and d'Aubigné chose to write in an impartial manner of events beyond his personal knowledge, yet in spite of the differences of experience and genre, for both men the dominant concern in these works is their experience of religious civil war. Both writers appeal to their faith and to their country in a double discourse of competing and ultimately irreconcilable feelings of cultural belonging. Neither was optimistic about Michel de l'Hospital's model of civic identity that put nation before religion. They favoured a model of community that was both confessional and national. However, the hopes they harboured and the solutions they conceived were already confined to the past when they took up their pens to write. For Léry, Brazil represents a missed opportunity, the safe haven from Catholic domination that might have been. For d'Aubigné, it was Henri IV who was the great hope, but his conversion shored up the status of Catholicism in France. Forced to choose between religion and nation, Léry and d'Aubigné opted for the former. These lines of division dominate the representations of Europe that their writings offer.

The preoccupation with religion and nation in Léry's *Histoire d'un voyage* and d'Aubigné's *Histoire universelle* demonstrate the twin challenges that the Reformation and growing national consciousness presented to overarching sentiments of unity in Europe. Léry does not articulate a sense of allegiance wider than that of France or the Reformed Church; he does not refer to Christendom; and, even faced with the alterity of the New World, he rarely thinks in terms of Europe. D'Aubigné does indicate the persistence of a wider sense of wider unity, but this ideal of Christendom is coherent only in the face of the Ottoman Empire, and elsewhere is internally beset by violence across religious and national divisions. Léry's *Histoire d'un voyage* demonstrates that as early as 1578 the notion of Christendom could be dismissed as irrelevant, whereas d'Aubigné's *Histoire universelle* points towards its continued political utility as late as the eve of the Thirty Years War. Preoccupied with a fragmented continent and a future in which division seems inescapable, neither text really indicates that Europe will develop as a marker of allegiance and identity. The eventual replacement of Christendom is suggested by d'Aubigné's phrase 'l'Europe [. . .] de toutes parts' (I, p. 24'; 'Europe [. . .] in all its parts'): 'Europe' is a term which arguably comprises plurality more easily, a whole constituted of many parts, and as such it is able to encapsulate the sense of fragmentation and diversity suggested by the very existence of plural discourses about the concepts of Europe and Christendom.

Notes

1. Michel de l'Hospital, *La Plume et la tribune*, ed. by Loris Petris, 2 vols (Geneva: Droz, 2002–13), I (2002), p. 399.
2. Olivier Christin, 'From Repression to Pacification: French Royal Policy in the Face of Protestantism', in *Reformation, Revolt and Civil War in France and the Netherlands 1555–1585*, ed. by Philip Benedict, Guido Marnef, Henk van Nierop and Marc Venard (Amsterdam: Koninklijke Nederlandse Akademie van Wetenschappen, 1999), pp. 201–14.
3. Loris Petris, 'Faith and Religious Policy in Michel de L'Hospital's Civic Evangelism', in *The Adventure of Religious Pluralism in Early Modern France*, ed. by Keith Cameron, Mark Greengrass and Penny Roberts (Oxford: Peter Lang, 2000), pp. 129–42 (pp. 140–42).
4. For example, John Hale, *The Civilization of Europe in the Renaissance* (London: HarperCollins, 1993), p. 3, and Mark Greengrass, *Christendom Destroyed: Europe 1517–1648* (London: Allen Lane, 2014), pp. 27–31. Greengrass argues that Christendom was reconfigured as Europe and was understood less as a faith community and more as the geographical extension of a set of values and a sense of superiority.
5. On d'Aubigné's understanding of 'histoire universelle' see Olivier Pot, 'Le Concept d'"histoire universelle": Ou quand l'historien se fait géographe', *Albineana*, 19 (2007), 23–65.
6. Jean-Raymond Fanlo has considered the similarities and differences of the two works in *Tracés, ruptures: La composition instable des 'Tragiques'* (Paris: Champion, 1990), pp. 243–88. He argues that both the *Tragiques* and the *Histoire universelle* were designed to justify the righteousness of the Protestant cause but using different means: the latter through reference to historical fact and the former through theology and imagination; the latter through wide dissemination and the former by narrow circulation to his coreligionists (pp. 245–47).
7. On changing understandings of history see Claude-Gilbert Dubois, *La Conception de l'histoire en France au XVIe siècle (1560–1610)* (Geneva: Slatkine, 1977), especially pp. 158–72. On d'Aubigné's *Histoire universelle* see pp. 185–95.
8. Frank Lestringant understands Léry's 1578 publication as part of a wider Huguenot literary project of refuting Catholic attacks: *Le Huguenot et le sauvage: L'Amérique et la controverse coloniale, en France, au temps des guerres de Religion (1555–1589)*, 3rd edn (Geneva: Droz, 2004), pp. 96–97.
9. For a study of Thevet's account of *France antarctique* in the *Cosmographie universelle*, see Tom Conley, 'Thevet Revisits Guanabara', *Hispanic American Historical Review*, 80 (2000), 753–81.

10. See, for example, *La Diaspora des Huguenots: Les réfugiés protestants de France et leur dispersion dans le monde (XVIe–XVIIIe siècles)*, ed. by Eckart Birnstiel and Chrystel Bernat (Paris: Champion, 2001) and Heiko Oberman, *John Calvin and the Reformation of the Refugees* (Geneva: Droz, 2009).
11. Agrippa d'Aubigné, *Histoire universelle*, ed. by André Thierry, 10 vols (Geneva: Droz, 1981–99), I, 76. Further references to this edition are given in parentheses after quotations in the text. There are several studies of the geography of the *Histoire universelle*: Claude-Gilbert Dubois, 'L'Organisation de l'espace dans l'*Histoire universelle* d'Agrippa d'Aubigné', *Albineana*, 19 (2007), 131–43; Jean-Raymond Fanlo, '"Mettre en ordre des choses tant desordonnees": Les enjeux politiques de la disposition dans l'*Histoire universelle*', in *Autour de l'"Histoire universelle" d'Agrippa d'Aubigné: Mélanges à la mémoire d'André Thierry*, ed. by Gilbert Schrenck (Geneva: Droz, 2006), pp. 195–207; Pot, 'Le Concept d'"histoire universelle"'.
12. Pot, 'Le Concept d'"histoire universelle"', p. 29.
13. On anthropomorphic maps of Europe, see Michael Wintle, *The Image of Europe: Visualizing Europe in Cartography and Iconography Throughout the Ages* (Cambridge: Cambridge University Press, 2011), pp. 247–51.
14. The idea that the Cossacks would protect Christian lands from the Ottomans and the Crimean Tatars emerged throughout western Christendom from the final decade of the sixteenth century; see Serhii Plokhy, 'Princes and Cossacks: Putting Ukraine on the Map of Europe', in *Seeing Muscovy Anew: Politics – Institutions – Culture: Essays in Honor of Nancy Shields Kollmann*, ed. by Michael S. Flier, Valerie Kivelson, Erika Monahan and Daniel Rowland (Bloomington, IN: Slavica Publishers, 2017), pp. 323–38 (pp. 337–38); on the history of the Cossacks in this period, see pp. 331–38.
15. D'Aubigné is referring to *La felicissima Armada que el Rey Don Felipe nuestro Señor mando juntar en el puerto de la ciudadde Lisboa en el Reyno de Portugal el año de 1588*, which was reprinted and translated across the continent. On this, see Meaghan J. Brown, '"The Hearts of All Sorts of People Were Enflamed": Manipulating Readers of Spanish Armada News', *Book History*, 17 (2014), 94–116 (pp. 107–08).
16. Jean de Léry, *Histoire d'un voyage faict en la terre du Bresil*, ed. by Frank Lestringant (Paris: Livre de Poche, 1994), p. 111. Further references to this edition are given in parentheses after quotations in the text.
17. For a detailed study of Léry's ethnographic or anthropological style in the *Histoire d'un voyage*, see Frank Lestringant, *Jean de Léry ou l'invention du sauvage: Essai sur l'*Histoire d'un voyage faict en la terre du Bresil (Paris: Champion, 2005).
18. Michel de Certeau considers that in Léry's hermeneutics, the binary of New World and Old World is transformed into a nature-culture opposition, whereby the savages are not truly other but the natural world is: *L'Écriture de l'histoire* (Paris: Gallimard, 1975), p. 260.
19. Phillip John Usher shows that in trying to make sense of a heterogeneous world Léry prefers the small scale of topographical description to the rigidity of cosmographical concepts: *Errance et cohérence: Essai sur la littérature transfrontalière à la Renaissance* (Paris: Garnier, 2010), pp. 139–74.

I argue throughout this book that Europe was such a rigid and totalising cosmographical concept.
20. Petris, p. 140.
21. On the role of Catholic writing in shaping public opinion and preserving France as a Catholic country, see Luc Racaut, *Hatred in Print: Catholic Propaganda and Protestant Identity during the French Wars of Religion* (Aldershot: Ashgate, 2002).
22. The Calvinists killed in Brazil were included in Protestant martyrologies, such as Jean Crespin's *Histoire des martyrs persecutez et mis à mort pour la vérité de l'Évangile*. See Silvia Shannon, 'Villegagnon, Polyphemus, and Cain of America: Religion and Polemics in the French New World', in *Changing Identities in Early Modern France*, ed. by Michael Wolfe (Durham, NC: Duke University Press, 1996), pp. 325–44 (pp. 326–27).
23. The peace of Cateau-Cambrésis ended the 1551–59 war between France and the Spanish Empire. It confirmed Spanish dominance on the Italian peninsula and was regarded by many as shameful for France. See Robert J. Knecht, *The Rise and Fall of Renaissance France, 1483–1610* (Oxford: Blackwell, 1996), pp. 237–39.
24. Fanlo, '"Mettre en ordre des choses tant desordonnees"', p. 205.
25. Olivier Pot, 'L'*Histoire universelle*, ou une poétique de l'événementiel: Réflexions sur l'invention d'un genre', in *Entre Clio et Melpomène: Les fictions de l'histoire chez Agrippa d'Aubigné*, ed. by Olivier Pot (Paris: Garnier, 2010), pp. 145–223 (p. 170).
26. Dubois, 'L'Organisation de l'espace', p. 141.
27. In a similar way, satirical works by French Reformers constructed an imagined community of fellow believers beyond the borders of France; see George Hoffmann, *Reforming French Culture: Satire, Spiritual Alienation, and Connection to Strangers* (Oxford: Oxford University Press, 2017), pp. 157–88.
28. On exiles' yearning for France see Hoffmann, *Reforming French Culture*, pp. 102–26.
29. Myriam Yardeni has examined the changing forms of national consciousness during the Wars of Religion in *La Conscience nationale en France pendant les guerres de religion (1559–1598)* (Louvain: Nauwelaerts, 1971).
30. Frank Lestringant has written on the idea of a Protestant refuge in America. See *Le Huguenot et le sauvage* and 'Genève et l'Amérique: Le rêve du Refuge huguenot au temps des guerres de Religion (1555–1600)', *Revue de l'histoire des religions*, 210 (1993), 331–47. There has been much debate on whether *France antarctique* was intended, when Villegaignon set out in 1555, as a Protestant refuge. Lestringant, for one, has argued that it was. On the other hand, John McGrath and Silvia Shannon have argued convincingly that Villegaignon's initial intention was to establish a fort to protect French commercial interests in the area: McGrath, 'Polemic and History in French Brazil, 1555–1560', *Sixteenth Century Journal*, 27 (1996), 385–97; Shannon, pp. 325–44. The Calvinists who set out for Brazil in 1556 may have interpreted *France antarctique* as a potential haven, contrary to the official intentions.
31. Certeau, pp. 257–68.

32. '[...] le mouvement de partance qui allait de *par-deçà* (ici, la France) à *par-delà* (là-bas, les Tupis)': Certeau, p. 250; '*par-deçà* (Genève)': Certeau, p. 259.
33. Janet Whatley has argued that Léry's allusions to cannibalism signal 'the utter breakdown of community in Europe': 'Food and the Limits of Civility: The Testimony of Jean de Léry', *Sixteenth Century Journal*, 15 (1984), 387–400 (p. 391).
34. Frank Lestringant, *Le Cannibale: Grandeur et décadence* (Paris: Perrin, 1994), pp.132–33. The 1585 and 1599 additions to chapter 15 can be found in the appendix of Lestringant's edition of the *Histoire d'un voyage*, pp. 571–95. On the development of successive editions of the *Histoire d'un voyage*, see Scott Juall, '"Beaucoup plus barbares que les Sauvages mesmes": Cannibalism, Savagery, and Religious Alterity in Jean de Léry's *Histoire d'un voyage faict en la terre du Brésil* (1599–1600)', *L'Esprit créateur*, 48.1 (2008), 58–71.
35. Andrea Frisch, 'In a Sacramental Mode: Jean de Léry's Calvinist Ethnography', *Representations*, 77 (2002), 82–106 (pp. 87–90); Michel Jeanneret, 'Léry et Thevet: Comment parler d'un monde nouveau?', in *Mélanges à la mémoire de Franco Simone*, 4 vols (Geneva: Slatkine, 1983), IV: *Tradition et originalité dans la création littéraire*, pp. 227–45 (p. 233). Conversely, it has been argued that Léry believed the Brazilians to be damned; see Anthony Pagden, *European Encounters with the New World: From Renaissance to Romanticism* (New Haven, CT: Yale University Press, 1993), pp. 42–47, and Lestringtant, 'Genève et l'Amérique', p. 334.
36. Hoffmann reads this and other references to France in the *Histoire d'un voyage* as an invitation to Léry's readership to examine critically their relationship to France, which contributed to a sense of placelessness among the reformed diaspora; see *Reforming French Culture*, pp. 127–56.
37. Wes Williams, '"L'Humanité du tout perdue?": Early Modern Monsters, Cannibals and Human Souls', *History and Anthropology*, 23 (2012), 235–56 (p. 252).
38. Frisch, pp. 90–91.
39. Lestringant, *Le Huguenot et le sauvage*, p. 80. Nor did Léry want to recreate France (as Catholic France) in the New World; see Jonnie Eriksson, 'Travelling Savage Spaces: Jean de Léry and Territorializations of "Antarctic France", Brazil 1555–60', in *Borders as Experience*, ed. by K. G. Hammarlund (Halmstad: Forsking i Halmstad, 2009), pp. 68–91 (p. 88).
40. Shannon (p. 329) has suggested that a reading of Léry's *Histoire* indicates that the Calvinists considered themselves a minority on the ship to Brazil and then on the island.

Conclusion: Writing Europe, Writing France

Montaigne's 'Des cannibales' begins with a critique of imagined geographies:

> Quand le Roy Pyrrhus passa en Italie, apres qu'il eut reconneu l'ordonnance de l'armée que les Romains luy envoyoient au devant: Je ne sçay, dit-il, quels barbares sont ceux-ci (car les Grecs appelloyent ainsi toutes les nations estrangieres), mais la disposition de cette armée que je voy, n'est aucunement barbare. Autant en dirent les Grecs de celle que Flaminius fit passer en leur païs, et Philippus, voyant d'un tertre l'ordre et distribution du camp Romain en son royaume, sous Publius Sulpicius Galba. Voylà comment il se faut garder de s'atacher aux opinions vulgaires, et les faut juger par la voye de la raison, non par la voix commune.[1]

> When King Pyrrhus went into Italy, after recognising the marshalling of the army that the Romans had sent to meet him, he said, 'I don't know what sort of barbarians (as the Greeks called all foreign peoples) these are, but the ordering of this army that I see is not in the least barbarous.' The same was said by the Greeks about the army that Flaminius led to their country, and by Philip when he saw from a hill the order and distribution of the Roman camp under Publius Sulpicius Galba in his kingdom. Thus it is necessary to guard against sticking to common opinions, and to judge them by the ways of reason, not by popular voice.

In labelling other cultures barbarous, the Greeks constructed an imagined geography that gave meaning to the boundaries of their world. Through the story of Pyrrhus, Montaigne focuses attention on the fictionality of such constructions. This description of a cultural encounter frames the whole essay, itself a meditation on cultural encounter, which challenges the reader to consider how they develop ideas about places and their cultures. Pyrrhus travelled to Italy and in encountering alterity changed his preconceptions. Montaigne's essay goes on to show that it is the act of sympathetic imagination, not travel in itself, that has this transformative effect. His positive assessment of the Brazilian other is based on imagination, that is, on his reading and his conversations.

The depiction of Pyrrhus in 'Des cannibales' serves as a contrast to the critical portrayal of cosmographers like André Thevet, who appears to Montaigne's readership as a traveller who learned nothing from his journey to Brazil and whose geographical imagination was unchanged by what he saw.

In 1585 François de Pavie, the baron of Fourquevaux, set out on a journey through the Levant, returning home via eastern Europe. In the account he produced of his travels, he wrote of the approach towards Constantinople: 'Le long de cestuy [destroit] de Trace, tant du costé d'Europe que d'Asie, dont il faict la separation, se voyent plusieurs grands villages, et chasteaux' ('Along the length of that [strait] of Thrace, on the coast of Europe as well as Asia, of which it separates the two, many large villages and castles can be seen').[2] Later, as he describes his sailing away from Constantinople, he remarks on 'deux chasteaux posez l'un en l'Europe, l'autre au costé d'Asie' (p. 202; 'two castles, one set in Europe, the other on the coast of Asia'). Pavie's journey constituted movement away from Europe and then back and through the continent. Constantinople is an end and a beginning of that continent, and his arrival and exit are characterised by his use of the word 'Europe': of its eight appearances in the text, five relate to the capital of the Ottoman Empire. And yet its use is strictly confined to its spatial designation. Constantinople does not, for Pavie, signify a boundary between two different civilisations. Upon leaving, he journeys to Kraków and Prague, places he finds just as unusual and foreign as the Ottoman world. It is the salt mines of Kraków that he calls another world: 'nuict est il toujours en cest autre monde, où il faut que la lumiere, et le fuzil vous suive tousjours' (p. 228; 'it is always night in that other world, where it is necessary to have a light and a flintstone with you all the time'). To Pavie, as for the travellers to the Levant examined in Chapter 4, Europe is only a spatial concept.

Montaigne's experience is different from Pavie's. He uses the phrase 'autre monde' ('other world') to refer to the Americas: 'cet autre monde qui a esté descouvert en nostre siecle' (p. 203; 'that other world which has been discovered in our century'). His conception of Europe, though, is more similar to Pavie's in that his rare uses of the word signify spatial but not cultural meaning. The only instance of the word 'Europe' in the *Essais* was examined in Chapter 2. In his *Journal de voyage*, an account of his journey through Switzerland and Germany to Italy and back, the word also makes only one appearance, when he compares the baths of Lucca with 'tutti li bagni famosi d'Europa' ('all the famous baths of Europe').[3] The use of 'Europe' in superlatives was not uncommon. The sole instance of the term 'Europe' in Rabelais' *Quart Livre* is as part of a superlative expression ('toutes les lunettes d'Europe'; 'all the glasses in Europe'),[4] but there it is tinged with comedy. Given that most of the ten appearances of the word in the plays of Shakespeare are as part of superlatives and that three of those are in the words of Falstaff (for example, 'I were simply the most active fellow in Europe'; *Henry IV Part 2*, IV. 2. 21–22),[5] it is clear that 'Europe' is sometimes used as a rhetorical figure for comic exaggeration.

The varied formations of Europe examined in this book have shown the diversity of influences on the cultural construction of the continent. Europe was produced according to personal experience, genre and purpose. Travellers who wrote accounts of their journeys explored geography in a manner different from that of cosmographies. Europe was not a significant idea in travel accounts that had some focus on human stories, namely Jean de Léry's *Histoire d'un voyage faict en la terre du Brésil* or the first three books of Nicolas de Nicolay's *Les Quatre Premiers Livres des navigations et peregrinations orientales*. Nicolay constructed an imagined geography of Europe in the fourth book in response to his description of Greece, a land he never travelled to, and his condemnation of the Greek people. An imagined geography of Europe as superior to the rest of the world is central to André Thevet's *Les Singularitez de la France antarctique*, which makes use of the narrative structure of a voyage but largely eschews personal experience in the interests of authorial self-fashioning as an expert cosmographer and of the promotion of French imperial ambitions. The scope of the cosmographies of Apian, Thevet and Belleforest – the whole world – necessitates usage of the term 'Europe'. It is a genre where an imagined geography of Europe is articulated in opposition to the other three parts of the world. Although Théodore-Agrippa d'Aubigné writes about the whole world in his *Histoire universelle*, 'Chrestienté' is found more frequently than 'Europe' in the text since religion is the main theme of the work. Ronsard, by contrast, favours 'Europe' in his poetry. More suitable for poetic metre and a term of classical origin, 'Europe' offers a conception of a Christian culture informed by Greco-Roman civilisation. François Savary de Brèves's treatises show a comfortable overlap between the imagined geography of Europe and the imagined geography of Christendom. It is in the thoughtful, speculative literature of Rabelais and Montaigne that the word 'Europe' is little used. Their works eschew dogmatic thinking and encourage reflection. An imagined geography of Europe, with its totalising and homogenising way of understanding the world and the people in it, was not relevant to their writing.

Place is another crucial factor in constructions of Europe. How Europe was imagined depended on the location of the writing subject, on the geographical location from which it was viewed. Europe considered from Calvinist Geneva did not look the same as Europe considered from Brazil. From each vantage point, there were different ways of viewing Europe according to the author's personal experience and motivation. In thinking about Brazil, Montaigne and Thevet represented Europe differently. In thinking about Constantinople, Ronsard and Savary de Brèves represented Europe differently.

Whatever location Europe was imagined from in French writing of the period, the place of France was involved in some way. The alterity of Brazil highlighted what people across the continent had in common yet also pointed to their political differences. The imagined geography of Europe in Thevet's *Singularitez* is constructed for the purpose of justifying French imperial ambitions. Similarly, Constantinople, like the New World, offered a location against which to define a unifying conception of the continent but also fuelled national ambitions. Ronsard uses Constantinople to project a fantasy of crusade, a victory for Europe with France as its head. The diplomat Savary de Brèves articulates a Europe shaped by opposition to the Ottoman Empire in order to defend the renewal of the Franco-Ottoman alliance that he negotiated. Fearing Spanish domination of the continent, he champions trade and cooperation with the Ottomans, representing Europe as a collection of diverse and fragmented polities. The fragmentation of Europe is the predominant view from Geneva. For Léry and d'Aubigné, the continent and Christendom are shattered by religious division. It is their attachments to their religion and to their country of birth that stimulate personal allegiance, but these do not align with geographical boundaries. Accounts of travel to Malta also stress personal attachments to nationality. As travellers move across boundaries they make sense of the world through the category of nationhood, which they use to identify the people and the places they encounter. Even cosmography, which places so much emphasis on continents as the pre-eminent symbolic divisions of the world, reveals the importance attached to national divisions. And only a Frenchman could have written, as André Thevet did, that 'la France estoit situee au milieu de l'Europe, comme le cœur de la Chrestienté' ('France was situated in the centre of Europe as the heart of Christendom').[6]

Many of the ideas of Europe that were included in French writing circulated more widely in the continent. Thevet's and Belleforest's cosmographies drew on previous works, like those of Sebastian Münster and Peter Apian. Notions of the fecundity and inhabitability of the continent can be traced back to ancient Greece. But French writing on Europe was also doing something that writing in other languages was not. Where

Walser-Bürgler's work has shown how a discourse of European integration was developed in Neo-Latin texts, *Writing Europe in Renaissance France* has demonstrated how the French vernacular drew on notions of continental unity to articulate the place of France within Europe and therefore to construct a vision of French nationhood.[7] To imagine the geography of Europe in French writing was also to imagine the geography of France. Representations of Europe were framed by concerns about France, from Savary de Brèves's defence of French relations with the Ottoman Empire and Thevet's support of French empire-building to Léry's and d'Aubigné's grief at the French Wars of Religion. Their attitudes to France and their reasons for writing about France determined the ways in which they wrote about Europe. The concept of Europe did not develop as an alternative to the nation state, but in productive dialogue with nationhood.

France and Europe were of such concern during this period since society was changing, and attempts to write France and to write Europe were the product of anxieties about this changing world. D'Aubigné's *Histoire universelle* and Léry's *Histoire d'un voyage* reveal a deep yet unattainable desire to practise their religion in a peaceful France. The literary works of Rabelais and Montaigne vividly dramatise the sense of uncertainty that their turbulent times provoked. The islands of Rabelais' *Quart Livre* give fictional form to these anxieties, and the book ends with the Pantagruelists sailing into an uncertain future. The 'nous' in Montaigne's 'Des cannibales' presents an inability to give a name to his cultural world. Other texts attempt to efface doubts, but these emerge nonetheless as unresolved problems. In his poetry Ronsard heralds a *translatio imperii* from Rome to France yet writes elsewhere of a France ravaged by civil war. Savary de Brèves publishes two ostensibly contradictory political tracts alongside each other, one focusing on the destruction of the Ottoman Empire, the other promoting cooperation. The cosmographies of Thevet and Belleforest precisely delimit the geographical boundaries of Europe and imbue the space with cultural meaning, but also reveal how the cultural and the geographical do not align, casting both Greece and Muscovy as within the spatial boundaries yet outside the religious ones.

In writing France and Europe, the authors considered in this book were imagining different geographies of the nation and the continent. Visions of a Europe fragmented along religious lines circulated with visions of a continent united spiritually under the rule of the French king. Visions of a Europe expanding into the New World circulated with visions of a continent shrinking as the Ottoman Empire spread. Europe, then, was a literary phenomenon, written and rewritten from different perspectives. Above all, though, the meanings of Europe shifted in accordance with the individual writers whose own travels, whether in reality or in imagination, gave them a particular perspective on the world, on Europe and on France. The Europe they each wrote was a contingent one, reflecting the varying audiences and purposes for which they were writing. Where other studies on the history of the idea of Europe have focused on a shared European way of looking at the world, *Writing Europe in Renaissance France* has demonstrated that there was not even a shared French view of the world, let alone a shared European one.

Notes

1. Michel de Montaigne, *Les Essais*, ed. by Pierre Villey and V. L. Saulnier (Paris: Presses Universitaires de France, 2004), p. 202. Further references to this edition are given in parentheses after quotations in the text.
2. 'Relation de François de Pavie, seigneur de Forquevauls, d'un sien voyage fait l'an 1585 aux terres du Turc et autres divers lieux de l'Europe', Paris, Bibliothèque Nationale de France, MS nouvelles acquisitions françaises 6277, p. 175. Further references to this document are given in parentheses after quotations in the text.
3. *Journal de voyage de Michel de Montaigne*, ed. by François Rigolot (Paris: Presses Universitaires de France, 1992), p. 174. Most of the journal is written in French, but there is a section composed in Italian.
4. Rabelais, *Œuvres complètes*, ed. by Mireille Huchon (Paris: Gallimard, 1994), p. 549.
5. William Shakespeare, *Henry IV, Part 2*, ed. by René Weis, The Oxford Shakespeare (Oxford: Oxford University Press, 1998), p. 226.
6. André Thevet, *La Cosmographie universelle d'André Thevet, cosmographe du roy, illustrée de diverses figures des choses plus remarquables veuës par l'auteur, & incogneuës de noz anciens et modernes*, 2 vols (Paris: Guillaume Chaudiere, 1575), II, fol. 508^r.
7. Isabella Walser-Bürgler, *Europe and Europeanness in Early Modern Latin Literature: 'Fuitne Europa tunc unita?'* (Leiden: Brill, 2021).

Bibliography

Primary Sources: Manuscripts

'Copies des "letres et despesches de Monsieur François Savary de Breves, pendant son ambassade de Rome depuis l'année 1608 jusques en 1614": Lettres de François Savary de Brèves, 25 juillet 1608–24 décembre 1611', Paris, Bibliothèque Nationale de France, MS fonds cinq cents de Colbert 351

'Mémoires politiques et diplomatiques de François Savary de Brèves', Paris, Bibliothèque Nationale de France, MS fonds français 18075

'Relation de François de Pavie, seigneur de Forquevauls, d'un sien voyage fait l'an 1585 aux terres du Turc et autres divers lieux de l'Europe', Paris, Bibliothèque Nationale de France, MS nouvelles acquisitions françaises 6277

Primary Sources: Books

Apian, Peter, *La Cosmographie de Pierre Apian, libvre tresutile, traictant de toutes les regions & pays du monde par artifice astronomicque, nouvellement traduict de Latin en François. Et par Gemma Frison mathematicien & docteur en medicine de Louvain corrige* (Antwerp: Gregoire Bonte, 1544)

Belleforest, François de, *La Cosmographie universelle de tout le monde, augmentee, ornée et enrichie par F. de Belle-Forest*, 3 vols (Paris: Michel Sonnius, 1575)

Boemus, Johann, *Recueil de diverses histoires touchant les situations de toutes regions & pays contenuz es trois parties du monde, avec les particulieres mœurs, loix, & ceremonies de toutes nations & peuples y habitans* (Paris: Galliot de Pré, 1539)

D'Aubigné, Agrippa, *Histoire universelle*, ed. by André Thierry, 10 vols (Geneva: Droz, 1981–99)

Du Bellay, Joachim, *La Deffence, et illustration de la langue françoyse*, ed. by Jean-Charles Monferran (Geneva: Droz, 2001)

Isocrates, trans. by George Norlin and Larue Van Hook, 3 vols (London: Heinemann, 1928–1945), II, trans. by George Norlin (1929)

La Noue, François de, *Discours politiques et militaires*, ed. by F. E. Sutcliffe (Geneva: Droz, 1967)

La Popelinière, Lancelot Voisin de, *Les Trois Mondes de La Popelinière*, ed. by Anne-Marie Beaulieu (Geneva: Droz, 1997)

Léry, Jean de, *Histoire d'un voyage faict en la terre du Bresil*, ed. by Frank Lestringant (Paris: Livre de Poche, 1994)

L'Hospital, Michel de, *La Plume et la tribune*, ed. by Loris Petris, 2 vols (Geneva: Droz, 2002–13)

Monluc, Blaise de, *Commentaires, 1521–1576*, ed. by Paul Courteault (Paris: Gallimard, 1964)

Montaigne, Michel de, *Journal de voyage de Michel de Montaigne*, ed. by François Rigolot (Paris: Presses Universitaires de France, 1992)

— *Les Essais*, ed. by Pierre Villey and V. L. Saulnier (Paris: Presses Universitaires de France, 2004)

Münster, Sebastian, *Cosmographiae universalis libri* VI (Basle, 1550)

Nicolay, Nicolas de, *Dans l'empire de Soliman le Magnifique*, ed. by Marie-Christine Gomez-Géraud and Stéphane Yérasimos (Paris: Presses du CNRS, 1989)

Rabelais, François, *Œuvres complètes*, ed. by Mireille Huchon (Paris: Gallimard, 1994)

Ronsard, Pierre de, *Œuvres complètes*, ed. by Jean Céard, Daniel Ménager and Michel Simonin, 2 vols (Paris: Gallimard, 1993)

Savary de Brèves, François, *Discours abrégé des asseurez moyens d'aneantir & ruiner la monarchie des Princes Ottomans* (Paris: [n.pub.], [n.d.])

— *Discours sur l'alliance qu'a le Roy avec le grand Seigneur, & de l'utilité qu'elle apporte à la Chrestienté* (Paris: [n.pub.], [n.d.])

— *Relation des voyages de Monsieur de Brèves, tant en Grèce, Terre Saincte et Ægypte, qu'aux royaumes de Tunis et Arger, ensemble un traicté faict l'an 1604 entre le Roy Henry le Grand, et l'Empereur des Turcs, et trois discours dudit sieur, le tout recueilly par le S.D.C.* (Paris: Nicolas Gasse, 1628)

Thevet, André, *Cosmographie de Levant*, ed. by Frank Lestringant (Geneva: Droz, 1985)

— *La Cosmographie universelle d'André Thevet, cosmographe du roy, illustrée de diverses figures des choses plus remarquables veuës par l'Auteur, & incogneuës de noz anciens et modernes*, 2 vols (Paris: Guillaume Chaudiere, 1575)

— *Le Brésil d'André Thevet: Les singularités de la France antarctique*, ed. by Frank Lestringant (Paris: Chandeigne, 2011)

Other sources

Abulafia, David, *The Great Sea: A Human History of the Mediterranean* (London: Allen Lane, 2011)

Anderson, Benedict, *Imagined Communities: Reflections on the Origin and Spread of Nationalism*, rev. edn (London: Verso, 2006)

Andrukhovych, Yuri, 'The Star Absinthe: Notes on a Bitter Anniversary', in *The White Chalk of Days: The Contemporary Ukrainian Literature Series Anthology* <https://www.whitechalkofdays.com/the-star-absinthe-notes-on-a-bitter-anniversary> [accessed 4 May 2023)

Armstrong, Megan C., and Gillian Weiss, 'France and the Early Modern Mediterranean', *French History*, 29 (2015), 1–5

Barthe, Pascale, *French Encounters with the Ottomans, 1510–1560* (Abingdon: Routledge, 2016)
Beaune, Colette, *Naissance de la nation France* (Paris: Gallimard, 1985)
Besse, Jean-Marc, *Les Grandeurs de la Terre: Aspects du savoir géographique à la Renaissance* (Lyon: ENS Éditions, 2003)
Birnstiel, Eckart, and Chrystel Bernat, eds, *La Diaspora des Huguenots: Les réfugiés protestants de France et leur dispersion dans le monde (XVIe–XVIIIe siècles)* (Paris: Champion, 2001)
Bisaha, Nancy, *Creating East and West: Renaissance Humanists and the Ottoman Turks* (Philadelphia: University of Pennsylvania Press, 2004)
Blum, Claude, 'Des *Essais* au *Journal de voyage*: Espace humain et conscience européenne à la fin du XVIe siècle', in *La Conscience européenne au XVe et au XVIe siècle: Actes du colloque international organisé à l'École Normale Supérieure de Jeunes Filles (30 septembre – 3 octobre 1980)* (Paris: École Normale Supérieure de Jeunes Filles, 1982), pp. 23–33
Bradford, Ernle, *The Great Siege* (London: Hodder and Stoughton, 1961)
Brafman, David, 'Facing East: The Western View of Islam in Nicolas de Nicolay's *Travels in Turkey*', *Getty Research Journal*, 1 (2009), 153–60
Braudel, Fernand, *La Méditerranée et le monde méditerranéen à l'époque de Philippe II* (Paris: Colin, 1949)
Broc, Numa, *La Géographie de la Renaissance (1420–1620)* (Paris: Bibliothèque Nationale, 1980)
Brotton, Jerry, *The Renaissance Bazaar: From the Silk Road to Michelangelo* (Oxford: Oxford University Press, 2002)
Brown, Meaghan J., '"The Hearts of All Sorts of People Were Enflamed": Manipulating Readers of Spanish Armada News', *Book History*, 17 (2014), 94–116
Burke, Peter, 'Did Europe Exist before 1700?', *History of European Ideas*, 1 (1980), 21–29
Buttigieg, Emanuel, 'The Maltese Islands and the Religious Culture of the Hospitallers: Isolation and Connectivity c.1540s–c.1690s', in *Islands and Military Orders, c.1291–c.1798*, ed. by Emanuel Buttigieg and Simon Phillips (Farnham, Surrey: Ashgate, 2013), pp. 39–49
Canny, Nicholas, 'A Protestant or Catholic Atlantic World? Confessional Divisions and the Writing of Natural History', *Proceedings of the British Academy*, 181 (2012), 83–121
Cassar, Carmel, *Society, Culture and Identity in Early Modern Malta* (Msida: Mireva, 2000)
Cassar, George, 'Malta and the Order of St John: Life on an Island Home', in *Islands and Military Orders, c.1291–c.1798*, ed. by Emanuel Buttigieg and Simon Phillips (Farnham, Surrey: Ashgate, 2013), pp. 75–83
Cave, Terence, *The Cornucopian Text: Problems of Writing in the French Renaissance* (Oxford: Oxford University Press, 1979)
— 'Epilogue: Time's Arrow', in *Pre-Histories and Afterlives: Studies in Critical Method for Terence Cave*, ed. by Anna Holland and Richard Scholar (London: Legenda, 2009), pp. 135–46
— *How to Read Montaigne* (London: Granta, 2007)
— *Pré-histoires, II: Langues étrangères et troubles économiques au XVIe siècle* (Geneva: Droz, 2001)

— *Pré-histoires: Textes troublés au seuil de la modernité* (Geneva: Droz, 1999)
— 'Ronsard's Mythological Universe', in *Ronsard the Poet*, ed. by Terence Cave (London: Methuen, 1973), pp. 159–208
Cave, Terence, ed., *Thomas More's 'Utopia' in Early Modern Europe: Paratexts and Contexts* (Manchester: Manchester University Press, 2008)
Céard, Jean, 'L'Europe en quête de son identité, selon les cosmographes de la fin de la Renaissance', in *Renaissances européennes et Renaissance française*, ed. by Gilbert Gadoffre (Montpellier: Éditions Espaces 34, 1995), pp. 53–67
— 'L'Image de l'Europe dans la littérature cosmographique de la Renaissance', in *La Conscience européenne au XVe et au XVIe siècle: Actes du colloque international organisé à l'École Normale Supérieure de Jeunes Filles (30 septembre – 3 octobre 1980)* (Paris: École Normale Supérieure de Jeunes Filles, 1982), pp. 49–63
Certeau, Michel de, *L'Écriture de l'histoire* (Paris: Gallimard, 1975)
Chakrabarty, Dipesh, *Provincializing Europe: Postcolonial Thought and Historical Difference* (Princeton: Princeton University Press, 2007)
Christin, Olivier, 'From Repression to Pacification: French Royal Policy in the Face of Protestantism', in *Reformation, Revolt and Civil War in France and the Netherlands 1555–1585*, ed. by Philip Benedict, Guido Marnef, Henk van Nierop and Marc Venard (Amsterdam: Koninklijke Nederlandse Akademie van Wetenschappen, 1999), pp. 201–14
Clendinnen, Inga, 'Cortés, Signs, and the Conquest of Mexico', in *The Transmission of Culture in Early Modern Europe*, ed. by Anthony Grafton and Ann Blair (Philadelphia: University of Pennsylvania Press, 1990), pp. 87–130
Colie, Rosalie, *The Resources of Kind: Genre-Theory in the Renaissance*, ed. by Barbara K. Lewalski (Berkeley: University of California Press, 1973)
Conley, Tom, *An Errant Eye: Poetry and Topography in Early Modern France* (Minneapolis: University of Minnesota Press, 2011)
— *The Self-Made Map: Cartographic Writing in Early Modern France* (Minneapolis: University of Minnesota Press, 1996)
— 'Thevet Revisits Guanabara', *Hispanic American Historical Review*, 80 (2000), 753–81
Conrad, Sebastian, *What is Global History?* (Princeton: Princeton University Press, 2016)
Cooper, Richard, 'Rabelais, Jean Du Bellay et la crise gallicane', in *Rabelais pour le XXIe siècle*, ed. by Michel Simonin, Études Rabelaisiennes, 33 (Geneva: Droz, 1998), pp. 299–325
Cowling, David, ed., *Conceptions of Europe in Renaissance France: Essays in Honour of Keith Cameron* (Amsterdam: Rodopi, 2006)
Creore, A. E., *A Word-Index to the Poetic Works of Ronsard*, 2 vols (Leeds: W. S. Maney, 1972)
Creswell, Tim, *Place: An Introduction* (Chichester: Wiley-Blackwell, 2015)
Curtius, Ernst Robert, *European Literature and the Latin Middle Ages*, trans. by Willard R. Trask (London: Routledge & Kegan Paul, 1953)
Dainotto, Roberto M., *Europe (in Theory)* (Durham, NC: Duke University Press, 2007)
Das, Nandini, and others, *Keywords of Identity, Race, and Human Mobility in Early Modern England* (Amsterdam: Amsterdam University Press, 2021)

Davies, Norman, *God's Playground: A History of Poland*, 2 vols (Oxford: Oxford University Press, 2005)
— *Heart of Europe: A Short History of Poland* (Oxford: Oxford University Press, 1984)
Davies, Surekha, 'America and Amerindians in Sebastian Münster's *Cosmographiae universalis libri* VI (1550)', *Renaissance Studies*, 25.3 (2011), 351–73
Defaux, Gérard, *Rabelais agonistès: Du rieur au prophète. Études sur 'Pantagruel', 'Gargantua' et 'Le Quart Livre'*, Études Rabelaisiennes, 32 (Geneva: Droz, 1997)
— 'Un cannibale en haut de chausses: Montaigne, la différence et la logique de l'identité', *Modern Language Notes*, 97 (1982), 919–57
Delanty, Gerard, *Inventing Europe: Idea, Identity, Reality* (Basingstoke: Macmillan, 1995)
Demerson, Guy, *Rabelais* (Paris: Balland, 1986)
Demonet, Marie-Luce, 'Raves, Rabbis et Raboulière: La persecution des Papefigues (Rabelais, *Quart Livre*, chapitre XLV)', in *Questions de littérature: Béroul, Rabelais, La Fontaine, Saint-Simon, Maupassant, Lagarce*, ed. by Jean-Michel Gouvard (Bordeaux: Presses Universitaires de Bordeaux, 2011), pp. 33–59
Desan, Philippe, 'Être Français à la Renaissance: L'expérience de Montaigne', in *Montaigne et l'Europe: Actes du colloque international de Bordeaux (1992)*, ed. by Claude-Gilbert Dubois (Mont-de-Marsan: Éditions InterUniversitaires, 1992), pp. 47–59
— '*Locus Narrandi*: The Place of Leisure in the Renaissance', in *Early Modern Visions of Space: France and Beyond*, ed. by Dorothea Heitsch and Jeremie C. Korta (Chapel Hill: University of North Carolina Press, 2021), pp. 405–20
Detering, Nicolas, *Krise und Kontinent: Die Entstehung der deutschen Europa-Literatur in der Frühen Neuzeit* (Cologne: Böhlau Verlag, 2017)
Detering, Nicolas, Clementina Marsico and Isabella Walser-Bürgler, 'Contesting Europe: Comparative Perspectives on Early Modern Discourses on Europe, 1400–1800 – an Introduction', in *Contesting Europe: Comparative Perspectives on Early Modern Discourses on Europe, 1400–1800*, ed. by Nicolas Detering, Clementina Marsico and Isabella Walser-Bürgler (Leiden: Brill, 2020), pp. 1–10
Detering, Nicolas, Clementina Marsico and Isabella Walser-Bürgler, eds, *Contesting Europe: Comparative Perspectives on Early Modern Discourses on Europe, 1400–1800* (Leiden: Brill, 2020)
Dickason, Olive Patricia, *The Myth of the Savage: And the Beginnings of French Colonialism in the Americas* (Edmonton: University of Alberta Press, 1997)
Dickson, Colin, 'Geographic Imagination in the *Essais* and Geomorphism in Montaigne Criticism', in *Geo/graphies: Mapping the Imagination in French and Francophone Literature and Film*, ed. by Freeman G. Henry, French Literature Series, 30 (Amsterdam: Rodopi, 2003), pp. 29–40
Dubois, Claude-Gilbert, *Essais sur Montaigne: La régulation de l'imaginaire éthique et politique* (Caen: Paradigme, 1992)
Dubois, Claude-Gilbert, *La conception de l'histoire en France au XVIe siècle (1560–1610)* (Geneva: Slatkine, 1977)

— 'L'organisation de l'espace dans l'*Histoire universelle* d'Agrippa d'Aubigné', *Albineana*, 19 (2007), 131–43
Dubois, Claude-Gilbert, ed., *Montaigne et l'Europe: Actes du colloque international de Bordeaux (1992)* (Mont-de-Marsan: Éditions InterUniversitaires, 1992)
DuPlessis, Robert, *Transitions to Capitalism in Early Modern Europe* (Cambridge: Cambridge University Press, 1997)
Dursteler, Eric R., 'On Bazaars and Battlefields: Recent Scholarship on Mediterranean Cultural Contacts', *Journal of Early Modern History*, 15 (2011), 413–34
Duval, Edwin, *The Design of Rabelais's 'Quart Livre de Pantagruel'* (Geneva: Droz, 1998)
— 'Lessons of the New World: Design and Meaning in Montaigne's "Des Cannibales" (I:31) and "Des coches" (III:6)', *Yale French Studies*, 64 (1983), 95–112
Duverdier, Gérald, 'Les Circonstances favorables à l'apparition d'impressions orientales pour l'Europe savante', in *Le Livre et le Liban jusqu'à 1900*, ed. by C. Aboussouan (Paris: UNESCO, 1982), pp. 175–89
— 'Savary de Brèves et Ibrahim Müteferrika: Deux drogmans culturels à l'origine de l'imprimerie turque', *Bulletin du bibliophile*, 3 (1987), 322–59
Eriksson, Jonnie, 'Travelling Savage Spaces: Jean de Léry and Territorializations of "Antarctic France", Brazil 1555–60', in *Borders as Experience*, ed. by K. G. Hammarlund (Halmstad: Forsking i Halmstad, 2009), pp. 68–91
Fanlo, Jean-Raymond, '"Mettre en ordre des choses tant desordonnees": Les enjeux politiques de la disposition dans l'*Histoire universelle*', in *Autour de l'*'Histoire universelle' d'Agrippa d'Aubigné: Mélanges à la mémoire d'André Thierry*, ed. by Gilbert Schrenck (Geneva: Droz, 2006), pp. 195–207
— *Tracés, ruptures: La composition instable des 'Tragiques'* (Paris: Champion, 1990)
Febvre, Lucien, *L'Europe: Genèse d'une civilisation*, ed. by Thérèse Charmasson and Brigitte Mazon (Paris: Perrin, 1999)
Filho, Celso Martins Azar, 'Nouveau monde, homme nouveau', *Montaigne Studies*, 22 (2010), 71–84
Fleet, Kate, *European and Islamic Trade in the Early Ottoman State: The Merchants of Genoa and Turkey* (Cambridge: Cambridge University Press, 1999)
Ford, Philip, *The Montaigne Library of Gilbert de Botton at Cambridge University Library* (Cambridge: Cambridge University Library, 2008)
Freller, Thomas, *Malta and the Grand Tour* (Malta: Midsea Books, 2009)
Frisch, Andrea, 'In a Sacramental Mode: Jean de Léry's Calvinist Ethnography', *Representations*, 77 (2002), 82–106
Glacken, Clarence J., *Traces on the Rhodian Shore: Nature and Culture in Western Thought from Ancient Times to the End of the Eighteenth Century* (Berkeley: University of California Press, 1967)
Gray, Floyd, *Rabelais et le comique du discontinu* (Paris: Champion, 1994)
Greene, Molly, *A Shared World: Christians and Muslims in the Early Modern Mediterranean* (Princeton: Princeton University Press, 2000)
Greengrass, Mark, *Christendom Destroyed: Europe 1517–1648* (London: Allen Lane, 2014)

Gregory, Derek, *Geographical Imaginations* (Oxford: Blackwell, 1994)
Gunn, Geoffrey C., *Imagined Geographies: The Maritime Silk Roads in World History, 100–1800* (Hong Kong: Hong Kong University Press, 2021)
Hale, John, *The Civilization of Europe in the Renaissance* (London: HarperCollins, 1993)
Hamilton, Alastair, 'François Savary de Brèves', in *Christian–Muslim Relations: A Bibliographical History*, IX: *Western and Southern Europe (1600–1700)*, ed. by David Thomas and John Chesworth (Leiden: Brill, 2017), pp. 415–22
Hamilton, Alastair, and Francis Richard, *André du Ryer and Oriental Studies in Seventeenth-Century France* (Oxford: Arcadian Library, 2004)
Hampton, Timothy, *Literature and Nation in the Sixteenth Century: Inventing Renaissance France* (Ithaca, NY: Cornell University Press, 2001)
Hanke, Lewis, *All Mankind is One: A Study of the Disputation between Bartolomé de Las Casas and Juan Ginés de Sepúlveda in 1550 on the Intellectual and Religious Capacity of the American Indians* (DeKalb: Northern Illinois University Press, 1974)
Hankins, James, 'Renaissance Crusaders: Humanist Crusade Literature in the Age of Mehmed II', *Dumbarton Oaks Papers*, 49 (1995), 111–207
Harley, J. B., 'Deconstructing the Map', *Cartographica*, 26 (1989), 1–20
Harp, Margaret Broom, *The Portrayal of Community in Rabelais's 'Quart Livre'* (New York: Peter Lang, 1997)
Harrigan, Michael, 'The *Navigations* of Nicolas de Nicolay and the Economics of Ethnology in the Early Modern Mediterranean Basin', in *Anthropological Reformations – Anthropology in the Era of Reformation*, ed. by Anne Eusterschulte and Hannah Wälzholz (Göttingen: Vandenhoeck & Ruprecht, 2015), pp. 541–56
Hartog, François, 'Barbarians: From the Ancient to the New World' in *Barbarism Revisited: New Perspectives on an Old Concept*, ed. by Maria Boletsi and Christian Moser (Leiden: Brill, 2015), pp. 31–44
Hausmann, Frank-Rutger, 'Comment doit-on lire l'épisode de 'L'isle des Papefigues' (*Quart Livre*, 45–47)?', in *Rabelais en son demi-millénaire: Actes du colloque international de Tours (24–29 septembre 1984)*, ed. by Jean Céard and Jean-Claude Margolin, Études Rabelaisiennes, 21 (Geneva: Droz, 1988), pp. 121–29
Hay, Denys, *Europe: The Emergence of an Idea*, 2nd edn (Edinburgh: Edinburgh University Press, 1968)
Heath, Michael J., *Crusading Commonplaces: La Noue, Lucinge and Rhetoric against the Turks* (Geneva: Droz, 1986)
— *Rabelais* (Tempe: Arizona Center for Medieval and Renaissance Studies, 1996)
Heitsch, Dorothea, and Jeremie C. Korta, eds, *Early Modern Visions of Space: France and Beyond* (Chapel Hill: University of North Carolina Press, 2021).
Helgerson, Richard, *Forms of Nationhood: The Elizabethan Writing of England* (Chicago: University of Chicago Press, 1992)
Heller, Henry, *Anti Italianism in Sixteenth-Century France* (Toronto: University of Toronto Press, 2003)
Hess, Andrew, *The Forgotten Frontier: A History of the Sixteenth-Century Ibero-African Frontier* (Chicago: University of Chicago Press, 2011)

Higman, Francis, 'Ronsard's Political and Polemical Poetry', in *Ronsard the Poet*, ed. by Terence Cave (London: Methuen, 1973), pp. 241–85

Hoffmann, George, 'Anatomy of the Mass: Montaigne's "Cannibals"', *PMLA*, 117 (2002), 207–21

— *Reforming French Culture: Satire, Spiritual Alienation, and Connection to Strangers* (Oxford: Oxford University Press, 2017)

Holland, Anna, and Richard Scholar, 'Introduction', in *Pre-Histories and Afterlives: Studies in Critical Method for Terence Cave*, ed. by Anna Holland and Richard Scholar (London: Legenda, 2009), pp. 1–14

Horden, Peregrine, and Nicholas Purcell, *The Corrupting Sea: A Study of Mediterranean History* (Oxford: Oxford University Press, 2000)

Hutchinson, Steven, *Frontier Narratives: Liminal Lives in the Early Modern Mediterranean* (Manchester: Manchester University Press, 2020)

Isom-Verhaaren, Christine, *Allies with the Infidel: The Ottoman and French Alliance in the Sixteenth Century* (London: I. B. Tauris, 2011)

Jardine, Lisa, *Worldly Goods: A New History of the Renaissance* (London: Macmillan, 1996)

Jeanneret, Michel, *Le Défi des signes: Rabelais et la crise de l'interprétation à la Renaissance* (Orléans: Paradigme, 1994)

— 'Léry et Thevet: Comment parler d'un monde nouveau?', in *Mélanges à la mémoire de Franco Simone*, 4 vols (Geneva: Slatkine, 1983), IV: *Tradition et originalité dans la création littéraire*, pp. 227–45

Juall, Scott, '"Beaucoup plus barbares que les Sauvages mesmes": Cannibalism, Savagery, and Religious Alterity in Jean de Léry's *Histoire d'un voyage faict en la terre du Brésil* (1599–1600)', *L'Esprit créateur*, 48.1 (2008), 58–71

Keller, Marcus, *Figurations of France: Literary Nation-Building in Times of Crisis (1550–1650)* (Newark: University of Delaware Press, 2011)

— 'France, Europe, and the Orient in the *Essays*: Montaigne's Dialectics' in *The Dialectics of Orientalism in Early Modern Europe*, ed. by Marcus Keller and Javier Irigoyen-García (London: Palgrave Macmillan, 2018), pp. 121–36

— 'Nicolas de Nicolay's *Navigations* and the Domestic Politics of Travel Writing', *L'Esprit créateur*, 48 (2008), 18–31

— 'The Turk of Early Modern France', *L'Esprit créateur*, 53.4 (2013), 1–8

Keller, Marcus, and Javier Irigoyen-García, eds, *The Dialectics of Orientalism in Early Modern Europe* (London: Palgrave Macmillan, 2018)

Knecht, Robert J., *The French Religious Wars 1562–1598* (Oxford: Osprey, 2002)

— *The Rise and Fall of Renaissance France, 1483–1610* (Oxford: Blackwell, 1996)

La Conscience européenne au XVe et au XVIe siècle: Actes du colloque international organisé à l'École Normale Supérieure de Jeunes Filles (30 septembre – 3 octobre 1980) (Paris: École Normale Supérieure de Jeunes Filles, 1982)

Lacore-Martin, Emmanuelle, *Figures de l'histoire et du temps dans l'œuvre de Rabelais*, Études Rabelaisiennes, 51 (Geneva: Droz, 2011)

Le Cadet, Nicolas, *L'Évangelisme fictionnel: Les 'Livres' rabelaisiens, le 'Cymbalum mundi', 'L'Heptaméron '(1532–1552)* (Paris: Garnier, 2010)

— 'L'Ile des Macraeons, ou les ambiguïtés du *transitus* rabelaisien (*Quart Livre*, ch. XXV à XXVIII)', *Réforme, humanisme, Renaissance*, 61 (2005), 51–72

Lestringant, Frank, *André Thevet: Cosmographe des derniers Valois* (Geneva: Droz, 1991)
— *Bribes d'îles: La littérature en archipel de Benedetto Bordone à Nicolas Bouvier* (Paris: Garnier, 2020)
— 'Cosmographes', in *Dictionnaire de Michel de Montaigne*, ed. by Philippe Desan (Paris: Garnier, 2007), pp. 256–58
— 'Europe et théorie des climats dans la second moitié du XVIe siècle', in *La Conscience européenne au XVe et au XVIe siècle: Actes du colloque international organisé à l'École Normale Supérieure de Jeunes Filles (30 septembre – 3 octobre 1980)* (Paris: École Normale Supérieure de Jeunes Filles, 1982), pp. 206–26
— 'Genève et l'Amérique: Le rêve du Refuge huguenot au temps des guerres de Religion (1555–1600)', *Revue de l'histoire des religions*, 210 (1993), 331–47
— 'Guillaume Postel et l'"obsession turque"', in *Guillaume Postel 1581–1981: Actes du colloque d'Avranches* (Paris: Éditions de la Maisnie, 1985), pp. 265–98
— *Jean de Léry ou l'invention du sauvage: Essai sur l'*Histoire d'un voyage faict en la terre du Bresil (Paris: Champion, 2005)
— *L'Atelier du cosmographe: Ou l'image du monde à la Renaissance* (Paris: Albin Michel, 1991)
— *Le Cannibale: Grandeur et décadence* (Paris: Perrin, 1994)
— 'Le Déclin d'un savoir: La crise de la cosmographie à la fin de la Renaissance', *Annales: Histoire, sciences sociales*, 46 (1991), 239–60
— *Le Huguenot et le sauvage: L'Amérique et la controverse coloniale, en France, au temps des guerres de Religion (1555–1589)*, 3rd edn (Geneva: Droz, 2004)
— 'Le Récit de voyage et la question des genres: L'exemple des *Singularitez de la France antarctique d'André Thevet* (1557)', in *D'encre de Brésil: Jean de Léry, écrivain*, ed. by Frank Lestringant and Marie-Christine Gomez-Géraud (Orléans: Paradigme, 1999), pp. 93–108
— 'L'Insulaire de Rabelais ou la fiction en archipel (pour une lecture topographique du *Quart Livre*)', in *Rabelais en son demi-millénaire: Actes du colloque international de Tours (24–29 septembre 1984)*, Études Rabelaisiennes, 21, ed. by Jean Céard and Jean-Claude Margolin (Geneva: Droz, 1988), pp. 249–74
— 'Paysages anthropomorphes à la Renaissance', in *Nature et paysages: L'émergence d'une nouvelle subjectivité à la Renaissance*, ed. by Dominique de Courcelles (Paris: École des Chartes, 2006), pp. 261–279
— 'Rabelais and Travel Literature', in *A Companion to François Rabelais*, ed. by Bernd Renner (Leiden: Brill, 2021), pp. 185–215
— *Une sainte horreur, ou le voyage en Eucharistie: xvie – xviiie siècle* (Paris: Presses Universitaires de France, 1996)
Lewis, Martin, and Kären Wigen, *The Myth of Continents: A Critique of Metageography* (Berkeley: University of California Press, 1997)
Lorcin, Patricia M. E., and Todd Shepard, eds, *French Mediterraneans: Transnational and Imperial Histories* (Lincoln: University of Nebraska Press, 2016)
Lupher, David A., *Romans in a New World: Classical Models in Sixteenth-Century Spanish America* (Ann Arbor: University of Michigan Press, 2003)
Mackenzie, Louisa, *The Poetry of Place: Lyric, Landscape, and Ideology in Renaissance France* (Toronto: University of Toronto Press, 2011)

MacLean, Gerald, ed., *Re-Orienting the Renaissance: Cultural Exchanges with the East* (Basingstoke: Palgrave Macmillan, 2005)

Malcolm, Noel, *Useful Enemies: Islam and the Ottoman Empire in Western Political Thought, 1450–1750* (Oxford: Oxford University Press, 2019)

Mansel, Philip, 'The French Renaissance in Search of the Ottoman Empire', in *Re-Orienting the Renaissance: Cultural Exchanges with the East*, ed. by Gerald MacLean (Basingstoke: Palgrave Macmillan, 2005), pp. 96–107

Margolin, Jean-Claude, 'L'Europe dans le miroir du nouveau monde', in *La Conscience européenne au XVe et au XVIe siècle: Actes du colloque international organisé à l'École Normale Supérieure de Jeunes Filles (30 septembre – 3 octobre 1980)* (Paris: École Normale Supérieure de Jeunes Filles, 1982), pp. 235–64

McCabe, Ina Baghdiantz, *Orientalism in Early Modern France: Eurasian Trade, Exoticism, and the Ancien Régime* (Oxford: Berg, 2008)

McGrath, John, 'Polemic and History in French Brazil, 1555–1560', *Sixteenth Century Journal*, 27 (1996), 385–97

McKee, Sally, *Uncommon Dominion: Venetian Crete and the Myth of Ethnic Purity* (Philadelphia: University of Pennsylvania Press, 2000)

McLean, Matthew, *The 'Cosmographia' of Sebastian Münster: Describing the World in the Reformation* (Aldershot: Ashgate, 2007)

Melzer, Sara, *Colonizer or Colonized? The Hidden Colonial Stories of Early Modern French Culture* (Philadelphia: University of Pennsylvania Press, 2012)

Ménager, Daniel, *Ronsard: Le roi, le poète et les hommes* (Geneva: Droz, 1979)

Micallef, Patricia, 'The Vision of the Island of Malta and its Role in the Transformation of the Order's Mission as Seen by the Seventeenth- and Eighteenth-Century Traveller', in *Islands and Military Orders, c.1291–c.1798*, ed. by Emanuel Buttigieg and Simon Phillips (Farnham, Surrey: Ashgate, 2013), pp. 115–25

Mignolo, Walter, *The Darker Side of the Renaissance: Literacy: Territoriality, and Colonization* (Ann Arbor: University of Michigan Press, 1995)

Miller, Peter N., *Peiresc's Mediterranean World* (Cambridge, MA: Harvard University Press, 2015)

Molho, Anthony, and Diogo Ramada Curto, eds, *Finding Europe: Discourses on Margins, Communities, Images* (New York: Berghahn, 2007)

Mosley, Adam, 'The Cosmographer's Role in the Sixteenth Century: A Preliminary Study', *Archives internationales d'histoire des sciences*, 59 (2009), 424–39

Mudimbe, V. Y., *The Idea of Africa* (Bloomington: Indiana University Press, 1994)

— *The Invention of Africa: Gnosis, Philosophy, and the Order of Knowledge* (Bloomington: Indiana University Press, 1988)

Oberman, Heiko, *John Calvin and the Reformation of the Refugees* (Geneva: Droz, 2009)

O'Brien, John, '"Le Propre de l'homme": Reading Montaigne's "Des cannibales" in Context', *Forum for Modern Language Studies*, 53 (2017), 220–34

Oddy, Niall, 'Crusade or Cooperation? Savary de Brèves's Treatises on the Ottoman Empire', *The Seventeenth Century*, 34 (2019), 143–57

Pagden, Anthony, *European Encounters with the New World: From Renaissance to Romanticism* (New Haven, CT: Yale University Press, 1993)
— *The Fall of Natural Man: The American Indian and the Origins of Comparative Ethnology* (Cambridge: Cambridge University Press, 1987)
— *Lords of All the World: Ideologies of Empire in Spain, Britain and France c.1500–c.1800* (New Haven, CT: Yale University Press, 1998)
Panaite, Viorel, 'East Encounters West: French Merchants and Islamic Law in the Ottoman Mediterranean (Late-Sixteenth and Early-Seventeenth Centuries)', *IRCICA Journal: A Journal on Islamic History and Civilisation*, 1 (2013), 47–91
Parsons, Jotham, *Making Money in Sixteenth-Century France: Currency, Culture, and the State* (Ithaca, NY: Cornell University Press, 2014)
Peronnet, Michel, 'Montaigne et l'Europe?', in *Montaigne et l'Europe: Actes du colloque international de Bordeaux (1992)*, ed. by Claude-Gilbert Dubois (Mont-de-Marsan: Éditions InterUniversitaires, 1992), pp. 61–71
Petitclerc, Isabelle, 'François Savary de Brèves, ambassadeur de Henri IV à Constantinople (1585–1605): Diplomatie française dans l'Empire ottoman et recherche orientaliste' (unpublished doctoral thesis, Université Paris IV, 1988)
Petris, Loris, 'Faith and Religious Policy in Michel de L'Hospital's Civic Evangelism', in *The Adventure of Religious Pluralism in Early Modern France*, ed. by Keith Cameron, Mark Greengrass and Penny Roberts (Oxford: Peter Lang, 2000), pp. 129–42
Piechocki, Katharina, *Cartographic Humanism: The Making of Early Modern Europe* (Chicago: University of Chicago Press, 2019)
Piterberg, Gabriel, Teofilo Ruiz and Geoffrey Symcox, eds, *Braudel Revisited: The Mediterranean World 1600–1800* (Toronto: University of Toronto Press, 2010)
Plokhy, Serhii, 'Princes and Cossacks: Putting Ukraine on the Map of Europe', in *Seeing Muscovy Anew: Politics – Institutions – Culture: Essays in Honor of Nancy Shields Kollmann*, ed. by Michael S. Flier, Valerie Kivelson, Erika Monahan and Daniel Rowland (Bloomington, IN: Slavica Publishers, 2017), pp. 323–38
Pot, Olivier, 'Le Concept d'"histoire universelle": Ou quand l'historien se fait géographe', *Albineana*, 19 (2007), 23–65
— 'L'*Histoire universelle*, ou une poétique de l'événementiel: Réflexions sur l'invention d'un genre', in *Entre Clio et Melpomène: Les fictions de l'histoire chez Agrippa d'Aubigné*, ed. by Olivier Pot (Paris: Garnier, 2010), pp. 145–223
Quinn, Frederick, *The Sum of All Heresies: The Image of Islam in Western Thought* (Oxford: Oxford University Press, 2008)
Quint, David, *Origin and Originality in Renaissance Literature: Versions of the Source* (New Haven, CT: Yale University Press, 1983)
— 'A Reconsideration of Montaigne's *Des cannibales*', *Modern Language Quarterly*, 51 (1990), 459–90
Racaut, Luc, *Hatred in Print: Catholic Propaganda and Protestant Identity During the French Wars of Religion* (Aldershot: Ashgate, 2002)
Ramachandran, Ayesha, *The Worldmakers: Global Imagining in Early Modern Europe* (Chicago: University of Chicago Press, 2015)

Robichaud, Denis J.-J., 'Renaissance and Reformation, in *The Oxford Handbook of Atheism*, ed. by Stephen Bullivant and Michael Ruse (Oxford: Oxford University Press, 2013), pp. 179–94

Romer, James William, 'François Rabelais and the New World: A Study of Geography and Navigation in Rabelais's Romance' (unpublished doctoral thesis, University of North Carolina, 1977)

Rothman, E. Natalie, *Brokering Empire: Trans-Imperial Subjects between Venice and Istanbul* (Ithaca, NY: Cornell University Press, 2011)

Rouillard, Clarence Dana, *The Turk in French History, Thought, and Literature (1520–1660)* (Paris: Boivin et Compagnie, 1940)

Rubiés, Joan-Pau, 'New Worlds and Renaissance Ethnology', *History and Anthropology*, 6 (1993), 157–97

Said, Edward, *Orientalism* (London: Penguin, 1978)

Sandberg, Brian, '"Moors Must Not Be Taken for Black": Race, Conflict, and Cultural Translation in the Early Modern French Mediterranean', *Mediterranean Studies*, 29 (2021), 182–212

Scholar, Richard, *Montaigne and the Art of Free-Thinking* (Oxford: Peter Lang, 2010)

Schule, Winfried, 'Europa in der Frühen Neuzeit – Begriffsgeschichtliche Befunde', in *"Europäische Geschichte" als historiographisches Problem*, ed. by Heinz Duchhardt and Andreas Kunz (Mainz: Philipp von Zabern, 1997), pp. 35–65

Schwartz, Jerome, *Irony and Ideology in Rabelais: Structures of Subversion* (Cambridge: Cambridge University Press, 1990)

Schwoebel, Robert, *The Shadow of the Crescent: The Renaissance Image of the Turk (1453–1517)* (New York: St Martin's Press, 1967)

Screech, M. A., 'The Death of Pan and the Death of Heroes in the *Fourth Book* of Rabelais: A Study in Syncretism', *Bibliothèque d'humanisme et Renaissance*, 17 (1955), 36–55

—— *Rabelais* (London: Duckworth, 1979)

Shannon, Silvia, 'Villegagnon, Polyphemus, and Cain of America: Religion and Polemics in the French New World', in *Changing Identities in Early Modern France*, ed. by Michael Wolfe (Durham, NC: Duke University Press, 1996), pp. 325–44

Smith, Darren M., '"Le monde est un logement d'étrangers": François Savary de Brèves (1560–1628), Diplomatic Agent in the Early Modern Mediterranean' (unpublished doctoral thesis, University of Sydney, 2022)

Smith, Paul J., 'Naked Indians, Trousered Gauls: Montaigne on Barbarism', in *Barbarism Revisited: New Perspectives on an Old Concept*, ed. by Maria Boletsi and Christian Moser (Leiden: Brill, 2015), pp. 105–22

—— *Voyage et écriture: Étude sur le 'Quart Livre' de Rabelais*, Études Rabelaisiennes, 19 (Geneva: Droz, 1987)

Soykut, Mustafa, *Image of the 'Turk' in Italy: A History of the 'Other' in Early Modern Europe: 1453–1683* (Berlin: Klaus Schwarz, 2001)

Starobinski, Jean, *Montaigne en mouvement* (Paris: Gallimard, 1993)

Strauss, Gerald, 'A Sixteenth-Century Encyclopedia: Sebastian Münster's *Cosmography* and its Editions', in *From the Renaissance to the Counter-Reformation: Essays in Honour of Garrett Mattingly*, ed. by Charles Carter (London: Jonathan Cape, 1966), pp. 145–63

Szabari, Antónia, 'The Ambassador, The Spy, and the *Deli*: Self-Representation and Anti-Diplomacy in Nicolas de Nicolay's *Navigations*', *MLN*, 131 (2016), 1002–22

Takeda, Junko, *Between Crown and Commerce: Marseille and the Early Modern Mediterranean* (Baltimore: Johns Hopkins University Press, 2011)

Tally, Robert T., Jr, 'Spaces of the Text: Literary Studies after the Spatial Turn', in *Spatial Literary Studies: Interdisciplinary Approaches to Space, Geography, and the Imagination*, ed. by Robert T. Tally Jr (New York: Routledge, 2020), pp. 1–10

Tally, Robert T., Jr, ed., *The Routledge Handbook of Literature and Space* (London: Routledge, 2017)

— *Spatial Literary Studies: Interdisciplinary Approaches to Space, Geography, and the Imagination* (New York: Routledge, 2020)

Tinguely, Frédéric, *L'Écriture du Levant à la Renaissance: Enquête sur les voyageurs français dans l'Empire de Soliman le Magnifique* (Geneva: Droz, 2000)

— 'Le Vertige cosmographique à la Renaissance', *Archives internationales d'histoire des sciences*, 59 (2009), 441–50

— *Le Voyageur aux mille tours: Les ruses de l'écriture du monde à la Renaissance* (Paris: Champion, 2014)

Tolias, Georges, 'Seuils de l'espace – seuils de pouvoir: les détroits dans la pensée cosmographique', in *La Renaissance au grand large: Mélanges en l'honneur de Frank Lestringant*, ed. by Véronique Ferrer, Olivier Millet and Alexandre Tarrête (Geneva: Droz, 2019), pp. 361–72

Tournon, André, *'En sens agile': Les acrobaties de l'esprit selon Rabelais* (Paris: Champion, 1995)

— *La Glose et l'essai* (Paris: Champion, 2000)

— 'Nargues, Zargues et le concept de trépas', *Réforme, humanisme, Renaissance*, 64 (2007), 111–23

Usher, Phillip John, *Errance et cohérence: Essai sur la littérature transfrontalière à la Renaissance* (Paris: Garnier, 2010)

— *L'Aède et le géographe: Poésie et espace du monde à l'époque prémoderne* (Paris: Garnier, 2018)

— 'L'Intertexte virgilien dans les *Singularités de la France antarctique* (1557) d'André Thevet', in *La Renaissance au grand large: Mélanges en l'honneur de Frank Lestringant*, ed. by Véronique Ferrer, Olivier Millet and Alexandre Tarrête (Geneva: Droz, 2019), pp. 119–28

— 'Walking East in the Renaissance', in *French Global: A New Approach to Literary History*, ed. by Christie McDonald and Susan Rubin Suleiman (New York: Columbia University Press, 2010), pp. 193–206

Van Den Abbeele, Georges, 'Duplicity and Singularity in André Thevet's *Cosmographie de Levant*', *L'Esprit créateur*, 32 (1992), 25–35

Walser-Bürgler, Isabella, *Europe and Europeanness in Early Modern Latin Literature: 'Fuitne Europa tunc unita?'* (Leiden: Brill, 2021)

Warf, Barney, and Santa Arias, eds, *The Spatial Turn: Interdisciplinary Perspectives* (London: Routledge, 2009)

Weiss, Gillian, *Captives and Corsairs: France and Slavery in the Early Modern Mediterranean* (Stanford: Stanford University Press, 2011)

Weller, Shane, *The Idea of Europe: A Critical History* (Cambridge: Cambridge University Press, 2021)

Whatley, Janet, 'Food and the Limits of Civility: The Testimony of Jean de Léry', *Sixteenth Century Journal*, 15 (1984), 387–400

Williams, Phillip, *Empire and Holy War in the Mediterranean: The Galley and Maritime Conflict between the Habsburgs and Ottomans* (London: I. B. Tauris, 2014)

Williams, Wes, '"L'Humanité du tout perdue?": Early Modern Monsters, Cannibals and Human Souls', *History and Anthropology*, 23 (2012), 235–56

— *Monsters and their Meanings in Early Modern Culture: Mighty Magic* (Oxford: Oxford University Press, 2011)

— *Pilgrimage and Narrative in the French Renaissance: The Undiscovered Country* (Oxford: Oxford University Press, 1998)

Wilson, Peter, *Europe's Tragedy: A New History of the Thirty Years War* (London: Allen Lane, 2009)

Wintle, Michael, *The Image of Europe: Visualizing Europe in Cartography and Iconography throughout the Ages* (Cambridge: Cambridge University Press, 2011)

Wolfe, Michael, 'Introduction: Becoming French in Early Modern Europe', in *Changing Identities in Early Modern France*, ed. by Michael Wolfe (Durham, NC: Duke University Press, 1997), pp. 1–21

Yardeni, Myriam, *La Conscience nationale en France pendant les guerres de religion (1559–1598)* (Louvain: Nauwelaerts, 1971)

Yates, Frances, *Astraea: The Imperial Theme in the Sixteenth Century* (London: Routledge & Kegan Paul, 1975)

Index

Abydos, 102
Aegean Sea, 104
Aeneid, 48
Africa, 3, 7–10, 15–16, 20–1, 23–5, 44–5, 49, 51, 66, 71, 80, 87–96, 100–2, 105, 107
   as cultural construct, 95
   diversity of, 95
   imagined geography of Africa, 10
Alexander the Great, 64–5
Algiers, 104
America (continent), 1, 3, 7–9, 16, 20, 25, 27, 43–51, 56, 88–9, 95–6, 107, 118, 120, 129, 136
   North America, 4, 43
   South America, 43–4
Anderson, Benedict, 4
Angoulême, 103
Antarctic France (*France Antarctique*), 43–4, 47–8, 51, 56, 114, 127, 129
Apian, Peter
   Cosmographia, 15
   La Cosmographie de Pierre Apian (The Cosmography of Peter Apian), 8, 15–17, 20–1, 24–5, 27–8, 32, 34, 36–7, 88, 137–8
Arabia, 104
archipelagic fiction, 18
Armenia, 104
Ash Wednesday, 121
Asia, 3, 5, 7–8, 15–16, 20–1, 24–5, 32, 52, 64–6, 71, 73, 77–8, 80, 88–91, 95–7, 102–3, 107, 117, 136

Asia Minor, 105
   East Asia, 8
astronomy, 16
atheism, 48, 122
Atlantic Ocean, 17, 20, 49, 129
Atlantis, 51–2
Augsburg Settlement, 124

Bachelard, Gaston, 6
barbarism, 6, 43, 46, 51–5, 64, 66, 75, 102, 106, 116, 128, 135
Barbary Coast, 92
Belgrade, 117
Belleforest, François de, 100
   Cosmographie universelle (Universal Cosmography), 9, 87–99, 106–7, 137–9
Berbers, 93
Bihać, 117
Black Sea, 52, 90
Bosporus, 62, 67, 78, 102, 107
Boemus, Johann, *Omnium gentium mores*, 46
boundaries
   between peoples/communities, 3, 19, 21–2, 74, 122, 138
   cultural boundaries, 21, 63, 96, 98, 107, 115–16, 139
   geographical boundaries, 6, 10, 20–2, 89, 96–8, 102, 107, 115–17, 138–9
   of Europe, 2, 20–1, 74, 87–90, 93–4, 97–100, 102, 115–17, 139
   of nations, 3, 21, 115, 125
   of place, 3, 138

boundaries (cont.)
  uncertain boundaries, 2, 22, 43–4, 57
Braudel, Fernand, 86
Brazil, 8–9, 43–57, 114, 119–20, 122, 127–30, 136, 138

Calabria, 64
Calvinists, 43–4, 113–31
Calvin, John, 121
Canada, 17–18, 27, 43, 56
Canary Islands, 45–6
cannibalism, 25, 52, 55, 128
capitalism, 1, 35
Cartier, Jacques, 43
cartography, 1, 5, 7, 16, 20
Catherine de Medici, 116
Catholicism, 4, 8, 21, 43, 48, 56, 74, 86, 96, 101, 105, 107, 113, 121, 124–7, 129–30
Cave, Terence, 6, 18
  method of pre-history, 6
Certeau, Michel de, 127
Chakrabarty, Dipesh, 7
Charlemagne, 65, 67
Charles V (Holy Roman Emperor), 70, 75, 87
Charles VIII (King of France), 54
Charles IX (King of France), 53, 64, 65
Christendom, 1, 4, 10, 29–30, 36, 48–9, 62, 63–5, 69–80, 87, 92–3, 107, 114–26, 130–1, 137–8
Christianity, 4, 9, 26, 28–9, 46–7, 49, 56, 65, 68, 73–4, 76–7, 79, 86, 92–3, 104, 120–3, 128
  confessional disputes, 113–31, 138
  split between Western (Latin) Christianity and Eastern (Orthodox) Christianity, 97–9, 106, 116
civility, 9, 24–5, 45–6, 49
climate, 15–16, 91–3, 119
  climatic theories, 91–2, 94
Colie, Rosalie, 6
Coligny, François de, 127
Coligny, Gaspard de, 127
community, 3, 16, 22, 24, 29–30, 32–5, 37, 54–5, 68, 74, 114, 119, 122, 125–30
  imagined communities, 4
Conley, Tom, 17
Conrad, Sebastian, 8
Constantine, 65
Constantinople, 9, 62–80, 100, 102–5, 136, 138
continents as cultural constructs, 5
Corsica, 70
cosmography, 8–10, 16–17, 19, 22, 36, 51, 87–8, 94, 100–1, 107, 115, 137–8
Cossacks, 115–16
Crete, 18, 32, 88, 96–100
Croatia, 117
cultural customs, 9, 46, 54, 65, 87, 90–7, 102, 118
cultural relativism, 43

Dainotto, Roberto, 2, 7, 99
d'Aramon, Gabriel, 103
d'Aubigné, Agrippa, 10, 138–9
  Histoire universelle (*Universal History*), 10, 114–20, 122–6, 130–1, 137, 139
  Les Tragiques, 114
Davies, Norman, 99
Denmark, 117
Desan, Philippe, 5, 50
de Thou, Jacques Auguste, *Historia sui temporis*, 114
Don River, 20
Dordogne, 51, 54
Du Bellay, Guillaume, 30–3
Du Bellay, Joachim, 63
Dutch Republic, 72
Duval, Edwin, 18, 29, 34

Egypt, 51, 100
England, 72, 75, 115
  Church of England, 28
ethnicity, 2, 6, 10, 96–8, 101–2, 105, 107
Euromaidan, 2
Europa (myth), 32
Europe
  as constructed through difference, 7, 95–6

as culturally produced, 2, 20, 137
as geographical signifier, 23–4,
  51–3, 56, 74, 77, 79, 90, 102,
  115, 119
as marker of cultural identity, 1, 3,
  62, 130
as object of allegiance, 1, 130
as rhetorical figure for comic
  exaggeration, 137
as set of values, 1, 8, 97
boundaries, 2, 20–1, 74, 87–90,
  93–4, 97–100, 102, 115–17,
  139
concept, 2–4, 7–8, 10, 20, 23, 43,
  45, 49–50, 52–3, 57, 62–5, 68,
  71, 76, 78–80, 86–8, 99–100,
  107, 114, 117, 119, 131, 136–7,
  139
eastern Europe, 136
heritage of classical antiquity, 26,
  30–2, 48–9, 65, 70, 79, 137
maps of, 1, 21, 115
potential futures of, 21, 36–7
south-eastern Europe, 126
split between geographical Europe
  and cultural Europe, 98–9,
  115–17, 139
supposed superiority to rest of
  world, 9, 24–5, 37, 44–6, 49, 56,
  67, 91, 102, 128, 137
unity of, 28, 36–7, 46, 48, 95,
  102–3, 108, 130, 138–9
word, 4, 7, 9, 17, 22–6, 36–7,
  43–5, 47–53, 56–7, 62–4, 69–73,
  77–9, 102–3, 105–6, 115–16,
  118–20, 126, 130, 136–7
European Union, 1, 2
Evangelical Humanism, 18
exile, 10, 66, 114, 129–30

Ferdinand I (Holy Roman Emperor),
  124–5
fiction, 3, 5–6, 9, 17–19, 21–2, 26–7,
  29, 36–7, 139
Florida, 43, 56
France
  alliance with Ottoman Empire, 64,
    70–1, 73–7, 80, 138–9
  as homeland, 103, 128

as universal monarchy, 67–8, 80
boundaries, 4, 10
colonial missions, 4, 27, 43–4,
  46–7, 49, 56, 138–9
civil wars / Wars of Religion, 4, 48,
  54–6, 69, 80, 107–8, 113, 120,
  126–7, 129–30, 139
Estates General, 113
glorification of France in poetry,
  63, 80
relations with papacy, 28, 35, 77–8
religious division, 21, 23, 55,
  113–31
rivalry with Habsburgs, 4, 67–8,
  75–6, 80, 138
St Bartholomew's Day Massacre,
  127–8
François I (King of France), 4, 32, 43,
  64, 70, 75
François II (King of France), 67
Frisius, Gemma, 15, 25

Gallipoli, 102
Geneva, 8, 10, 113, 119, 127,
  129–30, 138
genre, 3, 6, 8–10, 16–18, 51, 67,
  87–8, 100, 107, 114–15, 130,
  137
geography, 1–5, 7–8, 10, 15–19,
  22–3, 25–7, 34, 36–7, 49–56,
  63, 74, 87, 90–1, 94, 97, 105,
  107, 114, 126, 130, 137, 139
Germany, 99, 115, 124, 136
globalisation, 1
Gozo, 86, 104
Greece, 65–7, 79–80, 97, 99, 103–4,
  106–7, 137–9
Gregory XIII (Pope), 117

Habsburgs, 4, 64, 67–8, 70, 75, 80
Hampton, Timothy, 3, 4, 54
Hellespont (the Dardanelles), 102,
  105
Henri II (King of France), 18, 27–8,
  54, 67, 104
Henri III (King of France), 8, 66, 80
  and King of Poland, 8, 66
Henri IV (King of France), 77–8,
  125–6, 130

Héret, Mathurin, 44
Holy Roman Empire, 67, 117, 124
Huchon, Mireille, 18

identity
   Christian identity, 62, 68, 72, 114, 120–2
   civic identity, 130
   collective identity, 3, 53–5, 57, 113
   confessional identity, 55, 121–2
   cultural identity, 1, 72, 74, 105, 119
   European identity, 1, 62, 76, 130
   French national identity, 3, 54–5
   national identity, 87
   personal identity, 23, 55, 107, 127
   religious identity, 63, 107, 120
imagined geographies, 5–10, 17, 36, 43–4, 46, 49–50, 52–4, 57, 62, 69, 74–6, 86–8, 91, 95–7, 99–100, 102–8, 114, 116–17, 126, 128, 135–9
Islam
   anti-Islamic rhetoric, 62, 65, 69, 74
   excluded from imagined geography of Europe, 99
   relations with Christendom, 62–80, 86, 93, 104
Isocrates, 7
isolario, 18
Italy, 48, 53, 64, 92, 99, 115, 126, 135–6
   physical separation of mainland from Sicily, 94

Jeanneret, Michel, 33
Jesuits, 125
Jerusalem, 68, 100

Keller, Marcus, 4, 103
Knights Hospitaller, 64, 86–7, 93, 104
Kraków, 136
Kyiv, 2

Lampsacus, 102
landscape, 9, 16, 20, 24, 95
La Noue, François de, 70, 75

La Popelinière, Lancelot Voisin de, *Les Trois Mondes*, 89
Las Casas, Bartolomé de, 47
Laudonnière, René Goulaine de, 43
Le Havre, 44
Léry, Jean de, 43, 47, 51, 114, 138–9
   Histoire d'un voyage faict en la terre du Brésil (*History of a Voyage Made to the Land of Brazil*), 10, 114, 118–22, 126–30, 137, 139
Lestringant, Frank, 18–19, 100
Levant, 97–8, 100, 103, 136
Lewis, Martin, and Kären Wigen, 5
l'Hospital, Michel de, 113, 120–3, 130
literature
   and geography/cartography, 5, 17
   and history, 6
   and nationhood, 3–4, 63, 80
   and word 'Europe', 137
   definition of, 6
   French Renaissance, 3, 62, 66
   Neo-Latin, 2
   spatial literary studies, 5
locus amoenus, 16, 28
Louis XIII (King of France), 75
Lucca, 136
Lutheranism, 117, 120, 123–4

Malta, 9–10, 86–108, 138
   Siege of Malta (1565), 64, 93, 100, 118
Mandeville, John, 100
Mantua, 124
maps, 1, 16, 18, 20–1, 89, 115
Marseille, 100, 103
Maximilian II (Holy Roman Emperor), 117
Mediterranean Sea, 8–9, 18, 20, 52, 86, 88, 90–4, 96, 100, 103, 105, 107
Mexico, 46
Mignolo, Walter, 7
Monluc, Jean de, 70
Montaigne, Michel de, 6, 8, 47, 137–8
   cosmopolitanism, 49–50

'Des cannibales' ('Of Cannibals'), 9, 43, 49–57, 135–6, 139
'Des coches' ('Of Coaches'), 2–3, 54, 56
'Des destries' ('Of War Horses'), 54
'Du pedantisme' ('Of Pedantry'), 54
Essais (Essays), 3, 9, 49, 53–4, 56
Journal de voyage (Travel Journal), 136
Moors, 89, 92, 94–6, 101
More, Thomas, *Utopia*, 19, 22
Münster, Sebastian, 36–7, 88–9, 92–3, 97
  Cosmographia, 8, 16–7, 20–1, 24–5, 32, 87, 138
Murad III (Sultan), 117
Muscovy, 98–9, 107, 115–16, 139

nationhood
  affection for nation, 103
  consolidation of nation states, 1, 3–4
  national ambitions, 47, 49, 138
  national consciousness, 4, 8, 130
  national interest, 9, 28, 71, 77
  national sentiment, 2
  nation as object of allegiance, 125–31, 138
  discourses on nation and nationhood, 3–4, 10, 23, 62–4, 69, 80, 138–9
Neo-Latin, 2, 139
New Historicism, 6
New World, 1–3, 9, 18–19, 21, 25, 27, 35, 89, 114, 118–21, 127–30, 138–9
  European conquest of, 43–57
Nicolay, Nicolas de, *Les Quatre Premiers Livres des navigations et peregrinations orientales* (*The First Four Books of Oriental Navigations and Peregrinations*), 10, 87, 100, 103–7, 137
North Sea, 20
North-West Passage, 17–18

Orléans, 113
Orphic Argonautica, 18

Orthodox Christianity, 73, 79, 88, 96, 98–9, 105, 116
Ottoman Empire
  and concept of Europe, 8–9, 62–80, 96, 106, 116, 120
  expansion into Europe, 1, 20, 62, 64–8, 71, 75, 93, 97–9, 117–18, 126, 139
  hostilities with Knights Hospitaller, 86–7, 93, 101, 104, 118
  origins of the Turks, 97–8
  relations with Christendom, 62–80, 93, 123, 130
  relations with France, 64, 70–1, 73–7, 80, 138–9
Ovid, *Fasti*, 101

Pacific Ocean, 17
Palestine, 50
Pantelleria, 104
papacy, 27–8, 72, 77–8, 80, 126
  pope as head of Christendom, 4, 28, 121, 124–5
Paris, 8, 18, 67
Paul III (Pope), 124
Paul V (Pope), 77
Pavie, François de, 136
Peace of Stettin (1570), 117
Persia, 71, 104, 116
Peru, 25, 47
Phocaeans, 103
Piechocki, Katharina, 2
place (concept), 5, 6, 16, 23, 78, 116, 137
Pliny, 16
Plutarch, 30
Poland, 8, 66, 99, 116
Polish-Lithuanian Commonwealth, 115
Portugal, 53, 99
  Portuguese colonialism, 3, 27, 43–4, 46–9, 56, 120, 127, 129
postcolonial studies, 7
Prague, 136
Protestantism, 27, 36, 43, 55, 69, 72, 80, 113, 117, 122, 126
Ptolemy, 8, 32
  Geographia, 7, 16
Pyrrhonism, 51

Pyrrhus, 135–6

Rabelais, François, 6, 137
  Gargantua, 22
  Pantagruel, 22–4
Rabelais, François (cont.)
  Quart Livre, 9, 15–19, 21–37, 136–7, 139
  Tiers Livre, 22
Reformation, 1, 4, 10, 21, 23, 48, 67, 69, 114, 118, 127, 130
Reformed Christianity, 4, 121, 123–6, 129, 130
Renaissance humanism, 49, 64, 66, 100, 102
Rhodes, 86, 100–1
Rio de Janeiro, 43–4
Roman Empire, 49, 86, 135
  political ideas, 48
  Malta in Roman Empire, 93, 102
Rome, 21, 28, 35, 63, 67–8, 70, 77–80, 125, 139
Ronsard, Pierre de, 6, 9, 62–70, 78–80, 137–9
  'Bergerie', 69
  'Discours à G. Des-Autels' ('Discourse to Guillaume Desautels'), 69
  'Discours ou dialogue entre les Muses deslogées, et Ronsard' ('Discourse or Dialogue between the Homeless Muses and Ronsard'), 65–6
  'Exhortation pour la paix' ('Exhortation for Peace'), 68–9, 80
  La Franciade (*The Franciad*), 62
  'Les Isles fortunees' ('The Blessed Isles'), 67
  Le Troisiesme Livre des odes (The Third Book of Odes), 67
Rouen, 50, 53
Russian Federation, 20

Saintonge, 23
Saint Luke, 102
Saint Paul, 86, 93, 101–2
savagery, 9, 25, 45–6, 49, 51–4, 128

Savary de Brèves, François, 9, 63, 70–80, 137–9
  ambassadorship in Rome, 77–9
  Discours abrégé des asseurez moyens d'aneantir & ruiner la monarchie des Princes Ottomans (*Abridged Discourse on the Assured Means to Weaken and Ruin the Monarchy of the Ottoman Princes*), 71–6, 78, 80
  Discours sur l'alliance qu'a le Roy avec le grand Seigneur, & de l'utilité qu'elle apporte à la Chrestienté (*Discourse on the Alliance that the King Has with the Great Lord and on the Utility that it Brings to Christendom*), 71, 73–6, 78, 80
Said, Edward
  imaginative geography, 6, 7
  Orientalism 6, 7
Sestos, 102
Screech, Michael, 18, 27
Scythians, 97–8
Sepúlveda, Juan Ginés de, 47
Shakespeare, William, use of word 'Europe', 137
Sicily, 64, 71, 86, 92, 94, 100–1, 105
Solinus, Gaius Julius, *Polyhistor*, 100
space (concept), 1, 4–6, 8, 17, 20, 22, 54–5, 88, 115
  poetics of space, 6
  spatial turn, 5
Spain, 4, 68–70, 72, 75–8, 80, 90, 99, 115, 123, 126, 138
  Spanish Armada, 116
  Spanish colonialism, 2–3, 27, 43, 46–9, 54, 56, 127–8
Strabo, 91
Straits of Gibraltar, 18, 89
Suleiman I (Sultan), 64, 70, 75, 117–18
Sweden, 117
Switzerland, 114, 136

Tally, Robert, 5
Tanais, 18, 20, 90, 102

Tatars, 97–9, 115–16
Thevet, André, 44, 50, 107, 127, 136, 138–9
  Cosmographie de Levant (*Cosmography of the Levant*), 10, 50, 87, 100–3, 105–7
  Cosmographie universelle (*Universal Cosmography*), 9, 44, 51, 87–103, 107–8, 114, 137–9
  Les Singularitez de la France antarctique (*The Singularities of Antarctic France*), 9, 19, 43–57, 102–3, 119, 128, 137–8
Thirty Years War, 80, 130
Thrace, 136
topography, 18, 30, 34, 35
trade, 35, 86
  with Ottoman Empire, 73–4, 76, 78–80, 138
travel
  imagined travels, 8–10, 49–50, 79, 87, 105–7, 114, 140
  to Brazil, 44–5, 114, 120, 136
  to eastern Europe, 136
  to Malta, 87, 100–7, 138
  to the Levant, 100–6, 136
  to the Ottoman Empire, 62–3, 70, 74
  travel accounts, 10, 29, 36, 45, 51–2, 55–6, 87, 91, 100–7, 114, 136–8
treaty of Cateau-Cambrésis (1559), 68, 70, 123
Tripoli, 86, 104–5
Trojans, 48, 98, 103
Tupinambá, 49, 52, 114, 118
Tuscany, 51
Tyrrhenian Sea, 64

Vadian, Joachim, *Epitome trium terrae partium*, 102
Valladolid debate (1550–51), 47
Van Den Abbeele, Georges, 101
Venice, 70, 72, 96–7, 100, 117
Vespucci, Amerigo, 45
Villegaignon, Nicolas de, 43–4, 104, 121–2, 127, 129

Walser-Bürgler, Isabella, 2, 139
Wintle, Michael, 7